JOURNEY IN DEPTH

A TRANSPERSONAL PERSPECTIVE

Plate 1
Ian Gordon-Brown

Plate 2

Barbara Somers

The Wisdom of the Transpersonal

Other titles in this series by Barbara Somers and Ian Gordon-Brown
Edited by Hazel Marshall

The Fires of Alchemy: A Transpersonal Viewpoint
The Raincloud of Knowable Things:
A Practical Guide to Transpersonal Psychology
Symptom as Symbol: A Transpersonal Language

JOURNEY IN DEPTH

A TRANSPERSONAL PERSPECTIVE

BARBARA SOMERS
with
IAN GORDON-BROWN

editor
HAZEL MARSHALL

illustrations
IAN THORP

paintings
FRANCES CRAWFORD

ARCHIVE
publishing

MMXVII

First published in 2002 in Great Britain
by Archive Publishing.

This reprint published in 2017 in Great Britain by
Archive Publishing,
Shaftesbury, Dorset.

Designed for Archive Publishing by
Ian Thorp

A CIP Record for this book is available from
the British Cataloguing in Publication data office

ISBN   9780954271206   (hardback)
ISBN   9781906289423   (paperback)

Cover painting: 'New Sun' by Frances Crawford.
Also those in the text – all reproduced courtesy of the artist.
francescrawfordart@yahoo.com

Printed and Bound in England by
Lightning Source

DEDICATION

This book is lovingly dedicated
to the life and work of

IAN GORDON-BROWN

Plate 3

Awakening

CONTENTS

CHAPTER 1

INDIVIDUAL AS SEED   1
BARBARA SOMERS

The seed within.
The seed and psychology.
What happens to the seed ?
We can trust the process.
The seed of potential.
Breakthrough.
The gods of the nursery.
The shadow.
Masculine and feminine issues.
The wounded healer.

CHAPTER 2

ROOTS AND SEEDS   11
BARBARA SOMERS

The persona.
The ego.
The shadow.
Neurosis and psychosis.
Rejected attitudes.
Unlived life.

Unresolved conflicts.
Images of transformation.

What makes your heart sing ?
Nursery years.
Childhood.
Adolescence.
Adulthood.
Maturity.
Wisdom.
The call of the Self.

Rites of passage.
The healing wound.
Taking the hand of the child.
Befriending the child in the adult.
The language of the body.
The language of the nursery.
Avoiding interpretation.

The Mother archetype.
The personal mother.
The mother's viewpoint.
Mother's place is in the wrong !
The good enough mother.
The too loose hold.
The passive temperament.
The active temperament.
Gender identity.

The too tight hold.
Working with the mother image.

The Father principle.
The personal father.
The good enough father.
The authoritarian father.
The absent father.
The dead or vanished father.
The Father image.
Working with the father image.

Our place in the family.
The only child.
The elder child.
The second child.
The third child.
The middle child.
The youngest child.
Twins.
The death of a brother or sister.
Adopted and fostered children.
Step children.
Refugees and children who were evacuated.
The scapegoat.
Exploring the family.

Handling crisis.
Spirit of Place.

Power in organisations.
Working with people.

CHAPTER 9
THE MEANING OF ILLNESS :
AN INTRODUCTION TO SYMPTOM AS SYMBOL   157
BARBARA SOMERS
What is the meaning of illness ?
Ageing.
Crisis.
Illness.
The alternative approach.
Chronic illness.
Symptom as symbol.
Addiction.
The language of the symptom.
Listening.
The place of gathering.
The wise woman.
The journey.
The body.

CHAPTER 10
POLARITIES & THE TRANSCENDENT FUNCTION 173
BARBARA SOMERS
Paradox.
Projection.
The transcendent function.
Inner alchemy.
Gestalt with objects.
Using gestalt.
Hubris and inflation.
The transforming symbol.

CHAPTER 11
PROJECTION & COLLUSION   189
IAN GORDON-BROWN
Projection.

ILLUSTRATIONS

PLATES

NOTE
for Therapists and Counsellors
Barbara Somers

This book offers a perspective, a dimension, a Transpersonal way of working. It is also for the informed public outside the profession, for whom it will make a lot of sense: its theme is life.

The course in Transpersonal skills on which it is based was by nature ancillary to other counselling trainings: we recommended that counsellors had under their belts as much good basic training in other ways, skills and approaches as they could. It aimed to give an overall perspective, coming on top of a person's own approach to doing therapy. The hope was that it would add to and enhance their own natural style of working with people, offering some ancillary techniques. I hope for instance that you may be helped to pick the moment to go in at the imaging level, if that seems creative all round; or to hold a line, if that is what you wish.

However, the theory is only a springboard for the later work. Study any number of books, listen to any number of lectures, but you learn to counsel by counselling – by doing it.

FOREWORD

Naona Beecher-Moore

In the last few years a number of books have appeared about Transpersonal Psychology, but few have been written by those with years of experience both in life and in the study of the Transpersonal. In the 1970's Barbara Somers and Ian Gordon-Brown started a centre for transpersonal study. This came out of their lifelong work and interest in psychology in its many forms. They developed a method and a mode of teaching that was unique to them, drawing on their own personal study and their life-experiences, and they took the essence of this and distilled it into a new form of training.

This book, carefully edited by Hazel Marshall, is a distillation of that training. It will be extremely useful to therapists who have been working for some years, reconnecting them with their own original point of entry into this study and also affirming and adjusting many of the ways they now work. It will also be fascinating to those just starting on the path of psychotherapy, as it will give them insights that no other book that I know of can give them.

This book is easy to read, but it is not easy to forget. Sentences, paragraphs, thoughts, understandings and indeed its deep humanness will stay with you for some time; perhaps for ever.

Naona Beecher-Moore,
Middle Temple,
London

May 2001

INTRODUCTION
Hazel Marshall

Many of us have been desperately hurt and wounded in our lives. Torn between extreme opposites, we may feel ourselves to be flung and pulled in all directions: 'Either I stay with my partner and go mad, or I leave, lose the children and die of loneliness.' – 'Either I leave my job, go bankrupt and die of fear and boredom, or I stay in it and die of a heart attack.' We do not know that there can be a solution.

Just as the immune system heals the body, so does our inner wisdom heal the soul. Barbara Somers and Ian Gordon-Brown show in this unique book how the Transpersonal seeks to clarify the healing process : often we can find, given time, a third position beyond any two such awful polarities. It's a natural process, like the healing of a wound.

It's very important not to push this inner healing. Sometimes people try to stitch the opposites across, without exploring or allowing the third position. Our own inner world, when trusted, heals itself. However, it's tricky. That's why we need support in finding it for ourselves. It's not about other people telling us what to do, how to be. Barbara Somers and Ian Gordon-Brown encourage us to find within ourselves the quality and essence of our own innate wisdom, which can answer so many questions and problems. Thus, readers may find inside themselves what is often an astonishing awareness of their own wisdom and compassion.

This book is about inner development. Carl Jung likened the progress of our inner lives to the arch of the sun over a day, from its rising at our birth, through the high noon of our middle years, to its decline in the west towards the sunset of physical death. Yet often a man, in particular, is hardly recognised as changing in any significant way from the age of about twenty until he begins to deteriorate. He's commonly seen as remaining for forty years the same all through, on a railway line towards his end.

However, there is throughout a process of change and growth, a psychological opportunity for everyone. It can be seen as a quest; and while to be on a quest may not be comfortable, to be aware of life as a developmental journey may well lead individuals to move in and out of spiritual areas.

Barbara Somers and Ian Gordon-Brown, following Jung, help us to be discriminating about these areas. Mapping the territory in detail ('and the map is not the country'), they do not attempt to avoid the Shadow beneath, in contrast to some other approaches where a light-oriented preciousness may fail to grip the dark side, or may conflict with the aching, dark, destructive, excessive, violent parts of us.

Barbara and Ian met in 1970 and began to run workshops together. They founded the Centre for Transpersonal Psychology in London in 1973 and established the training there in 1978, running it together until Ian's death in 1996. The training offered a Transpersonal perspective on counselling and psychotherapy. Based upon its taped material, this book offers the reader the flowering of a unique British school. This is the first of a proposed series detailing their work, the transcription of mainly the early years of the counselling training they created and offered.

First a handful, then dozens, hundreds, thousands of people who met Barbara and Ian are out there now in Britain, Europe, America and further. Attending and re-attending workshops, filling great wonderful early conferences on London's Embankment, recognising each other with delight years later at further events, these people, scattered throughout Britain and overseas, know that something of pure gold is contained in this book: their lives are changed, they have come home.

It was Barbara and Ian's way of invoking the spiritual dimension, touching the soul, that made their work unique. The soul has become scarce in psychotherapy and in medicine. Trainee doctors, nurses, psychiatrists often claim to have lost the original impulse by which they were called. 'Our training brutalised us,' said one. 'As raw recruits,' said another, 'we could tell if a patient were lonely, terrified, grief-stricken: now we can give a long name to her disease, but we daren't name her feelings; nor could we.' It's a long time since we worshipped at grove and stream, mountain and waterfall. We have lost touch with the sacredness of all life, and the gods, neglected, have returned as diseases.

Barbara's work puts the soul back into its proper place, honouring, yes, the role of mind and reason, knowledge and will, yet knowing there is more. This journey in depth adds a dimension. The Transpersonal way is to ask, not 'What's wrong with me?' but 'What's right with me?' By learning to sense the symptom as symbol of the inner problem, the psyche's 'dis-ease', we may find our way back to wholeness. Here are intuition, the values of the feeling heart, the warmth of the hearth-fires of home. But not exclusively: both head and heart, reason and emotion, instinct and knowledge are needed if the soul is to come home in us, in our children and in our world.

Warning always, 'The map is not the country,' Barbara and Ian offered a rich treasury of charts of the unexplored inner territory into which people would be venturing. These maps, which make up the figures in this book, are theirs, though they drew on the work of Carl Jung, Abraham Maslow, Roberto Assagioli, the alchemy of the West and the mystery schools of the East.

Richly illustrated with case studies, this book is for caring people in the helping professions, both trainees and experienced practitioners who long for a different perspective on their lives and work. However, it's not only for professionals: it is for all who seek to know and befriend themselves, and thus each other. Full of stories about real people, it is for everyone who has known something of hurt or grief or betrayal, of the pain of loss, the excitement of the inner journey, the quest, the new birth that is itself a profound healing. That includes any one who loves or wants to love, befriends or longs to be befriended.

Hazel Marshall, Editor

Plate 4

Hazel Marshall
*in her garden at
Rock Bank*

AKNOWLEDGEMENTS

I wish to acknowledge my profound indebtedness to Barbara Somers
and Ian Gordon-Brown for the inspiration and opportunity which
made this book possible.

I am warmly grateful to very many people for their invaluable
support, help and advice, among them the following.
If I have left anyone out it was entirely accidental.

Sacha Abercorn, Pamela Allsop,
Monica Anthony, Alick Bartholomew, Naona Beecher-Moore,
Beata Bishop for proof-reading the early manuscript,
Sara Brain, Julie Brookes, Evelyn Bruce, Stasia Cain, Claire Chappell,
Frances Crawford, Marita Crawley, John Drew, Kenneth Evans,
Hossein Farhadi for endless patience with the computer.
Pauline Fieldhouse, David Fontana,
Celia Gunn for final proof reading, Leslie Kenton,
Jackie Kohnstamm, Alison Leonard, Aileen Lowndes,
Adrian Marshall, Sheila MacLeod, Elizabeth McCormick,
Peter Merriott, Suzy Millais, Melanie Reinhart,
Barbara Scott for a great deal of material help,
Kathy Smith for copious typing,
Anita Somers, Mary Swainson, Joan Swallow,
Reynold Swallow, Anthony Thorley,
Ian Thorp whose contribution to the book is incalcuable,
David Toms, Ruth White and Diana Whitmore.

Acknowledgement and thanks are due to the following publisher
for the use of the poem quoted :
Northumberland, Bloodaxe Books Ltd, 1990.
Connie Bensley, 'Progress Report', Cornwall, Peterloo Poets, 1981

Care has been taken to protect the identity of the people whose stories
appear in this book

Plate 5

The Offering

CHAPTER ONE

Individual as Seed

Barbara Somers

What makes your heart sing?

The seed within

I approach each individual with the understanding that within everyone is an original seed. That unique seed will grow in the soil in which it was impregnated and embedded, the darkness of earth, the shadow. Lodged in the matrix of the lower unconscious, it will grow out of the soil of infancy and childhood and begin to develop an everyday awareness. Thus I become 'I', the personal self in the everyday world, revealing my nature as I grow up into adulthood.

One of my most profound and basic beliefs is that the human seed is a *sound* seed. Its nature makes it grow to its own grain: an apple seed has to become an apple tree. If I am an apple pip, no power on earth is going to turn me into deadly nightshade or lesser columbine. My whole thrust will be towards the innate 'appleness' of my nature which should grow true and straight and, depending on the husbandry I've had in the nursery, presumably should flower and burgeon. Allowing for social accidents and impacts from the outside world, the tree will grow as it's meant to by nature, sooner or later putting out leaves and twigs and branches, and eventually bumps which turn out to be good, round, fruity apples. Some may be crab-apples – some may be damn great Cox's – but nonetheless it's allowed to become *apple*. People rush up saying, 'I've got these lumps and bumps all over me! Oh my God, there must be something wrong with me!' And I help them to see – apples; withered, shrivelled perhaps, yet no one has a right to stop them being apples. They learn to work with the 'appleness' of the apple seed, the 'lemonness' of a lemon pip, and not argue it.

This can happen if the child is not too badly inhibited, if its growth to its own nature has been enhanced. And of course it isn't usually like that at all; the majority of us don't have the background. But if we explore in depth the nature of the soil in which we were impregnated, mapping our individual origins, becoming aware of our parents and the images we have of them, we may indeed find we had a 'good enough' environment which got it roughly right when it wasn't getting it too badly wrong. The best sort of ground is certainly not disastrous, but neither is it perfect – that would be very bad preparation for the future. It's good enough. We'd always hope that a child would be born into a good enough environment; but not all have the possibility and opportunity. *Impregnated, not inhibited, individual organs*

good enough environment,

The seed and psychology

The seed is rooted deep in the 'lower unconscious', an area magnificently mapped by Freud. Our debt to him is immense. He explored it for the suppressed, undeveloped sides of our nature, revealing how far down we repress that which is not acceptable to our everyday consciousness. The lower unconscious is often referred to as the 'dustbin of the psyche'. Yet, if the material within the dustbin is well recycled, it can become compost out of which the seed of our new potential can grow.

Adler, in the same area, saw as a primary drive within the in---dividual the will to power, the will to overcome. He saw the person as an amalgam of body, mind and feeling, very much at the mercy of conditioning, environment and the traumas that occur in childhood. Again, brilliant; but we might ask, 'And then what?' There isn't much hope held out for the individual who's had a lot of that early wounding or damage.

The Transpersonal does hold out a hope. That's what draws us to it. The Transpersonal is that which includes the personal, but *also transcends it*. It emerged out of the Behavioural scene, where people were seen as reactive to their environment; out of the depth work with Freud, which opened up the person; and then out of the Humanistic movement which put the human being back into the centre, moving away from childhood and into the here-and-now of every day.

Carl Jung accepted conditioning and genetic inheritance, the social mores and the environment, as deeply important. But also, said Jung, there is another factor: within the lower unconscious lies the *potential* that hasn't yet emerged into consciousness. It must be taken into account. The original seed, born as a human being, bearing the factor of its own unique individuality, is the departure point. If it's an apple seed, it has to become an apple tree. And Jung believed it's a continuum: it came from somewhere, and it goes somewhere.

Lower unconscious, undeveloped self, A wounding damage

What happens to the seed ? *or the genetic*

What makes it grow away from its grain? Very many people have been cut back, distorted, *bonsaied*, pushed out of shape. It's as though they had fallen down into the wrong compost, landed in the wrong setting. Working with them, I discover that something happened which caused them to move away from their own inherent nature. They changed the way they grew –perhaps only slightly; they may have partly grown up first and (a bit late in the day) can readily come back to true, growing on relatively straight.

What goes on in the lower unconscious where the seed is rooted? What kind of figures come out? Using the Transpersonal approach, I ask, 'And how did that feel for you?' –'What does that remind you of?' This draws out the images and symbols which lie within every one of us. The moment we begin to look, a whole stream of images relevant to the person's underlying myth and meaning will emerge. The Self at the archetypal level, the One to which they must resonate, will send *Beware of inhibition afterwards* these streams of images down through the levels of consciousness until they strike into the outside world, emerging in dreams and in fantasy. There's a continuous dialogue coming from the Self as it mediates its meaning towards the individual in the world.

We can trust the process

This is my fundamental belief. Not asking someone to trust blindly in something they're not familiar with but, working with imaging, asking them to see what an extraordinary richness of light and dark can come out of it, I become more and more fascinated. And it's no dark fascination; I'm held and made more deeply reverent by this tremendous process working in everyone. My approach to these images within the individual lies under and over and behind the work. I start from certain basic assumptions:

Within every person, as well as the seed, is a Self with a large S. *Process of meaning* Life, as it manifests within an individual in the crises and experiences of human living, has *meaning*. Evoking the *images* within us can help us come towards this deeper meaning in our own lives, and in life at large.

It's important that we begin to see this for ourselves. Someone who helps the process will not superimpose their own images but evoke those which lie within us, so that we can begin to dialogue with our images and befriend them, ultimately being led back closer to our own original meaning and purpose. How far do we go? For some of us, it is enough to stay with the immediate problem (perhaps seeking help as we go through a particular crisis and towards a different view of the outer world) and leave it at that. But if the work penetrates more deeply, we're inevitably going to move from our view of the outer world towards the inner factors which underlie that view: our early scripting, our experiences in childhood, our expectations of life, of work, of relationships.

The seed of potential

And, too, there are the images of new potential within us. As someone moves into the lower unconscious I hope to bring out not just dark motifs, but *light* motifs. I ask people two often-unexpected questions: *What makes your heart sing, gives you joy?* and *When you were right at the bottom of your barrel, what brought you through?* Thus from the start we constellate the motifs of a new potential within, beginning by working from their strengths, from their light, in order to give them the courage to go into their darkness. So we start with the person's relationships, their adaptation to the outside world, their *persona* or mask; and with the one who wears it, their everyday self, their *ego*. It's only as the work deepens that we look to see who or what lies behind both; so we find the *shadow*.

This is fundamentally different from the approach of most classical analyses, which penetrate the inner, darker, more subjective side in order ultimately to come to some light motifs. I work from the light motifs right from the beginning, so as to take the light down into the darkness. Jung himself did this, so far as I understand; it seems to work extraordinarily well. People say (not in words, but the material is saying it), 'But I have a *healthy* component too!'

Breakthrough

There are many people around (more than one might imagine) who, 'breaking down', are in fact 'breaking up to break through'. I work with many of them, the two of us coming together over a common problem. We are walking together, holding a joint conversation, working with the seed, with the responsible person within. They may come back with, 'That doesn't ring bells with me', and then I ask, 'What *does* ring bells?' To say, 'Right, beech trees are the norm this year' is to make every apple seedling sick. The only 'norm' I'm interested in is the straight, true growth of the original seed. How do we find that within the person? To map the potential of growth within the original seed, I work with *their* images, with *their* nature. Eventually, by evocation together of their own inner impulse, we can discover who they are, where they need to go, what their face was before they were born. Once they're evoked and helped in this way, even people who have had labels slapped on them begin to understand the nature of their own seed. They take a stand on their growth and affirm it, in many cases responding to the deeper reason of their own life in a much less adaptive and more whole way.

By keeping a steady hold within myself, I hope to give that steadying, loving hold to them. Then they can begin to discover that, whether or not they fit into their outer environment, sooner or later they will have to move towards their own 'applehood'. A lot of our work together is to do with *gardening*, a gentle working with the seasons, helping them become their own horticulturalists able to do their own pruning – if pruning there has to be. Had it been dropped down in the Garden of Eden the seed would have followed a straight growth, as we've seen, and become a healthy tree and borne fruit. But few were born in Eden – and if we had been, would we ever have left the Garden? The majority of us, rather, have had experiences that run counter to developing who we are. In the thrust of the struggle to become who we are (willy-nilly, because 'who we are' will not let us go) the seed within us grows stronger than the personality's resistance against it. In that struggle perhaps we learn. This is how we gain experience.

The gods of the nursery

So together the two of us begin to map their earlier life. And they see that their parents were gods! This is true for every child coming out of the nursery. They realise how, later, the gods held them back, becoming dragons who had to be fought. Those who genuinely like and love their parents find it very difficult to realise that they once found those loving people frightening, authoritarian, restrictive, repressive. Others, those who have seriously considered their parents dreadful, awful, need someone to stand in and help them face and confront how they felt about that. The womb, which at a certain point sucks back consciousness, is bound to be seen as the consuming, devouring sea-monster, or the hole in the earth which drags them down. However they felt about their actual mother, that is what the mother image can feel like. So I have to hold a bridge as they deal, not just with mother, but with the *image* of 'mother' at a much wider, more collective level.

Or the father. It isn't just their own father. Poor, pathetic man he may have been, yet to the very small child he might have appeared a great ogre, a tyrant. Again it can be very difficult to look at this *father image*. Feelings of should or shouldn't, ought or oughtn't – guilt and duty and love and despair – all constellate. And I hope to stand in at this level, holding it: 'Yes, and this is the human experience, throughout history.' If I know enough about myth, legend, folklore and the background history of other peoples; lives, I can say, 'It's all right to feel that way, it's quite natural. At a certain point your father – or mother – will come down to size.' So they are helped ultimately to see their parents as human beings struggling along like everyone else. Not monsters. Not gods. Then they begin to relate to them (and to other parental and authority figures 'out there') in a totally different way. While all that's being gone through, I aim to stand and hold the bridge.

The shadow

Up it will come. It can be very, very shaking for someone to face such realities in their own nature. It's then that our care, respect, humour, and trust in the process begin to show. Standing midway between consciousness and the unconscious, I hope to hold it together for the person till at last they can begin to accept and take on their own light and dark, their adaptation to the outer world and the corresponding inner side of their life. So often the shadow, the 'inferior' side, is our great strength. If we can incorporate it in our total persona, in our attitude to the world, we're much richer, deeper, wider and more real.

Masculine and feminine issues

These will inevitably arise in the onward movement of such in-depth work: the masculine and feminine energies in all life. How does our own gender affect us as an essential energy? How does the other gender? What ideas and sense of the personal masculine and feminine have come through our parents? How are we affected by their view of what is Man and what is Woman? And then, how do masculine and feminine interact within us? Are they in combat, quarrelling – or do they dance together? They need drawing out: what's appropriate to us, how do we stand within the stream of these great energies? Does our sexuality fall into line with the essential thrust of our own nature? Eventually, as Jung described, there's the bringing of the masculine and feminine together into a marriage within each person, a conjunction, a dance. What is the nature of that interaction, that conjunction? Out of it, the true identity of the individual can be born – or reborn – in a new way.

I shall be looking from a Transpersonal orientation at the psychological, psychotherapeutic levels of these things (of being the seed in an individual; of being a child handling the mother and the father and the images of Mother and Father; of the Shadow; of the Masculine and Feminine within) and asking, 'What is the meaning implicit in it?' The experience we've already had –where we've come from, the earlier patterns, the implications of childhood – are very significant. But with Jung, I would ask a question just as important in terms of meaning, destination, vocation, purpose: 'Where are we *going*?' What do we *do* with the experience? Where is it taking us?

Sooner or later the two of us will explore together the question: 'What is your God?' Who are the gods? Perhaps it isn't 'God' for them. It may be *lack* of god, lack of meaning, lack of love, lack of a sense of journey. For others, the journey at a deeper level is the most profound thing of all; without it, their personal life would be without meaning. When archetypal symbols come in, early, late or midway, I help the person not to be carried away. There's a tendency to be overcome by these great symbols, feeling we *are* Mahatma Gandhi or the Virgin

Mary or the Christ. Many feel this way! But that is to *identify* with the Archetype. To be able to *relate* to the Archetype is different. To catch and hold those moments when the Self itself speaks (perhaps with a small, quiet voice, perhaps with a great, thunderous boom which turns our world upside down) is to be put in touch with something very deep and very profound: a religious, a peak experience.

It's to be hoped someone will stand in there with us and help us keep our feet in the world, still relating to our practical, realistic outer life while coming to a new kind of reality on an inner level. As we look at the roots from which we've come and how they affect the ego as personality, we hope never to forget the journey of the Self, whose nature both overlies us and forms the strata beneath us. The two, the Seed and the Self, are side by side, two voices in harmony. *Life* is the great therapist. The best work I can do is to get rid of my clients, helping them out to become their own therapists, walking alongside with respect and love, being with them wherever they are on their journey in search of *their* meaning, their dignity. Then, even if they come to the conclusion that there is no meaning, no journey, they can accept that. The therapy becomes a time for comparing maps side by side, honouring the dignity of what belongs to them.

The wounded healer

For that, a special kind of person is needed as therapist : someone with respect and reverence for the process. Paracelsus, echoed by Jung, said that only the wounded physician can heal. It requires people who have struggled and are struggling with their own lives; not those who have it made and, thinking they are all right, say, 'Now it's time to go out and help all those suffering people who aren't all right'. What's wanted are people who've received a creative wound. It's to be hoped some scar-tissue has grown over; but they've been hurt in the front line of life. Having been in difficult situations, they sense what being in the client's shoes must be like. They too are still struggling with what it is to be a decent, reasonable, sane human being. It's very, very difficult to be intensely human, to stay linked with the human family.

And every sensitive and feeling person gets wounded. No child can leave that Paradise Garden and the innocence of Eden without being hurt in the process. It's the wound of being betrayed by paradise, put out of paradise; and the angel with the flaming sword stops you getting back in so that you can experience life in the outer world, and eventually come back to a different kind of paradise. Children come out of Eden; the child-like go back into it, but it's after a long journey and by a different gate. Some have the kind of wound that bleeds and makes them weaker, enfeebling them until they begin to die of it; they need a very special kind of loving and caring, cherishing and comforting and carrying forward. Others have received a wound which becomes the most creative thing that's ever happened to them, from which they can get up and grow, opening to become understanding of other people's needs. Themselves on the journey, with wounds which they are turning over to the creative side, they too need companions.

I would say, with Paracelsus and with Jung, that the great medium is love. This is not about challenging people and causing them to defend themselves, nor banging at their boundaries and making them interact with each other. That's very valid, very important, but it's not what I wish to do. Most people become less defensive, let their guard down and feel free in an environment of lovingness, of real love, tough love; not the sentiment of love but the energy. The most we can do for anyone is to give them an even greater connection with the Self than they had in the beginning. That I recognise as the work. To stand in the way of that is to fall short of the work. They go out still holding that; enriched, maybe, by more understanding.

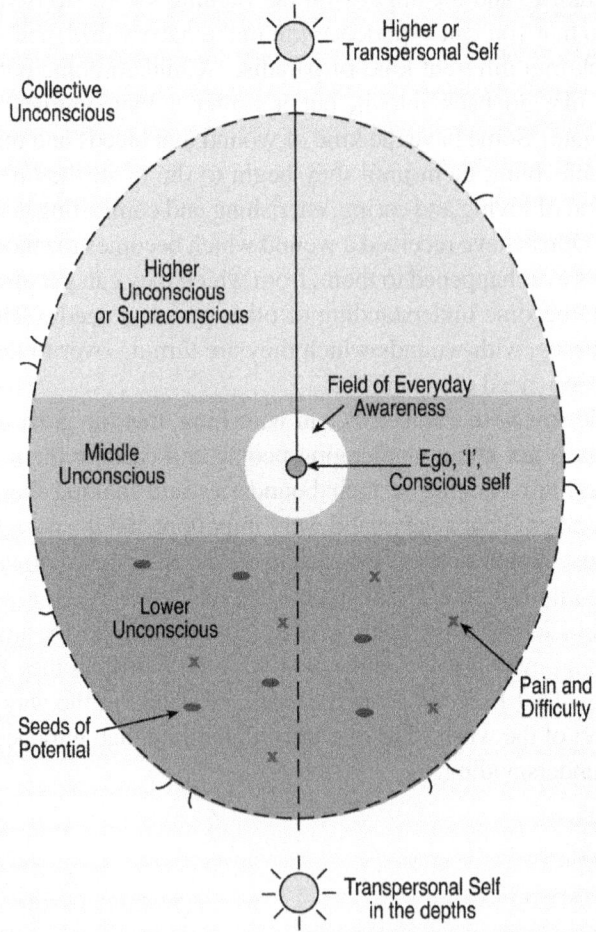

Figure 1   The Egg Diagram

CHAPTER TWO

Roots and Seeds
Barbara Somers

The Map is not the Country

This is adapted from Roberto Assagioli's egg-shaped diagram of the human being. He included the Lower Unconscious; the Field of Everyday Awareness in the Middle Unconscious, with the Persona and the Ego; up above lies the Higher Unconscious, or Supraconscious; and the map reaches out into the world : the hairy things are passages through the permeable membrane surrounding the individual egg, out into the Collective Unconscious. Assagioli mapped the Self at the top of the egg[1]. However, I would put the Transpersonal Self at the *bottom* as well. To make any real and vital sense, it's essential to have the Self also at the base, down through the Lower Unconscious.

How might our work of exploring it together (Transpersonal style) go? From the first meeting of client and counsellor we explore the outer world – how it is now for this particular person – and they bring their 'presenting problem'. Rarely can they define it exactly; if they could, they'd be more than half way to their answer. They give me the tip, and underneath lie the inner aspects of the problem. They may have trouble with recurrent negative patterns in relationships or with their own bad self-image; they may find it difficult to handle their job. Or they may say, 'Of course, I don't need counselling, but *he* does – she does'. People usually present matters of work, money, sex, relationship, personal and social bereavement, divorce, redundancy; or they bring depression, anxiety, psychosomatic factors. Many come in seeking the nature of who they are, their identity, and the nature of their journey. And we agree a contract to work with each other.

Listening at the level at which they present it, I do an initial mapping. I know that behind the appearances in the outer world lie all the levels available to an individual. The deeper we penetrate, the more we move from the objective outer into the subjective inner world.

---

[1]   See Assagioli, 1975, Page 17 .

The persona

At first the person will be talking from their ego or everyday self, the everyday I, the 'me' of the moment; and they'll be talking through their *persona*. Jung chose the word 'persona' for the outer mask; it comes from *personare*, 'to sound through'.[2] A beautifully-chosen word, it's the compromise between the demands of the outer environment and the inner structural needs of the individual. Greek actors would put their Etruscan masks before their faces; then a young man could play an old man, talking with his young voice yet holding an old man's mask in front of him. The persona is that bit of ourselves that we present to the world, the roles we play, the multiple faces we turn in various directions. These masks almost inevitably come up first, and appropriately so; we all need them as some sort of protection, so that the raw nature and truth of our being aren't immediately presented to everyone. It's a beautiful image of how we adapt to the outer world so that the inner self which lies behind can communicate.

I wonder what the pure and living inner spirit of a human being would be like if there weren't a mask over it? When Arjuna asked Sri Krishna to drop the veils from his face, which Sri Krishna obligingly did, Arjuna saw an abyss there – a chasm, and depths, and chaos and worlds and universes – and he very hastily asked him to put back his veils! At all levels we need our masks which make for natural interchange at a social level.[3]

A well-functioning persona accommodates in three ways: firstly, it has some bearing on how the inner person would like to appear in the outer world. Most of us have an outer mask that we like to present; this persona has to do with the needs and requirements of our particular time and space in history, our adaptation to our social environment. Some of us fight against it and wear the mask of rebel; some of us go with it and wear an

---

2 *Persona*, a mask used by an actor, a personage, character played by an actor, a person.
   Personare, to sound through; the large-mouthed mask of the actor was named from the voice sounding through it. Skeat, Concise Etymological Dictionary. Ed.

3 It's possible to map this with someone, exploring :
       the 'ideal image';
       the undervalued self-image;
       the overvalued self-image;
       how I would like to appear to others;
       how I do appear to others – or appear to appear to others –
       both in ways I like and ways I resent;
       what others try to make me into.
   And then, shaking them all off, to experience the freedom of that; and finally to get down to a real, a realistic, self-image.

accommodating one.

Secondly, the persona has to have some relevance to the physical and psychological capacities and limitations of the individual who wears it. Some try to wear masks which are unbelievably unfitting and get themselves into a fine old mess; others wear masks vastly *less* than they are inwardly capable of and thereby limit themselves.

And thirdly, everybody needs masks because they are the prime mode of communication, defending our vulnerable inner side and also making a mode of contact with the outer world.

The mask needs to be removable; a reasonably well-hung-together, healthy human being can take off the persona when they want. Some people can drop them and go very, very deep straight away. Some are plainly at home with themselves and can turn on different faces, show facets of themselves, adopt just for the moment the mode they choose to adopt and drop it at will. These are in pretty good nick. But others become chameleons, raising too many forms, changing faces immediately on the demand of the outer world. This is different from having the flexibility to choose, then drop, the mask.

Still others are rammed firmly into the one persona they wear; it's practically welded into the face they had before they were born. There are any number of reasons why a person gets stuck in the thing so it becomes rigid and inflexible and can't be removed at will. Take for example the teacher who's a teacher not only during the day, but in bed, on holiday, everywhere. Very often the person thinks they *are* the mask. Locked into their persona, into the outer world, they have no flexibility, no meeting, no intercourse at any deep or harmonious or flowing level with other people. They do everything in terms of their role, their function – their mask.[4]

A lot of my work lies in helping to make this persona less rigid; it needs to be flexible, adaptable, removable at will, just another skin. How far is it inhibiting the person's growth and need for change? Are those masks needed *now*? Sickness or health can be mapped in many ways, but the rigidity and immoveability of the persona is a very good

---

[4]   Jolande Jacobi has written that getting stuck in the persona can lead to the atrophying of innate potential, identifying with the image rather than with inner reality.   Then the personality stays repressed, undifferentiated and suffused with something almost menacing. This suppression leads invariably at mid-life to the risk of psychic disorder, whereas a persona that fits well is a key to inner health, enabling us to function well in the environment. See Jacobi, 1942, Page 30.

key to the state they're in. If it's fitting too tightly there's a dissonance between the outer person we see and the inner person we sense. Behind the authoritarian thunderer, for instance, we're aware of the original, shrinking individual who, wishing to put on that mask, got stuck in the wretched thing. There's total dissonance between inner and outer.

The more the mask is stuck, the more they are afraid to remove it, the more the person inside will be cowering. Ultimately it will run them, playing merry hell with every relationship. A person so stuck (the changeless expression, the same voice coming through) sees, like the Greek actor, through one eye-slit, not perceiving the incredible change and fluidity, the flow and the harmony of the world, nor the reality of other people. They see a masked world, and everybody else masked too. As the years go by and they become more withdrawn from outer reality, so the persona becomes more and more brittle. Perhaps they pass over into a breakdown – or maybe everyone around comes to recognise they're trapped in a neurosis.

So I *stand* with them, helping create an area of trust, holding a dialogue with the person who lies behind the persona until they choose to let it go. One of the marvels of imaging is that the person first holds up then puts down their mask. And they can be frightened if it's a rigid one. Because the inner, natural development has been cut back and unable to push through, there is a very vulnerable human being inside. They're shocked to the roots of their fundamental being by the face they suddenly see behind their own persona. Somebody who puts an enormous amount of energy into, say, being always good-natured and kind will be absolutely horrified when faced with their own anger and rage and violence and hatred.

One of the most tender and loving things I can do is to hold first one side and then the other until the two begin to come together, and what the person sees as the 'good' and the 'bad' begin to merge; then the light and the dark come together and are seen as two sides of one face. I say, 'There is neither good nor bad. There's inner and outer, there's light and dark, and it is a wholeness. If you didn't have the power to hate, you wouldn't have the power to love.' I help people accept the polarity within their own nature. It's beautiful to see how, even if they're 'very very good' and 'very very kind', after a while they will drop that front. And when they begin to face this, I pick on a growth-motif within them: 'Who are you when you're really *you*? What does it feel like?' I help anchor them to that. Then, more and more, they go out with a stance, an attitude to the world, to relationships, to people, which allows something of their light *and* their dark to come up at the same time. Then they don't always have to 'be good'; they can take a stand and speak up for themselves, recognising that in always being helpful or supportive they might be cutting back another person's development.

It may be long and slow; it can also be a very quick process. The images bring with them the energy necessary for the person to drop the persona. The moment they accept that it's just a mask, the moment they see their other face, they've already constellated that energy. For instance, one woman in a guided daydream felt herself to be in a hard shell. It was in the musculature: she held herself stiffly with a very rigid spine, the heroic, good person raising her head above all calamity, all the time, never going down into it. She considered it a very, very strong screen produced over many years by herself and other people. Then came a beautiful image: she heard a tap, and there was a woodpecker pecking at the screen. Recently married, she realised the woodpecker's eyes were those of her husband, who had contributed much to her seeing that the old persona was no longer necessary. A wonderful experience and realisation, there in a second.

The map is not the country, but the work is to reconstellate the images that come from every one of its levels, gathering them to a point or focus which ultimately becomes a reflection of the Self. Images come down from all times, all places; they come out of a consistent stream into the therapeutic flask of the work between the two of us. They may be poured down from the level of the ego, the 'I' who wears the persona; or from the Shadow. They may come from the masculine and feminine energies – the inner man and inner woman, the animus and anima – who pour down their own symbols and need to be taken into account as we look not just at the parents but at the person's *images* of the parents. Sooner or later, willy-nilly, from a still deeper level, the gods (the meaning and nature of the Transpersonal Self) begin to rain down the archetypal symbols which, underlying everything, hold that person's own myth and meaning.

Wouldn't it be marvellous if it happened just in that nice neat order! Of course, it doesn't. But eventually, if the work is well-rounded, the person begins to see the pattern of their lives, perceiving what has happened to them in a wider context. The more we bring the images into consciousness, map them back, gather them together, the more we constellate the Self within. When at last the ego begins to reflect that other Self, a line connecting the ego in the outer world and the Self at the inward level is drawn. It's to be hoped that, out there in the world, they sense the nature of the Self that has always been with them. Then inner and outer meaning begin to come together to make a round, a whole.

The ego

From the mask turned to the outside world, we move on to the wearer of the mask, to what Jung called the 'ego', the personality, the self with a small 's'. If we posit that it is the Self with a large S that is incarnating here as this individual, then it is the Self which is the arbiter of that individual 'me'. The little ego doesn't have the Self: *the Self has the small personality*, the 'I', the ego, to work through.

To understand the nature of the ego, I ask, 'Is the wearer of the persona at ease with him or herself, in good relation to the personality, the body, the mind, the feelings?' If not, disease, dysfunction and psychosomatic factors often show, because the one who wears the mask is at odds with the mask itself. We look at sub-personalities, often using Gestalt approaches, to explore the interaction between body, mind and feeling. We see how the body sometimes has to carry the dysfunction or gap between how we present ourselves in the outside world, and who we are behind those masks. Our medical history often reveals our life-story – and the life-story can reveal the medical approaches that may be required.

The shadow

Behind the persona and the ego lies the exact correlate, the balancing, compensatory side of consciousness, known in Jungian terminology as the *shadow*.

The shadow is that other face that lies behind both the mask *and* the personality, the complementary yet unknown part of us, the mirror-image. Where there's positive, there's also negative; where there's negative, there's positive. Passing through the presenting problems from the outside world, the person begins to make a confrontation with this opposite within. Looking in the mirror, they see a dark face looking back out at them, not the bright, light one they'd hoped for. They recognise that when they said, 'It's not me who needs counselling, it's him or her!' they were projecting on to the other. They see it's themselves they need to look at. This can be very frightening, even terrifying, confusing, bewildering, shaming, humiliating; their judgmental side can get in there, saying, 'I *shouldn't* feel like this, I oughtn't to feel like this! Why do I feel like this?' It's now that, listening, I need to come up to full stature.

One of my most glorious memories is of a highly intellectual woman who took everything up through her head. She dreamt consistently of a dreadful smelly old lady who followed her around – a real old drunken hag. The dreamer would be in a train going to her office or to give a lecture and 'sniff, sniff', lo and behold, there was this wicked old woman. She would follow the dreamer into the London Underground and on to the platform and start throwing off her garments. 'Suppose they think this dreadful old lady belongs to me!' She didn't see the point of the dreams. 'Absolutely ridiculous, totally meaningless! She's nothing to do with me.'

I said, 'Well, she does seem to have *something* to do with you, doesn't she?' By not myself rejecting the smelly old lady, I gently drew to this woman's attention that the image was coming not from anybody else, but out of her own psyche. 'Why not draw the old lady?' To anchor the motif by drawing it is to release the energy within it. To start with she refused. I accepted that this was her view at that moment, but when the dream turned up again and again, we set up a dialogue with it: 'What does it mean to you?' 'I couldn't ever bear to *talk* to a woman like that,' she said. 'Why does she keep haunting me?'

It's a holding process. I held the two together, drawing her attention to it, till she had to recognise and accept the possibility that the old woman was to do with *her*. She dreamed she had a dinner party for the people she considered most important, those she was trying most to impress; they were horrified when in came this dear old lady and climbed on to the table and began to dance the fandango. In another dream the smelly old woman was a laundress knocking at the dreamer's door and inviting her to put out any dirty washing. Sometimes the dreamer was hiding the old lady, shoving her into broom cupboards and up in attics. In one, the police walked in. Making a very rude sign to them, the old lady nipped out through the back door, leaving the dreamer stuck with the Law, trying to shield the wretched old thing.

We mapped her associations to the dream, drawing out what was relevant. 'Could there be an aspect of your nature that's trying to draw your attention to itself?' I used amplification, widening the framework of her individual associations to her own images. (It's to be hoped that the more we know of myth, legend, fairy tale, the more it helps. Widening the interconnections, linking the individual's particular experience with the whole of human history, can stop them feeling quite so alienated and isolated as many do.) This led her to look at her relationship to the world.

Another side of her nature was playful, laughing. Gently I passed books over to her. She began seeking things to help her understand. Highly intelligent, she couldn't help but see what some of her attitudes to authority had been. Had not a great deal of her life been locked off from her? She'd almost lost the ability to say what she really felt without worrying about 'them' and what 'they' felt.

So the old woman made the dreamer listen and hear her. Very early this dreamer had learned that 'everything that is instinctual and natural is dirty'. A part of her was being manifest and she couldn't get away. She came to see it as her 'shadow'. After a while, she and her shadow began to get on rather well. In yet another dream she opened her handbag and the old woman took out an egg and held it out to her. Then in a most beautiful dream, still keeping an eye open in case anyone saw them, they danced together. In private they were making friends. Through those images this very intellectual woman began to realise how much her own instinctual and feeling life had been cut away from her. She still behaved herself in public, but became far more real in private. And the old lady, starting out so smelly, degree by degree threw off her various veils and proved herself a wise person with a great deal to say. Her wisdom helped this person make relationships with men and her friendships have improved tremendously.

Jung said that it is essential to have your Shadow with you when you approach the mountain. He himself saw the shadow as being deeply positive, as well as negative. It's very often the strength of the shadow that makes us real. If we are all light and surface, without shadow, we are two-dimensional, not safe to be let out. In ancient cultures somebody who hadn't got a shadow was looked at very carefully: they might be a witch or a sorcerer. 'Only a ghost casts no shadow', said Jung. The trouble is that people who are striving hard and legitimately towards the path of light also cast longer shadows; the greater the light, the longer the shadow. But the shadow most definitely has a positive element.

Our work is concerned with the enrichment of the shadow, so that we become three-dimensional, not cardboard cutouts. The shadow is that which is *not in the light*, the full light of consciousness. In the Egg map

(Figure 1, page 10) it's associated with the lower unconscious. As we've seen, it is both positive and negative. It isn't just the correlate of the light, the repressed area, the unlived life, the pain which can no longer be held up in everyday consciousness and so has been pushed down into the lower unconscious. It also contains the seeds of that individual's very new potential which hasn't yet *been* up in consciousness. Where Freud called the lower unconscious the 'subconscious', I think of it as a compost bin; the rubbish put down into it recycles into very good compost. The seeds of new potential lying there can begin to sprout, growing in the darkness as seeds do in winter.

Suppose for example, as their way of getting around the world, someone is presenting the mask of clown, comic; what then of the inner? Suppose another is highly intellectually orientated, even tunnel-visioned about it; what about their undeveloped feelings? Are those coming out as sentiment, rather than being deeply felt? Suppose a third is too over-giving and sacrificial; what about their resentment? Are they feeling used, a victim? 'What about me?' Suppose yet another is concentrating so hard on being good and 'spiritual' that they're hardly fit for this world; what about the rigid, unloving, fanatical other side? It may be both a strength and a weakness, but it's in the shadow. A balancing out of the conscious and the unconscious cusps is needed: for the outwardly gentle, what about the inwardly raging; for the outwardly raging, what about the inwardly gentle?

As we've seen, a number of shadow figures personify not only repressed, unknown factors but also our new potential. The image is of something we long ago possessed but lost somewhere on the journey. It's lain quiescent, dormant through many years, sometimes through life, never surfacing before. Seeds of this new potential may just be coming into life, gathering energy in the unconscious, in the shadow side of ourselves. We'll see later that, if that potential has been blocked, the images can appear dwarfed, cut-back, misshapen, undeveloped, immature. Unlived life, thwarted growth, missed opportunities, unacceptable impulses and attitudes, all are muddled in together, not yet known in the light of consciousness. That's why they're called 'the shadow'.

I don't map the seeds of potential up in the supraconscious part of the picture; I put them down with what isn't yet in consciousness. The map is a continuum. Because it's two-dimensional, we sometimes miss the fact that there's continuous interaction between the lower unconscious and the supraconscious. The seeds of the new potential, down in the lower unconscious and yet to emerge, are drawn up by the energies of the supraconscious. The supraconscious is eternal, supernal; it reaches out into our whole being. The power of the Transpersonal Self is pouring into it all the time; presumably it much overbalances the lower unconscious.

I assume that the lower unconscious is part of the personal past of the individual; if it were possible to map the *whole* of their past, it would fill the whole of the lower unconscious. And there's a continuous feeding into the *collective* unconscious, which is endlessly refilling itself. That's why when people ask, 'How long will this work last?' the straight answer is, 'For ever'. No sooner have we worked through someone's personal unconscious than we begin on the collective unconscious –perhaps at the same time. In fact there's no end to it. But I'd hope to reply, 'Two or three years' – none of that nonsense of seventeen, eighteen, thirty years!

If a major block occurs, there's bound to be a certain amount of adaptation in the development of the individual, so that they can survive. The majority of us have had inevitably to adapt to our conditioning and we can adjust quite a lot without doing basic damage to ourselves.

What I find amazing, even artistic, in people is the degree to which they can accommodate. Even when our own natural growth has been almost completely blocked, we still hearken back to something within that knows how we're 'meant' to be. All right, we lose touch for a bit, but something helps to keep us to a straightish growth. Whether we have a reasonable, good enough environment – good enough parents, good enough help – or get bruised and bumped early on, or along the road, we still keep travelling. I think it's quite amazing how many people manage to come up into consciousness with relatively clear growth. From the lower unconscious they emerge into the everyday world where the personality is, managing remarkably well to approximate to who they truly are. Maybe they need nothing more than a little gentle, supporting affirmation – a little *gentling* –to recognise it and to take a stand on it. It isn't easy to be who you are.

Most psychologists have taken it that what's in the lower unconscious is suppressed, repressed and undeveloped material, that which is not acceptable to consciousness, all that we aren't – or don't want to be – in touch with. Indeed, the whole of Freud's psychology was involved in mapping that area of the lower unconscious. In analysis he would go back to the infantile stage, to the memories and locked-up traumas imprinted in the lower unconscious.[5]

Jung saw no reason to argue with that, but he did argue with what he saw as the over-emphasis on the idea that the child is simply open to, subject to, its conditioning. He felt that there was a factor in each person which could overcome their underlying conditioning; an innate quality in a uniquely individual seed. The conditioning of childhood is an overlay on the original, unique individual whom we are right from the beginning. The whole thrust of Jung's work goes towards this. He believed that we come from somewhere and go to somewhere. It's an excellent image. It's the lower area, which Assagioli terms the lower unconscious and Freud the subconscious, that Jung calls the shadow (as we've seen, 'that which is not yet in the light'). He saw that there's a shadow which is personal to the individual and also a shadow that's collective, which an individual shares with common human experience. Although there will be moments, early or late in our work together, when the collective shadow emerges, we're usually dealing with the personal shadow.

Neurosis and Psychosis

There's a lot said about neurosis and psychosis. What are they? Every healthy person has had to adapt, as we've seen, but some people have been so wounded, either early on or through later trauma, that their natural growth, pushed right away from its pattern, hasn't been allowed at all (Figure 2, overleaf). Some have had both a major early blockage and more pain or bruising later. Still the hurt shoot struggles up into everyday consciousness, though by all sorts of zigzags and turns and accommodations and movements. It may have come out into consciousness with a somewhat unexpected-looking growth; indeed, the shoot may look like a withered weed and give little indication of the 'appleness' of its nature. Then, too often, the person has these nice little labels slapped on: 'neurotic', 'psychotic'.

Somebody with a *neurosis* has enough ego-structure to lead a

---

[5] Alfred Adler was concerned with the will to overcome within each individual; the degree to which this was blocked by the parent constituted the original trauma of the child. In each case, the person was seen as an amalgam of body and emotions, at the mercy of their conditioning and their environment and of the traumas of childhood. Freud, on the other hand, put a great deal of stress on the child's sexual desire for the parent of the opposite sex. So too did Melanie Klein and Winnicott. This was one of the major differences and points of departure between Freud and Jung. Freud, the Kleinians and the post-Freudians tended to see the lower unconscious as negative *per se*.

relatively normal everyday life, except for the particular area of their 'complex', which is mapped down in the lower unconscious and can be triggered in the external world. The person manages reasonably well

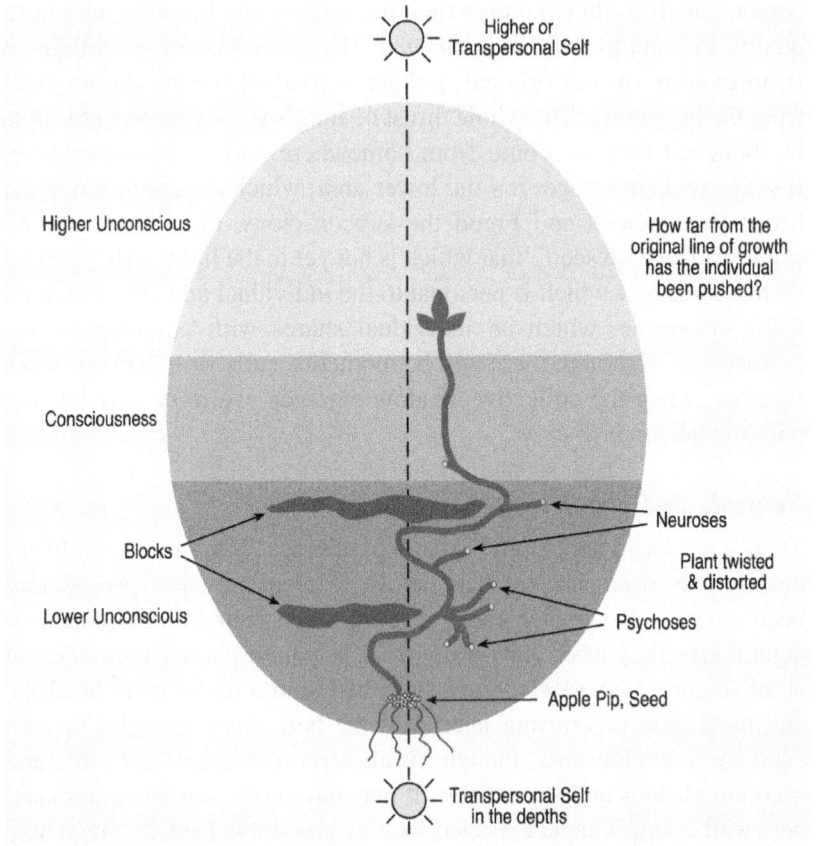

Figure 2   Wounds and Blocks

except when something sets off that complex within. Then it manifests as a neurosis. Somebody with a *psychosis*, on the other hand, has had such a degree of wounding or dysfunction, has had to adapt so far away from their own nature, that they are never able to build in enough ego-structure to hold them as a personality in the everyday world. They are the more caught down because so much of their energy is trapped back into the unconscious. Ego-strength would have helped them to emerge, but they haven't enough, they can't hold, they're inundated by their unconscious and it manifests as a psychosis.[6]

It is the inappropriate degree to which the shoot has been bent away that has caused the withering of the growth. To map the neurosis as an adaptation away from the straight growth of the seed, and the psychosis as the result of being pushed even further over – this is new thinking.

The labels 'neurotic' and 'psychotic' are often applied to those considered to be merely 'deviating from the norm'. I want to help get rid of these labels, which are absolutely meaningless. We have *people*. Under certain circumstances they react with what could be termed 'neurotic tendencies'. Then we can say, 'That's a person with a neurotic tendency'. But there's no such thing as 'a neurotic'. Equally, some people have been pushed into responding to the environment in a way that could be described as 'psychotic'; but there's no such thing as 'a psychotic'. They are just people.

This is how the majority of us grow: in certain areas we're hung up and when something is triggered we respond as we did at an earlier stage – we react like small children. We can grow up reasonably healthy and yet carry with us areas of adaptation abnormal to the true seed. Someone may, for instance, have been blocked by some figure of authority, perhaps a very strong father who, coming on heavy, prevented the natural growth of the child. The individual will have adapted to some extent but, growing towards adulthood, still have powerful feelings about authority. Certain conditions will trigger old memories of the father of their childhood. Then suppose, from that environment heavy with authority, they pick up another authority figure later – at school, perhaps. They may adapt even further away from their own growth. The normal reaction becomes abnormal; they respond that way to *any* authority figure. It has a very powerful pack, quite unlike an ordinary, healthy reaction. It flowers up into the everyday world as a neurotic reaction, and if it comes to dominate the life of the individual it can indeed be the beginning of a neurosis, triggered by any father-like figure.

---

6   To define it clinically: a neurosis is where the adaptation is abnormal under certain circumstances; a psychosis is where there's no ego structure, and somebody responds inappropriately to the environment the whole time. So someone with a neurosis responds inappropriately – at times. There's a trigger, energy needed for life is drawn down as it were magnetically to the original block, and they respond as if they were back in the past, rather than as they are now. Usually they adapt to their environment and it doesn't show – but under certain circumstances, it shows. And we aim to root the original seed right back, planting its roots down into the earth again.

Transpersonally, a neurosis may be seen as an adaptation which let us survive when we were bent away from our natural growth. If somebody who has a neurosis has an inappropriate response in certain conditions, reacting to certain people or things in a neurotic way, then our work is the narrowing of the gap between the natural response and the adapted response. We need to be able to see the particular line of growth their innate seed would have followed, and discover together how the adaptation they had to make pushed them away. Then they can see how they're now responding inappropriately. The Transpersonal aspect is that we develop a feeling for what is innate to the individual and what is adaptation enabling them to survive.

And it seems the psyche has a vested interest in getting the original seed to grow as it's meant to (see Figure 4, page 50) and any bending away is mediated through our images. These images are continuously being poured up to us from the lower unconscious, and not always via dreams or visualisations; images in films or books may grip us, something someone says may catch us.

There are other people who had such damage early on, such bruising, such wounding, such denial of who they were and so little chance to explore it, that the *root* growth of their nature began to get distorted. Lacking roots, they haven't really given themselves a sense of everyday awareness, nor put up into consciousness a shoot that even appears to approximate to who they really are; it's got turned over and sent back into the unconscious. We might draw them as pale green and drooping, pushed far from a straight, natural growth, far from their own innate, individual strength. Somebody with such psychosis has no ego-centre to rely on. They need a lot of cherishing, careful, loving work to help them rebuild the area wounded so early.[7]

It's going to take a lot of work, perhaps a number of lifetimes, to help people who have been labelled 'psychotic' to come back to who they were and are, to the stream of their lives. Yet it could be that in their so-called 'psychosis' is a normality and a strength and a vivid artistry which is all about the future. Some people labelled 'schizophrenic' may actually have an understanding yet to come into being, their language already

---

[7] Counsellors are unwise to deal with psychosis; it's too deep for a counsellor's abilities unless they're very, very gifted. It's the work of an analyst, and a highly skilled one at that. However, many counsellors can act as psychotherapists, even working quite analytically with unconscious factors in people who, except in certain areas where they begin to respond neurotically, do adapt reasonably well to everyday life.

drawing in the new images. In society, and I'm afraid too often in some of the therapies, we're dealing with the assumption that people need to be helped to ;readjust to the norm'. They're labelled 'abnormal' in terms of the so-called 'sane' world. But if the norm itself is insane, as in many ways it is, where does that leave them?

The majority of people seeking help are not 'psychotic', though there will be a certain amount of distortion somewhere in their growth. The health and wholeness within may also include pathology, yet pathology is *not* a necessary part of the journey. Health is wholeness; the seed was sound in the beginning. Maybe they've discovered themselves – maybe they've come in for reinforcement of the journey. Most of the work is about love, self-respect, the dignity of the human spirit. It lies in helping them to re-attune, affirming and strengthening them in taking a stand on who they *know* themselves to be.

Our ability as therapists and counsellors lies in our always working to re-attune *ourselves*, align ourselves more and more with who we are. We need courage to take responsibility for that, take a stand on it. Do we otherwise have the right to be out there? If ever we think we have the answer for another human being – or indeed for ourselves – we'd better pack it up and go and do something different. For, as we saw, we too are wounded. The concept of the Wounded Healer has so much become part of common jargon that we forget the implicit meaning behind it: the wound is valuable. It's the *wound that heals*, the wound that teaches, the wound that keeps us on our journey.

Contents of the shadow

Let's have a look at some of the contents of the unconscious, the shadow part of us. How do figures usually emerge from the shadow? We become most aware of them through dreams and active imagination. Images from the shadow often bring us messages about how what has happened to us has affected our natural growth and how we may have been forced to adapt away.

Rejected attitudes

Freud pointed out that these are held down in the lower unconscious. If, through the environment and conditioning of the past, parts of ourselves have become unacceptable to us, then we will have rejected them and figures telling us so will come up in dreams or imaging, or as sub-personalities. Exploring them through images we find thieves, dropouts, tramps, drunks, neglected animals, plants, children, objects, all telling us about our rejected, unacceptable attitudes, bringing out a side of ourselves which we prefer not to accept into consciousness. So our rejected, unaccepted attitudes show as images of *neglect*. The old woman in the dreams described above couldn't have been a more 'shadow' figure for the dreamer and yet in the exploration she represented the rejected and unacceptable attitudes of her own childhood, ready for befriending.

Unlived Life

Next we come to motifs which include anything maimed, dying, or dead. For also down here in the Shadow is the life we haven't lived, our undeveloped aspects for which no space was allowed. Here are bits of ourselves that were left behind; we didn't live them out at the time because they were too painful, or because we were totally unaware of them. Again, we were apple seeds dropped down where everybody around was an oak, and trying very hard to be oak trees too. The parts that weren't lived out were not developed and were abandoned often at a relatively primary, primitive level. They appear as crippled, dying, damaged things. Anything cut back – dwarfs, hunchbacks, gnomes; dreams of darkness, trapped places, helplessness, loss of the use of feet or hands or tongue or eyes; dreams or images of maimed children, crippled animals, damaged birds or trees or plants – all have to do with undeveloped aspects and unlived life.

A woman had a dream of a corpse and a robin. It's the most beautiful example I know of the seed speaking to a person of their unlived life and undeveloped aspects. She came to me in her fifties; since she was twenty-two she'd been having a recurrent and frightening nightmare. Of Jewish extraction, she'd been a child in Europe under the Nazis. Before she was three, all the people in her young scene had vanished one by one. She later discovered they'd gone into the gas chambers. The entire family was wiped out except for one aunt who was only fifteen or sixteen, little more than a child herself. She'd managed to get this little girl into the underground and out through Europe, across the sea and into England. By the time she was four she'd arrived with her young aunt in an alien country with an alien language, cut off from all their roots. Her later childhood and adolescence was spent in one room with her aunt, a single tap on the landing and a shared lavatory; and night after night she would wake from sleep to hear her aunt weep and weep and weep – waking to this endless weeping. A terrible background.

She pulled herself up by the bootstraps and managed to get herself very well placed in the Civil Service. But such a large part of her was locked back into the pain of the past that she was really a shell of a person. Together we worked through her persona and her ego. She'd managed excellently in areas involving work and she showed a very commendable front to the world. But the moment she came into a relationship, because of all the disappearances from her life and because most of her energy was still locked back with that endless weeping, her own sense of poverty and inner emptiness rose up and she felt there was no hope for her.

To add to it all, when she was twenty-two, up came this nightmare. She dreamt, not of a nice clean skeleton but of a decaying, rotting corpse coming out of the grave with the grave-clothes hanging from it, and it stood at the end of her bed. She would wake up sweating all over, sometimes screaming, horrified at this awful thing. And for the previous eighteen months, since she'd been coming to me, the thing had not just stayed at the end of the bed – it had begun to come close! Grinning and leering it would move nearer, leaning over her.

And then it began to appear in the daytime, emerging in her imaging as a sub-personality. 'Am I going mad?' she asked me. It was horrible dealing with that corpse: she was so absolutely averse to it. But we stayed with that one motif. Getting her to relate to it, and by degrees visualise it – having to work from the feet towards the centre of it – well! And eventually she was able to confront it, even approach it – I won't say 'befriend' it, but at least to set up some sort of dialogue with it, if only by looking at it. And finally she was able to visualise herself putting her hand out and touching it. And what was her horror when it collapsed and she could see inside it! And suddenly there was something inside....

It was a robin sitting on a nest of eggs. It said to her, 'Why did you keep me waiting all this time? I couldn't have kept these eggs warm much longer if you hadn't come to me now – at last!' By degrees her robin – and it was *her* robin – told her what was in the eggs and why they were there: 'Whatever happened to your music? You once thought you'd like to play an instrument –' She certainly loved music, but it was ages since she'd so much as listened to any. 'What happened to your love of art? Just to look at paintings once gave you a sense of fullness, when you felt so empty inside; but you never do that now. Why don't you occasionally go to the country, as you used to? Once, you thought you might like to make friendships, but you don't do it.'

The robin showed her that she was jeopardising her whole future, missing out on the essential nature of herself and her various talents. Music, friendship, relating, art – all and more – the robin had kept alive for her in the eggs. The robin became distinctly more forceful as it showed her these things, saying to her in its own language (which came out of *her* psyche), 'It is not you who are empty. The emptiness is because you will not let go of the dead past. You are using it as a defence against making approaches to people, against opening up to music and to feeling. It is you who won't let the corpse go back into the grave and rot away; it's you who's kept raising it out of the grave. It's you who keeps bringing that motif into your life.' It was a great moment when I said, 'Whatever happened to the corpse?' and she said, 'Oh that – it blew away in the wind, but you see there's this *robin*...' It was her scene, her robin, her egg.

We started our work together by looking not at human relationship but at her relationship to music and art. Later, we moved a little towards the interfaces of friendship, till she could take the first difficult steps. Without any question, because of the pain and the degree of block within her, she would always have the greatest difficulty in relating. For her, relationship meant total commitment: somebody out there had to rescue her from her past and her past from her. Otherwise she didn't dare take the risk at all. Her robin helped her, step by step, to walk this very difficult bridge.

A normal human approach has a great deal to commend it, given that we're working on ourselves and aware of our own unconscious hassle (for instance, we may be anxious for the person to get well, or to be successful). Our ability without fear to hold the tension of light-dark, good-evil is terribly important, infinitely more important than anything we may say. It's our quality of being able to face whatever may come. That horrible, hideous corpse eventually showed the robin. When she was describing it to me I really had to centre myself to stop the horror that she felt, which was practically in the room. I could smell that corrupting flesh, I could see that corpse as she described it to me – the damn thing was standing between the two of us! But later she said that the quality I had of 'not looking disturbed by it' was very important to her. Our acceptance of such things is very often the first threshold; cross it, and we're working equally with the person and the image.

Unresolved conflicts

These, too, are down in the shadow. They aren't always our own conflicts; they can be inherited. They tend to come up in images that attack: attacking animals, thugs, burglars, break-ins, situations with overtones of violence, danger, fear. This kind of image has a very powerful feeling of energy, unlike the passive feeling of unlived life. There's a lot of energy in attack and defence. Impotence to act or be able to do anything about it may be there: immobilisation, entrapment, but with violent implications.

I knew one very mild man, an architect of about fifty, a truly *gentle* man, for whom violent films had a horrible fascination. He never missed the latest James Bond. He couldn't bear to watch when the real violence set in, disappearing frequently to the gents, but he saw 'Jaws', and he saw 'Dracula'. He said, 'If it were pornography in Soho I could understand it; but it's the local flea-house. I hate these films, but I can't keep away!' He didn't have dreams, or said he didn't; but the images were flashing at him from the television and the cinema screen and he couldn't escape.

James Bond eventually helped him make the breakthrough! It took ages, but in the end he saw that his own anger was attacking him. He'd been living out of old scripts, playing out in current life the impotence he'd felt in his childhood. He'd had a very difficult environment. His parents were very good, which is not 'good enough' – they were too good by half. They'd given a gentle, quiet message: 'We never lose our tempers here; we never say anything that isn't nice.' Never allowed to voice anything natural to him, from birth he was in a place where nothing can grow – it has to try and adapt. The message was, 'Placate people, particularly authority figures; live outside and behind the scenes; never let it be seen who you are.' Everybody was very kind to him but he knew that if he didn't adapt he was going to be rejected and unacceptable. How can a child under five allow himself to be rejected and unacceptable? He'd be sawing off the very branch on which he was nested.

Despite the push to 'be good' and buy his place in the world, the environment was fortunately reasonable enough to allow some ego-strength to build up. But he went on adapting, becoming extremely gentle. In his own home, later, nobody ever said what they felt either. If they really felt anything, they went away in a most gentlemanly fashion and dealt with it alone – like going to the lavatory.

And now, over and over, that is where he went. He couldn't hold it in any longer. When anybody even remotely triggered that original background he would go into spasms, rushing to the lavatory. His body, producing inflammation and digestive troubles, was helping him recognize how much he was being adaptive. He thought it was diarrhoea. But he was suffering from a rage and an unknown violence. He had to claim that unvoiced anger and make it his own, recognising that he had inherited the conflict; it was his parents', not his. (It's enough to have our own conflicts without taking on those of our parents. Yet a child very often becomes the container for their unresolved conflict and treats it as if it were his own.) He had to be helped to drop the burden.

If later this man had hit setbacks which again constellated that first authority-block, he might well have been pushed further away from his real growth and been in danger of developing a complex. With such a neurotic tendency he would have seen everywhere a blocking authority figure saying, 'You're only accepted if you're good!' Fortunately he didn't. He met a male teacher who did allow him to speak what he meant and felt, telling him, 'I didn't think you had it in you. Good for you!' He realised he could be acceptable even when he was being 'bad'. Thus he managed not to have a neurosis. Had it been otherwise he might well have done so, or even been pushed right over into psychosis.

How does someone in this situation deal with his parents in the present? If he's fifty, mother eighty, does he still have to adapt? Let's suppose she's a dreadful old crab, forthright, extremely down-to-earth, standing absolutely no nonsense either from him or from his father. Relatively, she's almost at death's door. What's he to do about her?

Oddly enough, he doesn't have to do anything about her. He sorts *himself* out. Learning to update his adaptive behaviour, being less caught in to his past relationship with her so that he stops reacting as if he were still a child, he begins to treat this elderly 'old bag' as an adult. Strangely, if people are related to as adults, they sometimes respond! She may be too far gone; perhaps this is her destiny for another lifetime, or the continuum of consciousness or whatever. But locked, blocked, impossible, irreconcilable knots do open up in the most extraordinary way when one of the elements moves towards the creative. The relationship is like an alembic, an alchemical flask in which a change in one element becomes a catalyst for change in others. We're dealing with his image of his mother, not with the mother herself; the task is to bring the image down to size. If, after talking with him for some while, I'd happened to meet his mother, I might have been astonished to find some innocuous little woman. And if she had indeed been an old bag, really draining him, and if he had in fact been living as if he were still in the nursery even though he was fifty, then wasn't it time he grew up, got out of the nursery and related to her as a human being?

Images of transformation

Another thing to look for is the transformation of new potential. Jung tells how images frequently come up which have to do with this transformation: the fairy-tale toad turns into a prince when kissed; the old washerwoman hands an egg to the dreamer (above). A fertile egg is very often a sign of transformation. So too are dreams of being pregnant, of crossroads, bridges, circular shapes, a butterfly, a white bird, a jewel, a living tree. Out of the lower unconscious come these images of potential which, when explored, take us back closer to the person's original growth. My aim is to help them get in touch with that shadow material, bring it into the light, befriend it and use the energies of it in current living.

So we help both the other and ourselves to accept the light *and* the shadow, the reality and importance of the outside world *and* the reality and importance of the inside world, until we realise that there is no difference between those two realities. The personality and the Self become one and the same. We can't rush the process, but we can say that the apple tree was already implicit within the apple pip. Jung believed that the whole process of individuation may be to bring us back to who we were in the beginning – plus the experience.

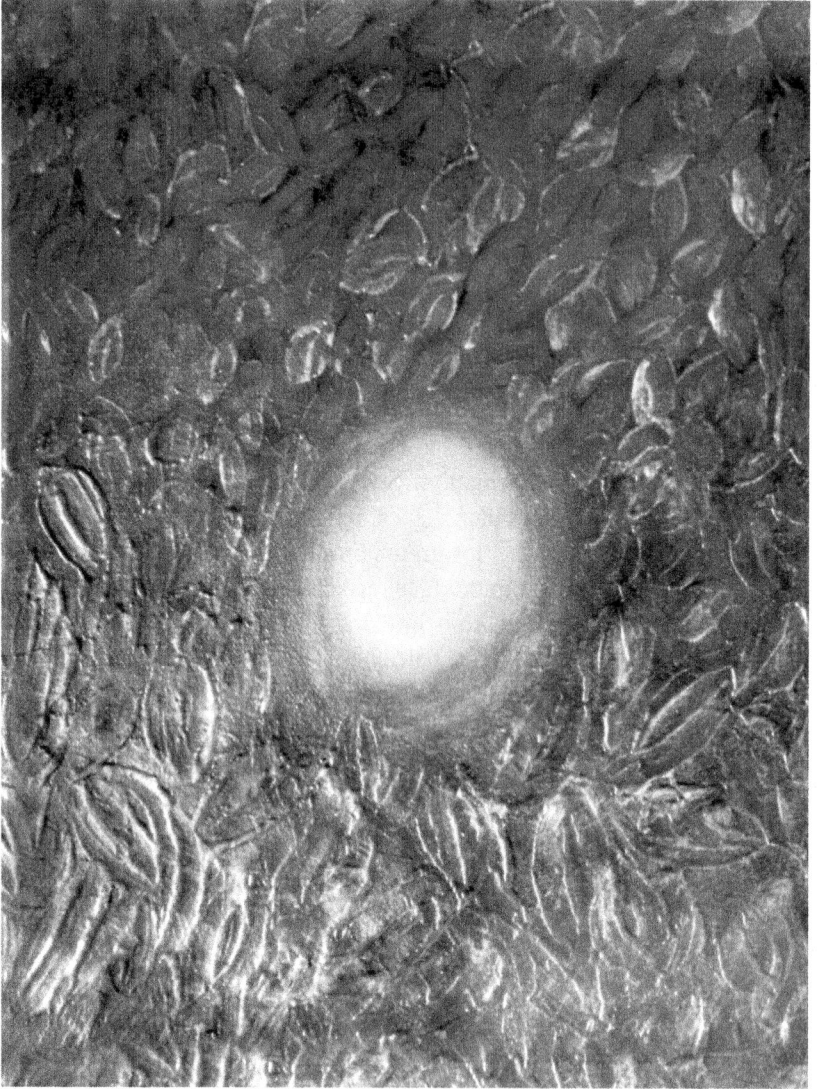

Plate 6

World Egg

CHAPTER THREE

The Child in the Adult
Barbara Somers

People talk about their 'castrating mother', their 'tyrannical father'
and though Mother may have become a bumbling old dear
and Dad be doddering in his dotage,
yet still the child feels itself to be contending with the gods

Deep in themselves, individuals have an incredible sense of their own identity. The seed very often speaks through, and they somehow know it. Children trying to survive in the world, whether friendly or alien, show an extraordinary artistry. Working with children of around five or six, I have often been amazed by their sense of 'who I am'. They might have no other measure for what love is, but they know when they are in an unloving environment. They might have no measure of what their rights are in terms of human dignity, and yet they have that dignity deep within themselves, implicit. It isn't moved away or tarnished, however painful their experience might be.

There are definite physical stages in our development, and ideally a psychological process also goes on in more or less perfect accord. We might think people would have polished off the business of the nursery by, say, twelve, but they haven't, not in the psychological sense. Physically, a baby is a baby and it won't be anything else until it's over three years old and begins to turn into a child. Later comes the stage at which it is neither child nor adolescent. Then inexorably – north, south, east and west – at about twelve, adolescence sets in. So too does *physical* adulthood at about twenty-five. But which of us *psychologically* will by then have hit 'adulthood', be totally separated from the parents? Many of us are still at the childhood stage; indeed, how many have actually left the nursery? While some wonderful part of nature has made all these stages happen physically, a lot hasn't been cleared away behind. So we meet people who are psychologically at a much earlier stage than their years. Adults may arrive in their thirties, fifties or whatever, but over and over there has been some hurt, wounding or damage along the ego-Self axis (see Figure 3, overleaf) and we find that it happened in the very early stages.

So in comes the Child in the Adult. That child will speak in big language, like the early Greeks. They were gods, those nursery figures: your Hecate, your smiling Zeus, Sun-eating Chronos. This is why it's so tremendously helpful to know something of the elaborative material of myth, folk tale, legend – all that wonderful knowledge and understanding of the human psyche, there in our fairy tales, our story-telling. Children need not to be deprived of it. Story-tellers used to go from place to place telling their stories and people everywhere recognised the characters: 'That's just like my mother!' – 'My father's like that'. In a wider sense, those are the gods!

It's nearly always parental *images* that we have to deal with, rather than with the parents as they are now. People talk about their 'castrating mother', their 'tyrannical father'. Those are the images, and though Mother may have become a bumbling old dear, and 'tyrannical' Dad be doddering in his dotage, it's the image we're talking about. The child feels itself to be contending with gods. In the nursery we were indeed under the pantheon of the gods; their whim could change everything. Talking to the Child in the Adult we hear that theme.[8] We still carry that language deep down in our modern psyche.

I profoundly believe that there is also in every individual some sense of an underlying pattern, an inner cypher of the Self. It's like a DNA coding of the Self, an instinctual drive towards meaning and purpose whether we choose it or not. Obviously, consciousness varies. It may take a lifetime to become even remotely aware of it, and many people never do. I was trained to believe that the personality was the be-all-and-end-all of everything, that an individual is *only* a personality. That's nonsense! I couldn't work in a place where our conditioning is held to be all that affects us, for better or worse. It is so appallingly unfair. I couldn't live in a universe where I believed we had one shot, one life, and while some people started practically at the goal, others had from the beginning such massive handicaps.

What makes your heart sing?

Jung brought out of the early philosophies and religions the idea that in the beginning was the Self; not that the personality has the Self, but that

---

8 If you don't want to read all of the fairy tales, at least read Marie-Louise von Franz on the subject: 'The Evil in Fairy tales', 'The Feminine in Fairy tales' – a treat and a joy. And 'The Inner World of Childhood' and 'The Inner World of Choice', by Frances Wickes.

the Self has the personality. Not that we are seeking the journey, but that the journey has us, and causes us to seek it. That idea is present in many people. *'What makes your heart sing – what brings you to your joy?'* People are rarely asked those questions. Yet when they are (even having come through horrendous backgrounds, never experiencing joy for more than a moment), they may have a sense of it: a glimpse of a tree, the first falling of a leaf, an ant on a window-sill, will carry them through many years. Sometimes it's *because* of the horrendous backgrounds. Prisoners have been kept going by less.

There are extraordinary 'ordinary' people everywhere who have a sense of something greater. When they remember that, re-attune to it, take it in as a possibility, the two journeys begin to interact. In accidents, meetings, books, moments of crisis, they begin to sense that otherness. They speak of human dignity, of what is fair and what is unfair, what is appropriate and what is not, the presence of love and the lack of love. It's immensely profound. For some people it takes a long time; for others it's not in the least relevant, though they may come into counselling (I

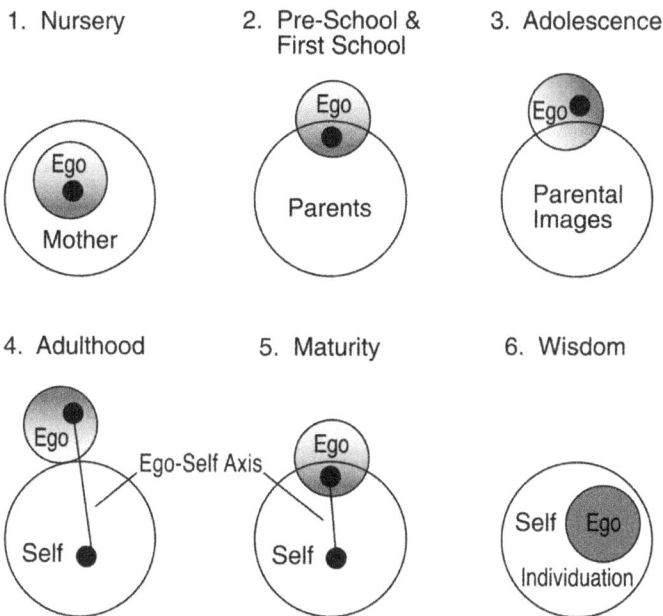

Figure 3   Stages of Emergence

never touch anything remotely to do with the Transpersonal unless it's appropriate for that person.)

Let's start off from a useful, straightforward, uncomplicated map of Edward Edinger's [9] which I've elaborated into the Emergence Map.

One	Nursery.	Ego within Mother.
Two	School.	Ego moving out from Parents.
Three	Adolescence.	Ego separating from Parental Images.
Four	Adulthood.	Ego completely separate.

Here the Self takes over from the parental images and I've added the fifth and sixth figures at the end:

| Five | Maturity | Ego merging again with Self |
| Six | Wisdom | Ego within Self |

Edinger effectively put something very subtle on to a two-dimensional figure and much can be gleaned from it, but I use it in a different way: it's a picture (a description rather than a definition) of the emergence of *consciousness* in the child, and its continuation into adulthood. It shows the progression of the relationship between the personality or ego on the one hand, and the Self on the other. [10]   Note how the ego-Self axis is less 'pulled out' at the stage of Maturity than it was in adulthood.

Nursery years

Stage One shows the years from birth up to about five.[11] The picture is of the mother as Self, containing the Child –containing the ego of the child. The first nine months out of the womb are very similar to the nine months of growth within it. Freudian, Kleinian and Jungian schools of psychology agree about this: the child's nature, certainly in its first nine months, but primarily in its first three to five years, is held in an extension of the placenta of the womb. The child shares the subjective life of the mother; it is still tied to her by a *psychological* umbilicus. Regression

---

9   See Edinger, 1972, Page 5. Edinger gave only the first four diagrams and did not refer to Mother, Parents or Parental Images.

10   I use the word 'ego' in the Jungian sense, as the everyday self. It's at the centre of the Egg Diagram: that sense of the personality 'I' – my name – 'me'.

11   This area has been brilliantly mapped by Freud, by Melanie Klein, by Winnicott, by a number of very fine therapists – Michael Fordham and others – and in the Jungian stream by Dr. Frances Wickes in the United States. The total subjective identity of it is very particularly worked over. One of the best books on that early period is 'The Maturational Processes in the Facilitating Environment' by Melanie Klein – if you can read the title, you can presumably read the book!

work done with adults, going back to birth experiences and the first years of their childhood, helps to confirm that mother is indeed at the other end of such a psychological umbilicus. The boy baby is thus contained within the feminine, within the mother, the past, the unconscious; so too is the girl baby.

There are fine therapies around the emergence of personality-consciousness and they're the best we have to go on: brilliant stuff, regressive work, returning to the nature of the relationship between child and mother. (And quite often a person isn't talking about their personal mother at all; somebody else provided mothering and was for them the nurturing surrogate – grandmother, nurse, aunt, sister.) Insofar as it is possible to map the nature of the child's emergent consciousness, as these great analysts and therapists have done, it appears that the psychological umbilicus by which the child is tied to the mother breaks a lot later than does the physical one. Research done on very small children strengthens this hypothesis. Winnicott believed that the mother and the child share both conscious and unconscious nature right from the beginning, even in the intra-uterine months when the foetus was developing into a child, a baby to be born.

The last figure, Wisdom, is very similar to the first, the Nursery, showing the ego as being wholly contained once more, but now within the Self. In the interim stages there develops a *spiritual* link or umbilicus, like that between infant and mother, joining the ego-personality and the Self, and now, with Jung, I'm positing that in these early years the mother stands in for the Self. She is Sun, Moon and stars to the child; she is the universe; she is meaning and purpose; she is the arbiter of whether it lives or dies. The child is completely dependent upon her; she, or her substitute, is all. His total dependency upon her forces the child to have that shared centre as a personality.

Nonetheless, in the Jungian concept and in the ancient traditions of East and West, the child already has within it the seed of the Self, one *not* to do with the mother. And the seed has a totally unique nature. Though the matrix in which our apple pip finds itself may not be appropriate for the *personality*, yet it may have been actually chosen by the Self: another of those open questions to which no one knows the answer. Jung posited that the Self chooses the mother, the setting, the environment, the very DNA coding that we inherit.

The child obviously needs containment during that first tremendous period of growth. Its physical development and the linking up of its nervous system are quite phenomenal in the first nine months after birth. It begins to approach and experience and cognise its world in a particular order: first through the senses of touch and taste – its little hands, feeling out, make contact with its world; and it has that rudimentary taste-bud on its lip which helps it turn towards milk, towards taste, before fading away. A little later come smell, then hearing, then sight. Very tiny babies are very, very much related to the mother, re-playing life in the womb.

Then, at about nine months old, it's as if something characteristically goes 'click'. It's as if the child doesn't 'get born' till this key moment when it moves away from the total subjectivity of those first nine months, its eyes come into focus and it begins to see a world out there as well as the world in here. Sorting the subjective from the objective, it begins to develop small islands of ego-consciousness.

If the child is lucky and in a good enough environment, it begins to be *outlined* and defined through its skin. The love-child is held and touched and stroked, and starts having a sense of being separate, as well as contained by its environment. With adults trying to redefine and value themselves, one often has to encourage them to stroke themselves (put oils on themselves in the bath, get a sense of having a right to be in a body), an outlining through sensuousness. Neither the too tight hold nor the too loose hold allows the child to be defined clearly enough; it's the 'good enough' hold, in Winnicott's inspired phrase, that allows the child a sense of definition.

In the work of Winnicott and others, 'transitional objects' are very important from nine months to three, four or five years old. At first, the child has developed neither a personality nor an ego-sense. It's still involved with the self of the mother and its own natural self. Toys help hold the child as it emerges from that containment in the unconscious, beginning to establish little ego-identity points – giving himself his name, 'Tommy', feeling herself 'Anna', having a sense that a little bit of identity belongs to it. Toys help the child to tolerate that later parturition. It begins to tell the difference between inner and outer; holding its teddy-bear, it moves away from a totally subjective relationship towards recognising itself as having an objective reality. And it isn't always a soft, cuddly toy – it can be a stone or a brick; you name it, the child will find it, carting around something to give it a sense of identification with the outside world. Very particularly at night, it needs that familiar object to be bedded down with. It's very subjective to the child, and easy to over-look. I've known people who, having lost their toy, their *familiar*, didn't have it replaced and it's as if part of their own being had been taken away.

One man had to watch as his favourite teddy-bear was pulled apart by his cousins. Brought up to be willing always to sacrifice everything to other children, he had to tolerate this treatment of a bear who was terribly important to him. At the age of sixty he began discovering how much it still hurt – and how much he needed a replacement bear! It's amazing the number of adults I send out into the toy department; pretending they're getting it for a grandchild, they take it home for themselves. He bought a small bear to keep in his pocket for times when the child was uppermost. The child in us is extraordinarily omnipresent; healthy, spontaneous child it may be, yet it often runs our life.

Up to three years old, not only toys but play and fantasy become tremendously important. So far as we can tell, children very easily identify at a subjective level with the objective world; the teddy-bear *is* them, but the teddy-bear is also part of the outside world. Up to around three, certainly up to five, they *become* the train, the dragon, the pirate – they become Mummy and Daddy. Children brought up in orphanages, or fostered out, or whose parents are so sophisticated that they feel toys aren't necessary, have a noticeable hole left in the psyche. This is often filled with fantasy playmates, fantasy toys, which have a tremendous value, as we'll see. But the child's fantasy life tends to stay inward-turned.

Childhood

At Stage Two (Figure 3) – at school, from about five onwards – the child has to emerge from that first total subjective interaction with the mother. I've drawn Stages Two and Three with the ego emerging from that womb-like containment. For 'Mother' I've put the word 'Parents'. An Ego/self-axis is beginning to emerge; the ego itself, the little person, is beginning to draw to itself a centre of identity which, although it's still tied, isn't quite as connected or identified with the mother as it was.

At this childhood stage, the *father* or his equivalent is extremely important for both boy and girl. Certainly by the age of five the child needs the 'otherness' of the father as counterpoint to its identity with mother. Her hold, so nurturing and sustaining, so much needed when the baby was helpless, has to become more background as the ego begins to emerge. To help it away from the natural dominance of the feminine, the child needs the masculine, which allows it to emerge into the outer world, letting the nursery drop into the background. So the world of the mother becomes the world of the parents. The Self end of the ego-Self axis is still rooted in the parents – whoever the parents are – but a small ego is beginning to emerge, a little sense of ego-identity, of personality. During that period the ego in the developing child goes out and looks for other parent figures, other authority figures, in the world of school and beyond.

Freud wrote graphically and dramatically about the triangle set up at about five, dramatising it as the Oedipus triangle (the boy-child falls in love with the mother and then fights the father as foe) and the Electra triangle (with the girl falling in love with the father and fighting the mother). Well, it's good Greek drama! It's certainly telling if somebody in their thirties or forties is still caught into that triangle; then you can say, yes, here's an Electra or an Oedipus complex. But, like Jung, I believe the point was made too strongly. It's a natural stage of development through which any healthy child will pass, and the father or male figure needs to come in to act as earthing terminal to the closed circuit of mother and child.

Now the child, with a growing sense of personal identity, begins to set outside authority figures in counterpoint to the parents at home. Bridging from the subjective life of the nursery over into the objective world, it forays out, still needing the parents and the nursery as background. The subjective moves inward into the background, the objective becomes the 'real' external world out there, and the child begins to move between them.

When it's around five or six, a healthy, natural, normal development includes very strong dreams: what we would call *nightmares*. The stage of nightmare is absolutely natural and normal as the external world meets with the child's own inner world; children of various cultures (and I've worked with Malay and Tibetan and Chinese children) all seem to have dreams at about this age. The outer and inner worlds collide, throwing up images which, though frightening for the child, can also be fascinating. It's now that our favourite, or unfavourite, figures from books come alive. Blind Pugh walks up the garden path! It's immensely vivid. We can smell Old Pugh, hear his tapping stick; it's just dark enough not to be able to see him because he's dressed in black. I try to help people later to reconnect with the vividness of the dreams and impressions they had as children, with that very sharp imagery.

Next, in the normal educative process, the external world overlies the internal, subjective world. The child is given an impetus away from the nursery. It's a natural stage. Though obviously it can be bent too far away from the inner, the child now belongs in the outside world.

Adolescence

If all of that is successfully accomplished, if the child is supported in an appropriate way in its adventures in the outer *and* the inner worlds, then it can move on to Stage Three: Adolescence. By puberty the young person's own ego-centre is less 'enwombed' and standing clearer. Still being fed from the parental background, the ego reaches much more into the external world. The parents become Parental Images, so named because the images are still there, to be projected elsewhere. The young person is still connected with them and still linked (though with less overlap) to the nursery, but now, from about twelve to eighteen, can explore and come back.

The emergent young person now experiences other authority figures and there is often considerable struggle. The parental background is felt to be constrictive, restrictive; the parents (or parent) are less supportive and more like threshold dragons to be fought. The push-and-pull thrust of the individual begins to emerge. Many of us remember from our own adolescence how, while longing to break away, we still wanted our washing done and our rent paid and our feet under an appropriate table. And how can the parents be, in all that? The young person caught by and pulling away from them expects to be housed, contained and looked after, and to kick them in the teeth at the same time. It's very graphic, both the tie and the impulse to kick against the tie. Some kick a lot more radically than others but, if the ego is to emerge clear of the nursery and come out naturally into adulthood, there has to be a *fighting* stage. The hero's quest, the heroine's quest, is to battle with the parental dragons; seeing them as threshold guardians, the hero has to dare go through that threshold to leave the nursery.

Having done that, adolescents have to widen the relationship with *themselves*. Very frequently, the parents' image is projected out to teachers, authority figures, peer-group leaders. Young people now are more likely to relate to leaders within their own groups than to older figures, but the same projection of the parent is there. In adolescent gangs the pecking order is very clearly marked by their rites and initiations; the group itself becomes the *alma mater* – cults, religions, philosophies.

Adulthood

If the young person has escaped fully from containment in the mother-lode, the pure metal can begin to come out of the original matrix. For adolescence we used the term 'Parental Images'; now in Stage Four, Adulthood, the ego stands clear. 'Mother', 'Parents' and 'Parental Images' can be replaced with 'the Self' with a large S. This is a Jungian map. The ego is now in the outside world and the potential of the Self lies behind, standing beneath where once the mother and the parents stood. The ego-Self axis is extended to its fullest. The personality is (or should be) at its most conscious in the outside world. And by natural development there is a potential line of communication between that small Ego and the larger Self.

If it's successfully achieved, the young person moves into the clear to become the true *adult*. Still resting upon tradition and background, yet their identification in the outside world grows stronger and stronger. While, as Jung believed, the extension of the ego-Self axis is still rooted and anchored within the parental images, the functioning end of the axis is now their own. There's less interaction, less crossover, less cross-contamination; they're no longer dependent upon mother, parents nor friends. (Otherwise – are they adult?) The ego is emerging as an individuating principle in search of its own myth and meaning. The person is withdrawing projections, releasing the parental images from within, becoming their own authority, their own parenting figure. Psychologically, this is a positive statement. Standing full stature, they take responsibility for their life.

However, though psychologically and spiritually capable of handling the external world, they may yet be a long way from consciousness of the Self. For it's now (between perhaps twenty-eight and thirty-five, when the ego-Self axis is most extended) that the Self characteristically begins to speak: 'Aha! This is possibly going to be a useful vehicle in the external world.' The voice becomes quite strong by about forty-two (hence, perhaps, the typical midlife crisis). The question is: 'What does the Self require from the personality?' rather than: 'What does the personality require from the Self?' We may now be in line with the nature of the meaning of our lives and why we came into this incarnation. That certainly takes quite a few years, typically from thirty-five to forty-nine. We need to become our own authority, take full responsibility for our own life. Then the Self begins to move forward in the individuation process.

People often have intimations of the Self from very early on. As children, they may have had a far greater sense of the Self within than ever they did of their outer background. The more alienated they felt from that background, the more likely they were to turn to the nature of the Self. Yet if they're to become adult they will have to incarnate their inner vision, embodying it in the external world. Some may readily accept that they come from the Self, that the Self is trying to come into a personality. Feeling that they are a Self incarnate, their lives will certainly help them to deal with the reality of the external world. Others may never have had a sense of the Self, but now grow towards a quest for purpose and meaning – if only through the lack of them. Whichever way people come, if they're to be truly adult this will have to happen. Then their personality-centre will begin to be related to that other Centre, the potential of their own nature. The seed (separate from, although very much embedded in, their experience of the past) holds their meaning and purpose, answering the question, 'Why am I here?'

Maturity

Stage Five, maturity, is necessary to the map if we are to do Transpersonal work. The ego-Self axis is less pulled out now than it was in adulthood; the two centres come closer together and begin to relate. The movement is inwards again, towards a degree of containment, this time not by the mother but by the Self. The 'I out here' becomes more conscious of that Self within. There is an area of meeting, a cross-threshold, where the small ego in the outer world and the Self in the inner begin to meet and set up a dialogue. And so we become dependent upon something Other, something greater, another authority.

With true spiritual maturity the Self begins to be the power and action in the ego-Self axis. Although the parents, the tradition, the background may all be more or less important (they were, after all, our rootedness and, as experience, mustn't be thrown out), now the personality is drawn less and less by them and more and more by the Self. Gradually, another kind of rooting is taking place.

Many who never had a mother or a father in the background find it imperative to discover something else to parent and nurture and nourish them. I have always found it incredibly, mysteriously amazing how, even as very small children, people have managed to re-parent themselves from nature, from the archetypal image of what they felt their background ought to be. The Self has, always and ever, nourished and helped them.

These are very often years in the labyrinth. A true adult may have developed a very powerful sense of who they are as a personality. It can be a great struggle to feel themselves – as many do – being drawn inexorably to something else. 'Well, blow that for a game! I was just thinking I'd got it hung together, and suddenly here's this pull to something *different*. I don't know myself these days!' They aren't doing a regression to the original parents, but making a movement towards the fundamental progenitor of their lives.

Wisdom

Perhaps this is the title for the last stage. The ego is now contained, fed by the placenta, nourished within the womb of the Self. Wisdom is often shown in Chinese and in Jungian psychology as the *Ouroboros*, the great world-dragon biting its own tail. The ego is entirely contained within the Self, the two centres coinciding, so that there is a total identification of the person out there with the person in here; they become one again. I felt it necessary to put Stage Six in to round off the map but, need I say, not many people who come into that final picture come in for counselling – at least, not into my counselling room! This would be what the Chinese call 'the true man of no rank', the one who stands in the outside world and more and more becomes an instrument in that world for the Self within. As Jung said, they came to themselves. Accepting themselves, sacrificing their own will, they were reconciled to adverse events and circumstances. They had submitted themselves to the will of God. It could be said of them that they had made their peace with God.

These are the final stages in the movement towards individuation, with an increasing sense that the Self is what life is about. Perhaps the whole journey in the round is what Jung called the individuation process: we come from the Self, we go through the experiences of personality, and we return to the Self at the end. We come from eternity, we pass through ephemeral life, and we return to eternity.

The call of the Self

In the old Eastern, Indian tradition out of the Upanishads the Self is seen as a diamond, the adamant diamond. Each experience of the personality, each incarnation, is but the light hitting that eternal diamond. The personality is a ray coming off a single facet of it. It's also said that in each lifetime the personality doesn't have to accept that incarnation if it doesn't want to; it doesn't matter. So the seed might in the beginning have come from that eternal diamond and run a shoot like a thread through all our developmental years. As Jung would term it, a flower sprang from the eternal rhizome.

For most people it's been quite unconscious. However, some have been aware that the experience of their life is a thread which, at about these years of maturity, begins to pull them home. That is the underlying possibility that Transpersonal psychology takes into account. We are looking both at the personal journey and at this journey of the Self. It's a continuum, and people coming in to us are at various stages along it. Some are in the pull of the return to the original womb, their ego struggling to be contained there still. Others are drawn towards this higher identity. People come in at sixes and sevens, at all stages. Through their images, I help them to discover the main part of the work that needs to be done. Perhaps there has been a break-point at any one of these stages, and damage or bruising. Perhaps they didn't emerge at the appropriate time and need help with the re-patterning.

The brilliant work of the Freudians, Kleinians and Winnicottians helps people return to the very basic building-blocks of who they may become, and rehabilitates them, recycling their experience so that it can come forward and be more appropriate to who they are now. My sense is that a lot of that work stops at Stage Four, at Adulthood. But for many people the work isn't about looking backwards; it's a movement on. Their wounding certainly needs to be taken into account; it could be that early wounding that eventually put them in touch with this inner journey.

There may be no wounding at all. It's always possible to have been undamaged, untouched; to have had perfect parents in an ideal setting and to have been understood, seen and heard, discerned from the very moment that we emerged. It would be very valuable. I haven't met too many people like that – but then, I suppose I wouldn't! But there must be some, and I thank God for them for the continuation of the human race. It's very difficult to remember that there are people perfectly natural – and by God they're healthy! For them therapy, counselling, analysis are not only contra-indicated; they can be poison.

But, as we've seen, some others have come from disastrous environments through the most terrible, appalling backgrounds and settings. Yet, working with them, listening to *their* story, their history, helping them to trust the seed and to discover through their own language the meaning of their lives, or the lack of meaning of their lives, I am amazed at what people can do with a disaster. One man said, 'When I look back over the debris of my broken life, I realise that it can become the underpinning of the new road that I shall travel.' He was able to put it into words; many just can't.

So I accept the hypothesis that the seed is sound, that from the beginning it has a meaning and a purpose running as a thread right through the nature of the person's life. There's the good of life, the bad of it, the problems, the joys. But there is another story too. The person can be put more in touch with that other story. And very often it will give meaning to the journey, take on the pain, lead them and guide them. It's in helping them to be led by that thread that I make myself redundant.

A lot of people don't want the thread. Very resistant to the meaning and depth of their lives, they come in and back off, come again and back off again. Like shy animals, they're drawn out of the maze of the wood towards – something? – and retreat again. They are pulled, and pushed. In some, the personality end of the axis is so weak that it can't hold the tension. A lot of help, support and nurturing, if not re-parenting, is required; at least they need an appropriate seed-box, until they can gain strength to begin to become who they are.

Others are fighting for their hard-won ego-personality; why should they give it up to something they feel is bugging them? Suddenly recognising that if they covet the thread they may lose something of their personal identity, or have to let go the defences and accommodations that have kept them going, they turn and spit in the eye of God. These are people who in the middle years said, 'Please, please give me a meaning and a purpose in life!' But it's not funny when it begins to happen: eventually we have to take responsibility for it. Very few human beings want responsibility.

But many of us have felt that we had the thread – for a moment – perhaps particularly in the darkness of traumatic pain. And then, mostly, life came in and we lost it. But that doesn't mean it vanished. Very often it became unconscious, went underground; life on the outside was too fractured, too demanding, even too joyful, for us to attend to that thread. However, for increasingly many people it becomes essential to do so. *It* has *them*, and keeps moving towards them, until one day it comes into their hands. These people come because – thank God, thank God! – they feel they have lived the whole of their lives in a strange country, trying to learn a language that wasn't their own and suddenly something has happened: a book's fallen off the shelf, they've run into someone, and they hear the language of their homeland. Just bumping into one person who truly speaks that language can give them the courage to go on, and lead them on the journey a long, long way.

Plate 7

Earth Fire

CHAPTER FOUR

Working with the Child in the Adult
Barbara Somers

Breaking up to break down is different
from breaking up to break through

As we've seen, the people I work with are nearly always caught in a tension somewhere in the middle of the Emergence map. If they're happily around the Maturity/Wisdom end of it, they don't need to come in, and if they haven't started it at all, they're not ready for counselling.

Rites of passage

These used to be set up at the thresholds of at least three distinct stages: emergence from the nursery; emergence into adolescence; emergence into adulthood. The majority of the wisdom schools also allowed for the movement towards maturity, which drew the person on from that third threshold and into the inner mysteries: the fourth threshold was *becoming* the inner mysteries. Nowadays we don't have the outer forms of those rituals, yet it seems there is an inner thrust, psychologically as well as physically, for us to go through each of these sequential stages. Many people are caught in a two-way pull, in the conflict and tension of the middle ground. Again, our nature seems to be pushing us towards the next stage, yet our experience of the past holds us back.

Figure 4 on the next page shows how layers of subsoil cover the *Original Seed* in the matrix of the lower unconscious in each individual. For each layer I've given a query, a question to be mapped:

Inherited Traits – conflicts within innate nature? We map how far what the person has inherited from parents and background is in conflict with the innate nature of their seed. If it is in fair harmony, the child sings in his cot. Watching nature – clouds, trees, earth – he knows, 'That is just like me'.

Scripts of the Nursery – conflict with parents' scripts? We explore 'them', the parents or major figures for the child, and their social mores, culture, class. We note their do's and don'ts ('Do this – but don't do that!') and any double messages ('Tell the truth – but don't say things like that!) How did they react to the child?

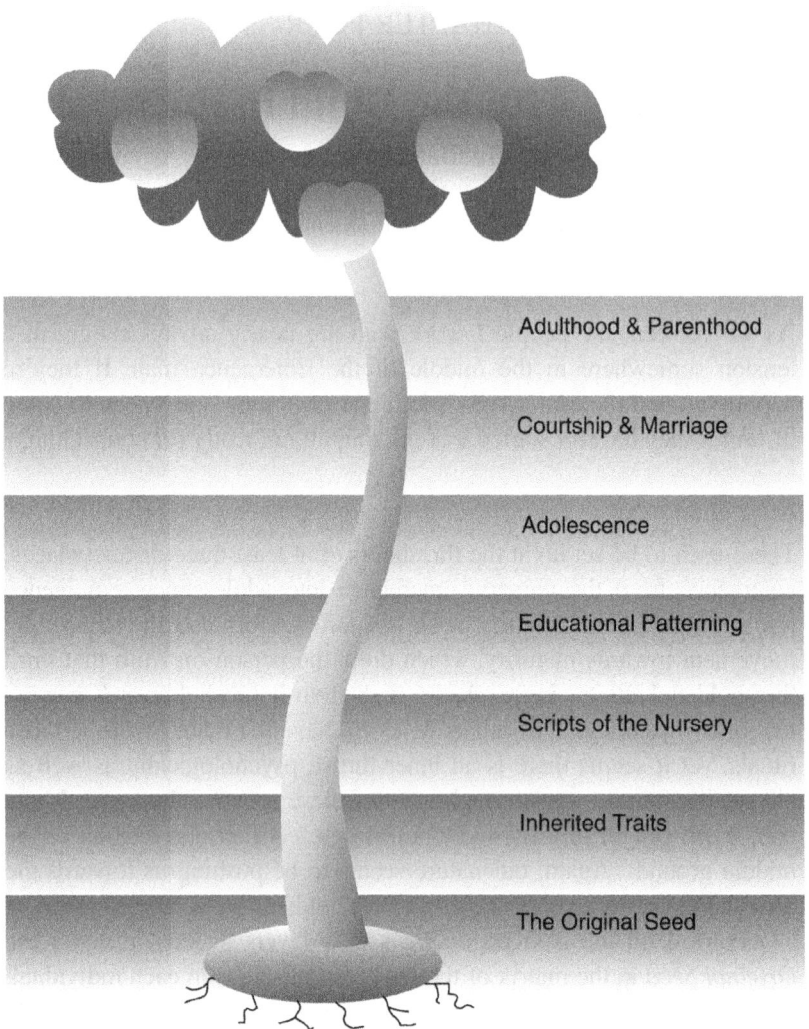

Figure 4 Natural Shape of Development

Educational Patterning – conflict between authority figures? Was
.what the child heard in its first educational experience, from children or
adults, in conflict with the parents' scripts? Did the authorities tally with
each other? The child had to learn to resolve that tension.

Adolescence – conflict with peers and siblings? Our self-evaluation is often inherited from things people said to us about us; it's not who we actually are. Our self-images may have been laid on us from way back. As our body-image began to change and sexual energy to come forward, the question will have arisen: 'Who am I?'

Courtship and Marriage – conflict with the background? Did all this go with the parents' script, or was it reactive? What were the stereotypes of masculine and feminine? Is the person now a conditioned product?

Adulthood and Parenthood – free choice? How far is our adulthood still structured for or against 'them', the adults we knew in childhood? Do we raise our children according to what we think parenthood ought to be – what we were conditioned to think it is?

All those layers of soil tend, in a perfectly normal, healthy, well-functioning person, to silt up the innate seed within. If the silting is too heavy, or if there's too much weight on one side, then we adapt away from our own innate nature and move, as we've seen, towards areas of neurosis. Was there a conflict between messages given inside and messages given outside? Or between scripts of school and scripts of the nursery? Was there a conflict between mother and father which we might have inherited, which appeared later as a self-conflict?

One man came in seeking the innate nature of his own being. Together, we looked at the strata built up over the original seed, working back through them to find out who he really was. This man was forty-three, in industry; married for twenty-two years, he had daughters of nineteen and sixteen and a younger son. The problem a person brings in is only partial, the tip of the iceberg (if they could state the problem they could probably solve it). The trouble he had brought was the heavy stutter this boy had developed at the age of seven. Could I suggest a therapist for his son? Believing it was somebody else's problem, he wanted to talk about 'them out there': the son. Gently I said, ' – And how about you?' 'Well, my marriage is a bit problematic – my wife's a very difficult woman, you know…' Again, 'them out there'. 'Anything else?' 'Well, I do have these migraines – I'll talk about them another time – you see, it's my son's stutter…' Only the migraines would he accept as his own.

So we talked about his son. 'Yes, I can recommend a therapist' (and the therapist worked extremely well with the child in a very short time). 'Perhaps there are things in his environment that need to be looked at?' I said.

I asked my two questions, 'What gives you joy?' 'Music. Mozart… and New Orleans Jazz – oh, and driving at speed.' Gently, gently I asked,

'When you hit the bottom of your barrel, what keeps you going?' 'Stubbornness!' he said. 'I'm too shit scared to stop grinding on.' (I thought to myself, 'Never presume *you* know what stubbornness is!') 'Let me say this: I have no imagination, I never dream, and I certainly can't visualise. That's it!' ('Got to work with this man!' I thought.)

What were his *inherited traits*? And what was the background soil where the original seed grew? He'd been born in South Africa of Polish-Jewish parents, not very orthodox. They'd moved out from the pogroms in Russia and he was first-generation South African, Jewish in black Africa, 'a minority within a minority'. His father was a solicitor's clerk. 'Not a very good one,' he said, 'gentle, shy, intellectual, second-rate, unsure, introvert'. Father was always reading and listening to music. 'He was silent, and he had migraines.'

What were the *scripts of the nursery*, the messages coming across from his parents? 'Could you get the *atmosphere* of your father?' (a very good question when you're mapping the child). 'Cloudy grey, and the sound of music – Bach and all that intellectual stuff', he said. 'He doesn't think much of emotions' (a very typical comment: doesn't *think* much of emotions).

And his mother? When he'd been simply remembering her, she was 'emotional, fiery, sentimental and ambitious'. On the other hand, visualising her ('Sense it atmospherically – ') he said, 'She's like a hot oven, sometimes full of goodies, sometimes empty, and totally unpredictable'. (He didn't know he was visualising – he can't visualise!) There had been two messages from his mother: first, 'Get out there and *do* something, make a man of yourself (your weak, wet father never did!)'; secondly, 'Whatever you do, don't make trouble!' (Her parents had experienced Russia and the pogroms, and she might be considered an alien in this place.) A double message: 'Get out and do something – but don't make trouble.' So on the one hand, the silent, withdrawn, introverted father, shy and musical, unsure of the man's role, undervaluing the emotions; on the other, the mother, unpredictable, fiery, sentimental, extravert, wanting to fight for causes, valuing the emotions but fearing their effects, blowing hot and cold.

And that just about exactly defined this man's own situation; he'd inherited and carried forth both these things. 'I tend to cool my emotions with my mind. I seek relationship but avoid commitment. I'm ambitious but I always pull out just when I'm going to make it. I go into a state of lethargy. That's when I get migraine.' With mother hot and fiery but sometimes empty and father cool and distant, he was in a right old mess there, sometimes cold, sometimes hot. This was also true sexually, with his wife. The images are often very, very exact. These were the scripts, the double messages, the do's and don'ts of the nursery, of *them*, the parents.

So by five, two layers of soil had already gone over the seed (the inherited traits, and the scripts of the nursery) each conflicting with his own innate nature. A bit more soil went over with the *educational patterning* he had. From about seven he'd been aware, through feeling and intuition, of the tension of South Africa. 'It's black and it's white,' he said. 'It's savage and it's beautiful, it's music' – and then, suddenly frightened of going on, 'Oh, it's just Africa!' With his natural sense of justice and fair play, he'd begun battling for the underdog; after all, he was in 'a minority within a minority'. Remembering his mother's double message, at first he kept the battles at the verbal level; introverted like his father, he was frightened of physical pain and aggression. So the other boys accused him of cowardice. So he got into fights; then his mother beat him up with her tongue: 'Make no trouble!' A lovely closed circuit! Where do you go from there? You've got to be a man among the boys, so you have to fight. And you're terrified of it. And if you do fight, mother knocks verbal hell out of you at home.

'I felt both a coward and the need to be a hero. I was frightened of my own powerful emotions. I went up into my head and became an intellectual good-boy'. His deeper feelings were very passionate, very strong; he would 'cool it' in order to handle them. He began to see everything in extremes: if it wasn't this, it must be that. I asked, 'What did you do to help yourself?' 'I went out and watched the animals.' Up came the voice of the poet he had denied so furiously: 'I lay on the land and drank in the beauty of it all.'

Migraine often goes with a split between head and heart. Fighting for causes – not being able to follow it through – migraine. The headaches which started then became very apparent later on.

At eight or nine he went to school in England. He hated being sent away from Africa. He felt deeply, he cried at night under the bedclothes, and he dreaded anybody knowing he was upset. He detested aggression. 'I felt feminine inside and the female inside was stronger than the male outside,' as he eventually said (he didn't use that kind of language at first).

He also detested rough games, feeling the whole pack was bearing down on him personally. Boxing he loathed, pretending to be knocked out because he couldn't bear it any longer. However, he was very good at high jump and short races. 'I could turn in a sprint because they were all after me!' He dreaded admitting his love of music and poetry; they'd think him a sissy – they didn't rate music and poetry much at that school. Extremely frightened that they would know he was frightened, he was more split off than before, in quite a bad way.

He couldn't relate to the stereotyped masculinity at the school, having a heterosexual dislike of the homosexuality manifested there. 'I majored up in my head even more,' he said. 'I put poetry, music, feeling and all that sort of stuff underground.' It's much easier for someone to find out what they are not than what they are. Jung's typology is useful here [12]; we found that originally he had been strongly *feeling* and *intuitive*, so that *sensation* – the ability to get in touch with the external world – was less well developed, and *thinking* least of all. If he'd found somebody to meet and bring out the feeling and intuitive sides of him too, he might have been all right. But he didn't. The school was against all that, and hammered sensation and thinking, games, sports and the mind, the stereotyped masculine values he couldn't go with, the worst in education. All he could do was spin the wheel of the four functions so that sensation came to the top: being able to get things anchored, learning about woodwork, handicrafts, trees (he liked working in the garden), running faster, leaping higher than anybody else. Thinking (his fourth function) was way down the list; he struggled desperately with his exams and he worked and he worked and he worked, 'too shit scared to stop grinding on'.

Thus his own wheel was spun, and by degrees he was pushed further and further away from the natural growth of the seed. Very often children are turned on the wheel in this way. It's not as bad as it sounds; there is a redemptive possibility. If we are to come in touch with all four sides of our nature, the wheel must be turned back. I played back to him his feeling for Africa, his sense of beauty, his love of nature, his deep under-standing of people. 'Yes, it's possibly so,' he admitted. I explained that, though he couldn't express his own measure of feeling and there was no place in his environment for intuition, yet he was high on feeling, and he was intuitive.

---

12   C.G. Jung, 1921, Chapter 10. We relate to the world by four Functions, two of Perception (Sensation and Intuition) and two of Judgement (Feeling and Thinking). The Four Functions can be represented diagrammatically as the four spokes of a wheel which has the Self as the hub at the centre.

He came to see the conflict between his father's cool intellect and grey absence, and his mother's fiery, blow-hot, blow-cold unpredictability, and he knew he didn't want to take on either of those two forms.

We moved together into the period of *adolescence*, and then of *courtship*. He'd been deeply attracted to feminine women – surprise, surprise! – unconsciously searching 'out there' for the feeling and intuition so pushed down in him. However, afraid as he was of the missing factor deeply repressed in his own nature, he was also frightened of such women. He admired them, but at a distance; they were 'out there', untouchable. So instead he had begun consciously to seek 'boyish women' (his words). 'They were adolescent, good at games, with good minds, ready to fight for ideas'. He'd related to them as brother and sister, 'for fun, for sexual play,' he said. 'It didn't go deep, but I felt all right with those women.' Of course he did, they were reflections of the self he'd become in the world, majoring in the two functions he'd developed in himself. He was compromising with his own persona and ego. The bodies of a different kind of woman frightened him, reminding him too much of the aspects he'd lost. He was making an adaptive compromise.

Then at twenty-one he was proposed to! Because he didn't like to say No – 'don't make trouble, darling!' – he married. And whom did he marry? A maternal, ambitious woman, who wanted him to be a man while treating him like a child. In other words, he married his mother. She gave him the adaptive set-up he needed. Though not safe in the long run, as history will relate, for the moment he was threatened by nobody he couldn't handle. He stopped playing games with adolescent girls. 'It's time you settled down and became a man'. He was so cut off from what he was really about that he chose – or rather, he happened to stumble into – a career in industry. By the time he was thirty-six, with two daughters and a son, he was still living up in his head, pushing feeling, poetry and music aside. His wife was a woman to guarantee that he wouldn't easily regain touch with the seed.

But it's not in the nature of life to let that happen; the seed has a tendency to grow to its own shape. After a little while things began to occur. A bad organiser, he hated groups and collective strength, and he hated 'them'. But he enjoyed industrial relations and union fights, and now he discovered he liked people very much, having an intuitive sense about them. Good, dutiful, loyal, orderly, well-mannered, discreet, he'd never really been allowed off the leash. But now, because he was such a good negotiator and fighter, his employers let him out and he began to travel. His wife (pushing and ambitious like his mother) was quite happy about that; it left her free, while his success gave her the background she wanted.

But during the next three years, lo and behold he was 'horrified' (the number of times he used that word was fascinating) to find himself seeking out other women on his travels. He had several affairs. 'Is there any connecting link between these women?' I asked. 'Yes, they have a lot of feeling – they all love poetry – we go to concerts.' Duty conflicted with morality. He hated the double life he was leading (his passion for justice again). Initially horrified, he became amused to see that the further he was from home, the more likely an affair, while the nearer home, the more he modified his behaviour. 'Who is watching out for you?' I asked. 'My wife!' Guilty and screwed up with fear of the coming confrontation, he tried very hard, but he 'couldn't help it'. 'All right, so we are incompatible, but it's not as bad as all that,' he said. 'It's just I can't live at home with her.' Terrified she'd find out, he searched the more obsessively for these other women. And he couldn't make love to his wife. It was a good day when he said, 'I suppose if I thought of her as my mother – you don't make love to your mother, do you?' I said, 'Well, no, better not...'

He got on well with his daughters, liking them and his son very much, treating them as people. But around this time his own headaches really came out. We mapped those migraines. 'They come as I go away; I don't have them on the trip back'. He visualised himself leaving home in an aircraft: 'I'm going into an area I love and am fascinated by. *I'm so happy to be there that I feel terrible*! I don't know what to do with it – it all gets cramped up in my head.' Then, coming home, 'I'm a good boy now, it will be all right, *Mother will have me back*'.

Well, as inevitably happens, his wife, alerted by the change in him, found out and there was a confrontation. 'What are you *doing* on these trips?' He made a fine old mess of his reply, and the whole thing came out. She declared, 'If you think you'll be allowed around our girls just when they're adolescent, you've got another think coming!' This was the most awful thing she could possibly have said. He told me he was 'absolutely screwed up, shattered, shamed'. Hardly knowing what to say, he stuttered, 'It was monstrous – absolutely monstrous – and unfair, and un- – unjust, I – I – I'll n –never forgive her!' And then he told me that

that was the time when his son's speech impediment had begun!

For him who 'never dreamed', dreams now started pouring up. He dreamed of a small black boy who turned out to be his Shadow, the lost, unloved child within himself, the naughty boy, a little figure continuously dancing in and out through the dreams. There was also a lumbering, brainless figure he called Caliban, who was good with trees and plants. This he felt was his undeveloped feeling side, unacceptable, kept down at a very primitive, bestial level, coming up as a monstrous figure. He later found that Caliban's power to do magic and let plants grow was also part of himself. *'People* ought to grow like this,' he said, 'green fingers with people.'

The horror of being debarred from his daughters! Punitive authority figures, the KGB, the secret police, came into his dreams; he was impotent, tied down by 'them', trapped, amputated, always having to fight back. At first he saw 'them' as his wife; only by degrees did he realize that she too was a helpless victim. He said, 'Poor kid! Perhaps she's got more in common with me than I've known.' By learning his own map he learned a bit more understanding of her. These figures were part of himself; he had to take them back. He promised her he'd 'be a good boy', he would conform all right! No, he wouldn't have any more affairs (and he had *not* had any more affairs). And his migraines were getting worse and worse. He said to me, 'I just hate myself, I really hate myself!'

Into his dreams came an almost-unseen woman whom he was trying to rescue. She took many forms: showing her back-view, she would look over her shoulder at him and dive into the water, or vanish laughing into the wood, a beautiful belly-dancer teasing him to sexual frenzy before rushing off and leaving him, always just a second before he could reach her. A figure out of the unconscious often starts by showing its back, the unconscious side. He came to realise that this figure from whom he was locked away was the hidden feminine within himself, the *anima*, his own very young, held down, feminine side coming out at an adolescent, teasing stage. The woman who is 'not-mother', she was the object of his quest, the holder and container of his intuitive and feeling sides. She was living out for him in dreams the bit of himself that he hadn't known how to handle, as were those 'feeling women' he'd been unconsciously drawn to and afraid of in adolescence.

But when his wife cut him off from his daughters (and he felt she might have a point) he was 'horrified in every possible way'. The migraines became crucifying, the boy's speech troubles worsened, and now there came into his dreams a man who was both fighter and healer. Aggressive against 'them', he was also gentle, quiet and capable. More and more the dreamer saw this figure as an aspect of himself: the strong fighter for causes, tender as well. His father, out of touch with his own masculine side, had given a pattern of masculine weakness; now he realised it was neither weak nor second-rate for a man to be feminine, as his mother had suggested. The fighter-healer was part of his own style; he had a lot to learn about what it is to be masculine.

In many of his dreams his son appeared, the inarticulate aspect of his own confused child. He began to talk with his son about the child's own real feelings, and by degrees the stutter eased out. The boy had been wondering where his father was; now, he came to see him as both tender and strong. Finding he had somebody to talk to, he admitted he too didn't like school games. Seen and appreciated, both in his inherited traits and in the differences in him, the boy knew his feelings had been heard.

Where to go next? The imaging suggested more work with people, using his own therapeutic qualities and understanding. Totally un-expected – to him and everybody else – was his new talent for producing plays. Music, yes; but amateur dramatics? In a dream, Caliban and the little black boy played together in an African landscape. He danced with them, but then stood back saying, 'No, that isn't my scene'; watching, he saw the shape of the dance. A producer was needed for the local theatricals; 'I'll have a go at it'. He found he loved it. He wrote a couple of song scripts and had them sung in his plays.

It was no miracle. He took up personnel counselling in a management consultancy firm, taking a pay cut and bringing the marriage conflict into the open. His wife was furious. They were very different characters and the marriage was certainly up for question. Among other things he had to learn to confront her. With the release of his own feminine side he could choose to relate to her feminine side. He set the pace of understanding. Every event, every relationship spoke to him about the nature, the pattern, of his own seed. Above all he saw that the seed had stayed true to itself.

The thrust of the seed is always pushing us forwards, and our crises often make us explore and take a stand. Without such life experience this man might have stayed fixed on the wheel, but he 'left the nursery', risking its turning. He still had a long journey to go. He began to make friends with the migraines, realising what caused them, recognising he'd been cut off from part of his nature. And the split began to come together. Valuing thinking, he learnt to anchor things in a new way; valuing feeling and intuition, he lifted the taboos against them. Led back more and more to the nature of his own original seed, his own Self, he saw a pattern in his life as a whole. Away from that pattern for forty-three years, now 'fate' had brought him back closer and closer to it.

Talking with someone caught back in this way, I as counsellor need to stand in at the Self end of the ego-Self axis, and begin to mediate the need to come to the appropriate stage of growth. If they're caught back into adolescence, I hold the other end as a parental *image* – this time an encouraging one – helping them over the threshold, neither actually nor tacitly holding them back. If they're caught back at school age, I may play the part of *parent*, holding, sustaining and encouraging them to go out and make forays of exploration, and so may have to take the projection of the parent for a period.

If the individual didn't really emerge from the nursery at all, never got their own ego-centre into the outside world, the parents will be very active within their psyche. Rarely does a counsellor have to deal with that extreme *participation mystique*, where the child and the mother still share absolutely the same ego. It's analysts who see people in that condition, as do psychologists and psychiatrists who may take them into care. Then the analyst has to be container for an ego so undeveloped or so damaged, so wounded that it has remained in or gone back into the foetal position.

The wound

Breaking up to break down is different from breaking up to break through. Somebody might come in with an addiction to drink or drugs, for instance, and you must know whether they are blotting themselves out because they want to return into the oblivion of the unconscious and hide, or whether it's the search for a new insight and a new vision that's pulling them back. Much of what's called 'regressive' or 'clinical' is an unconscious effort by the individual to reconnect broken links and emerge into the present. Very often it becomes apparent, through the imaging, that somebody's illness or dysfunction or strange behaviour is an effort to explore, cleanse and bring some of these old hurts and wounds to light so that a certain amount of scar tissue can grow over them. I myself could not now work in a way that paid no regard to the images of the people involved, because I wouldn't wish to have to make my decision about where they're coming from and where they're going. *They* will tell *me*, I hope, as we work with imaging – and very often they will tell me what they *don't* know.

In this connection, a little girl I know is a good example of how a hurt, a deep wound, was shown in behaviour that could have gone on to become a malfunction at a later stage: a woman came and asked if I could suggest a special school for her disturbed daughter. I said I couldn't, but would she tell me about her daughter? She was six and a half and had been behaving very oddly. The educational psychologist, suggesting the special school, had said, 'Yes, definitely disturbed, obsessive behaviour!' I asked the mother to bring the child along. I watched her play; she seemed to me a remarkably undisturbed child! I asked her mother about the nature of the disturbance. 'She keeps tying things together. Every single thing she comes across, she ties. She ties the dog-leads together, she ties up the fringes on the lamps.' This had been called 'disturbed, obsessive behaviour' by the psychologist. Nobody had asked the straight question which one would ask the child (or, come to that, the parent): 'What is happening in the home environment?'

It turned out that the parents were separating. So what was their daughter doing? Re-constellating for herself that which was being cut and parted! Here is a small child naturally and spontaneously trying to make whole that which was severed. And very frequently I'll find such a six and a half year old within a so-called 'disturbed' adult at a much later age, and see that the disturbance is not necessarily a regression, but a movement towards health.

The mother, the child and I explored backwards into the past. I wasn't sure from her behaviour that the mother wasn't further back than the child. I asked, 'Has she got a plaything, a toy?' 'She did have, once,' said the mother. 'When she was about eighteen months she had a yellow squirrel, but she lost it.' 'What happened to it – was it replaced?' 'Oh no! She was too old for that sort of thing by then!' Occasionally I allow myself the indulgence of getting angry! I said, 'For God's sake, if she can't have a toy when she's a child, when can she have one? What is "grown-up" and what isn't?' I suggested they went to a toy-shop and – if it wasn't too late by then – see if her daughter would choose a toy. Then the mother should duplicate it, getting two of them.

The little girl chose a pair of pandas. The two went everywhere with

her. Though they were soft toys she would dunk them in the bath, and
mother was so 'well brought up' that she absolutely hated this – perhaps
why her husband was going away. But, by degrees, the disturbed
behaviour began to stop (well, you'd expect it to with a child who took
two pandas out in the pram and slept with a panda on either side of her).
What had been displaced was replaced; otherwise by adolescence and
adulthood it might have become an hysterical displacement.

So with the Child in the Adult; holding the Self's end of the ego-Self
axis, we explore the nature of the wound. We are looking out for the
degree of bruising or hurt that occurred, early or late, along the axis. If
capable of it, the therapist may stand in for the Self as priest-healer,
mediating the nature of the Self to the person, helping to draw them
forward to the full potential of their own nature, which makes it very
Transpersonal counselling.

The healing wound

The Jungian school and the Freudian, Kleinian school part company over
the subject of hurt, damage, wounding. I find the latter approach very
depressing. The implication is that if you didn't have the right soil for the
seed to begin to grow, or if your conditioning didn't give you a chance to
make it at any particular age – well, you have no hope. The map stops
there.

Jung's emphasis, possibly his over-emphasis, was on the difference
between the damaging hurt or wound, which causes someone to bleed
and die of it, and the healing wound out of which our greatest creativity
can grow. 'Only the wounded physician can heal' was first said, as far as
we know, by Aesculapius and then by Paracelsus. In our modern times,
Jung spoke of Chiron the Centaur, wounded in the thigh;[13] out of that unhealing hurt grew his wisdom, his understanding, his sensitivity, his
power to heal. Jung made continuous reference to the fact that in the very
place where one is bitten and poisoned by the serpent, there also is the
healing. 'Wounding' is a strong word, but I've seen many people –
counsellors, therapists, analysts among them – grow, over the years, from
the wound in them.

Given the opportunity, people pin-point with absolute infallibility the
ages at which the wounds occurred. They know. Ask, 'How old do you

---

[13] Chiron was accidentally wounded with a poisoned arrow by his pupil and admirer, Heracles. Ed.

feel?' and they will tell you; if they say, 'I was three and a half', they were three and a half.

We're not always dealing with one child within the adult; in certain circumstances a number of 'children' will be constelled. We may have around us three or four of them at different stages, still interacting in current living. We all like to think ourselves adult, but in fact bits of most of us are caught back at earlier stages, and very often it's they who decide what we're going to do, how we're going to respond.

Taking the hand of the child

Here's a story of how a friend, a woman of mature years, wanted to buy a blouse. Holding a very important place at work, a pioneer and a leader, she was a wonderfully energising, supportive, remarkable, vivid person, who had herself helped a lot of inner children to grow up. However, as a child she'd been consistently abused in her brother's school, used as a sex object by any number of boys, and it had crucified her own feminine nature. Inside herself was a frightened, terrified child. Now, she'd just about had enough. 'I hate myself!' she said. Soon to do a television interview about her work, she'd seen in the boutique window a very lovely blouse, just exactly what was wanted. 'But I couldn't go in!' she said. There'd been nobody there but a couple of puffy-nosed ladies lording it in their shop, but she had not been able to bring herself to walk in.

She was terrified of the impact inside herself. We talked. By going back through the images, asking, 'What does that sort of thing remind you of?' we anchored the child, and the particular hang-up. Soon she found a young child within. Saying 'Hi!' to each other, they made friends. As her adult self, she was able by degrees to take hold of the child's hand. She realised she was linked with a child who couldn't just walk into a shop without someone saying, 'Look I'll hold your hand.' So, in imaging, she held the child's hand: 'Come on, we want that blouse. I will take you into the shop'. And they both went in. Next, she went to the actual shop and walked in, holding on to the child. Once in, of course they both had to handle it! But they got the blouse and belted out again. She felt marvellous for having been able to do it.

The child had been split off from herself, from her own validity, from her own being. It's extraordinary how we can reconnect, by these slow degrees, that which was split. Somehow we have to make the link. The best link in the world is with the adult person, who takes the hand of their own child and recreates and works from that link. Once again, it's the recreating of the Self-ego axis.

The Child in the Adult sees from a child's-eye view; there's a tendency to overblown language, over-large images. We need to move our eye-level down to the height of the child talking with us. A fifty-three-year-old, for example, exploring something that was very difficult when he was twelve, needs the eye-level of both of us to come down to explore that twelve year old world. He may imply that it ought not to be like that, but it *is* like that; the twelve year old is re-constellated at that moment, as alive as ever. By seeing the present situation from the viewpoint of that child, accepting it as a reality of *now*, we help them accept that there is a child in them which, given the right trigger, responds exactly as it did at twelve years old – or four years old or two years old.

When the four year old bobs up in an adult's life, the person reacts as if they were four. I then aim to reconnect them with the child *before* it became hurt, so that they can say, 'It's all right, there's two of us here. It may have been rough for you when you were four, but I'm here now.' That interaction and dialogue sounds simplistic but it's very, very fundamental and, like most simple things, highly effective. The person can bring forward into current living the energy locked back at four years old by reaffirming the child: 'It's all right to come out, I'm here now.' A lot of the work is to help them parent their own child, to comfort it. I will often use a cushion; for the adult sitting on the sofa, the cushion beside them can become that hurt and damaged child.

It often happens that parents substitute the child for what they haven't worked through themselves. Another man of about thirty three had what he called 'a humiliation problem'. In certain circumstances he would blush desperately, though he could see no pattern in feeling so humiliated. He'd been born in the Colonies. 'My father was all for huntin', shootin', beat-up-the-tigers-and-let's-have-'em-for-a doormat,' and while his older brother was like the father, his mother was very sensitive. Since her marriage was unsatisfying, she turned my client into her replacement lover, telling him, 'This great brute of a man goes and kills all those beautiful animals. You're not like that!' He was very, very interested in animals, always touching them, thinking them beautiful, and the sight of blood made him throw up. Certainly he was naturally a very intuitive, feeling person – but not quite to that extent. By the time he was four he was playing with paper dolls, and would have chosen to carry them around with him but that obviously, with his father and brother there, he couldn't. So he turned to painting and art, using a great deal of colour. Already the natural impulse of the child was to redeem the polarity, the tension between himself and his father and his mother.

In connection with the feeling of humiliation, he remembered vividly his father 'beating him with a rawhide whip for having run away from a fist fight'. As it turned out, he hadn't been beaten with the rawhide whip, though his father had threatened him with it (by working on the imagery of it we found it was a fantasy beating). He was completely out of tune with his English school and, of course, very much tied to his mother. Hitting the stereotyped masculine there drove him even further away from his natural development, though not into his feminine side, which wasn't all that strong. His feminine was his mother, and every time he imaged it, up she came. Needing him in her life, she hadn't let him go; sad for her, but very sad for him.

When we came into one another's lives he was very unsure of his own gender. Perhaps he was bisexual? We worked on what that meant to him; he felt it to be a problem. With men he always went into the humiliation mode, and, when we looked at it, with women too. We started flipping back through the images. He brought out key points right back to those first five years with mother: 'Those great big brute men go out and kill things. But you're not like that, dear'. At about six and a half, when his father should have been leading him over towards the masculine, he was instead threatening him with the rawhide whip: 'You aren't like your brother, you aren't like me, you little sissy!' So he lacked even more any sense of his own gender.

By the time I met him, he was a film set designer. This is a fascinating and very, very clear example of someone choosing a vocation, a career which re-constellated his earlier position and brought it up in a new way. Dealing with film sets, he was given the freedom to make the characters move as he wanted and to provide the background against which they moved. He dressed them as he had designed the clothes for his paper dolls, using a lot of colour. In this setting he felt himself to be both masculine and directive. Need I say, the producer whom Life provided was very macho, just like his father! The terrific fight he had with this man was not with rawhide whips, but it wasn't far short.

Two images came up for him, as we worked on his sense of humiliation. First he flipped back to a scene he'd completely forgotten, when at about five and a half he'd been at a mixed infants' school and – lo and behold, again the polarity! – for some game the little boys were lined up on one side and the little girls on the other. And a big bully-boy came along and whipped my client's trousers down. And there he was, exposed in front of all those girls! He ran away and hid and cried, and there was a lot of teasing about it. Telling me this story, which he'd completely forgotten, he started to cry again. He felt very embarrassed, crying in front of me. I gave him a cushion, saying, 'What would you have liked to do with that child?' He said, 'Somebody should have gone and comforted it'. I said, 'Would you like to go and comfort it?' He obviously felt an absolute idiot doing it, but he started to comfort the cushion, and he got very involved with this cushion. We worked over it a couple of times, going through the whole scene until he was more confident about comforting the child.

I quite often ask people to bring photographs of themselves at key ages. His memory of himself at that time was as 'a ninny, a sissy, an effeminate milksop'. But (and over and over you come across this) that was the overlay of what other people had said about him. The photographs didn't show it at all. They showed a dirty-kneed, upright little boy, pretty fair and square to the earth. He was astonished to see he'd been that kind of boy at that age. We looked at even earlier pictures to compare, and there was the same emergent little character. It was only later, at school, that the photos began to get closer to what other people had laid on him.

Flipping back through the album, a second image came up whose nature he'd never been able to understand. At school, aged thirteen or fourteen, he'd been brought in to play cricket as thirteenth man. His parents were visiting, it was the school match and he was batting, which wasn't his style. He could never explain why it was, but the bowler moved towards him in such a way that my client came out from the batting crease and cracked him over the head with his bat. NOT what you do on an English cricket pitch, least of all with your parents there.

There was the most horrendous hoo-ha. 'You can shoot who you like, but you do not hit the bowler with a bat or you get expelled!' And by God he was expelled! Then he began to understand the humiliation picture, though it did not seem to have a direct bearing. His memory was of that rawhide whip, but his imaging was taking him back to two other eras: age five and a half, and age thirteen. He recognised that the bowler had reminded him of the bully-boy who pulled his trousers down. For the first time in his life he began to understand the connections: on top of being called 'milksop', he had this peculiar behaviour-pattern which had got him expelled from school. So the images took us back exactly where they wanted us to go.

Befriending the child in the adult

Sometimes, although it's unconscious, the adult may have a fairly considerable dislike of the habits and patterns of the child within. People think they hate themselves, but what they're hating is their own childish behaviour. When (in imaging) we constellate the child, we discover that it experiences the adult as hating it! This brings into focus the inner conflict. People may hate themselves for, say, cringing in front of an authority figure, but it's the poor little cringing child who feels it's being hated. It's a matter of acceptance; first beginning to recognise that child, then befriending it, and eventually – maybe – coming to love it, which takes a little more time. At last the child may come to trust the adult a bit, and release its energy into their life.

Many of us 'don't remember' with our heads what it was like as a child. There's usually a very good reason for that, but when, with the images, we work through the feelings, it's amazing how much someone may recall that they didn't know they did. We remember a lot more than we think; we cannot presume that we forget. The memory isn't just the imprint in the mind; the very young child takes it in through the body, through the feeling, through the atmosphere, through taste, a sudden smell – 'What is that smell?' – and up it comes again. We register everything, though not in our heads. Working with this can cut in right under the mind to these earlier stages, which were absorbed subjectively, through sensation: ancient, ancient memories…

One man had a phobia about the smell of chrysanthemums. He had no idea why. He was also having rows with his wife; they'd had an awful argument the night before. I wasn't choosing to work on chrysanth-emums as we began with imaging. I asked, 'When have you felt like this before?' Inwardly, we went back through a whole series of stages till he reached the age of about four. He said he didn't consciously remember anything earlier than that, and certainly we could get no further by talking about it. But through imaging he went back to an evening when he'd been on his way down to get a glass of water and heard his mother and father having a row. He didn't know what to do; he hovered on the staircase, he crept down and looked in – and there was his father, apparently throttling his mother.

In fact, as this adult now realised, he was probably shaking her. She'd been having an affair, as was later known. But from the child's point of view his father was strangling the life out of mother in the dining room. Both of them were shouting, which he wasn't used to – another family where negative feelings were kept well under. Although, young as he was, he'd been aware of 'things going on' in the environment, the child was shocked.

I asked him about the room. Imaging it in detail, he gave an absolutely clear picture, down to the colour of the carpet (he later checked this out with his mother). He remembered the curtains, the crackling of the fire, the feeling of the room, how he felt in his pyjamas standing looking through the crack in the door. And, quivering in a vase under the impact of father shaking mother, was a trembling bunch of yellow chrysanthemums! An impact image of that moment was indelibly within him, not in his mind but in his body. Now, had I talked only to his mind he wouldn't have recalled that (though it might have come out under hypnosis or drugs). It was the image that took him back and re-evoked the impress that had been made on him. His body had held the memory of the whole trauma. It was that that came up when he smelt chrysanthemums, giving him his sense of panic – his phobia.

The language of the body

Memories are also locked in the musculature. I either use body-work myself (working on stance, for example), or I suggest the client go to an expert to help release what has been locked – not in the head; the mind forgets, but the muscles remember. Talking to someone, I often see their body go into some typical reaction: they may cradle one side of their body; quite often they rock. You can arrest a moment like that: 'Just what is your body saying now?' It's the movement of the defended child. It's worth remembering that, before about four, consciousness of feeling and body aren't well-differentiated; it's all one kind of sensation. For many, the earliest memories go back to about three; we can't get back beyond that in consciousness, nor in feeling, nor in images. But in terms of body sensation we go way back beyond that, and this may help us understand some of the root problems.

The father of one woman was in the Navy and was killed at sea when she was three. We kept going back in memory to the effect this had had on her mother, and therefore on her own environment (remembering that between birth and five we still share an ego-centre with our mother). Something I'd observed over a few sessions without really noticing it was that she moved her mouth like a rabbit, moving her top lip down. I became fully aware of it only when we were talking about that three-year-old period. 'What are you doing with your top lip?' I asked, and she said, 'I can't explain it – I've just got this very odd tingling feeling'.

We checked out the feeling: in effect she'd been taking in the environment through her top lip. For the first three months, a baby has little sensitive buds on the lip which vanish after weaning. Her memory of taking in the environment of her mother without her father was being communicated across to us by her top lip – crazy though it sounds! I was very slow in the uptake: it was only after about three meetings that I started questioning her 'rabbiting' expression. We'd been talking about her life at three to four years old, but much earlier on, her top lip had been telling us to look right back to the breast-feeding period, between birth and three months. When we did, she found that the father's death was the confirmation of a feeling her mother had had when he first went to sea. His death by drowning, and the telegram that told this, was no more than a confirmation of her mother's adult expectation (checked out later). And there was her top lip quivering!

The memories are there, imprinted. The child's memory of the very early period is all touch; it's impressed in the fingertips, in the feeling, in the sensation; it's there in the top lip and the taste buds, it's there in smell. As far as we're able to judge it, a child's sense of smell is much stronger and closer to the animal in the first year of life than it ever is again. Later functions overlie it, replacing those earlier survival factors. This woman was forty-seven and had had three children, but her top lip was communicating something. Through its images, the *body* will take you to what the child in the adult was feeling. The head may rationalize; it's the most marvellous instrument – wonderful – presumably about the whole emergence of consciousness. But it's an awful disguiser too, veiling as much as it reveals. We have to work with the total person. If I can't get in through the head, I will go in through the images, and through the body.

Talking about simplistic things: as a child, another woman had had a lion called Lena. Lena had vanished off the scene. It was a large, untidy family and Lena had been taken away, presumably passed on to somebody younger than herself. Asked about the atmosphere and ambience of the nursery, she said, 'Total chaos!' 'What was the counterpoint to total chaos?' I asked. 'Lena! I'd forgotten all about that lion!' We began to work with Lena the Lion. With a cushion for Lena we were able to go back and map her childhood and the whole chaotic atmosphere. She couldn't handle it; an introverted child, frightened, in a very extraverted family.

I said, 'Let your body take the position that you were in during those first years.' Going back now to two and a half, by degrees she curled up, took the cushion, slid off my couch and went behind it. I went after her – we did the rest of the counselling round the back of the furniture! She was right down, and I went down with her – the best way to help a child if you want to understand it is to get down to its eye-level. I was working along with her; as she came up by degrees, we both came up. I asked her if she'd like to take the cushion away with her. 'I'd look an absolute fool walking through London with a gold and black cushion, wouldn't I?' she said. 'Would you?' I asked. 'Who says so?' She took that cushion out under her arm and went off carrying it.

She bought a lion – her own choice – and called it Lena. At first, she used to arrive bringing a bag with a long tassled tail hanging out. It sounds crazy but it was her reality, it brought her back to the one hold, the one 'transitional object' that had held her – 'between chaos and being wiped out,' as she said – and enabled her to begin to stand. From that one thing we were able to work forward. No longer did she have to carry the lion around with her; when she went out into chaotic adult situations she could just say, 'Hi Lena!' And she'd come back to Lena again at the end of the day: 'Hi, Lena.' She doesn't need Lena now. Lena is back inside her where she belongs. But, my goodness, what a journey we went, and how grateful I was for that lion!

The language of the nursery

As we listen to what the child in the adult says, out come the shoulds, the oughts, the double messages, the dos and don'ts: 'It's an absolute pain in the neck!' they say. 'I can't stomach it.' 'I feel totally hog-tied.' 'It's like banging my head against a brick wall.' The language takes us back through the stages, very often to a burden the person is carrying; it may be appropriate, or it may now be inappropriate – like the parents' unfulfilled expectation of them. I ask, 'Whose scripts and viewpoints are these? Are they *still* your responsibility? Haven't you enough aboard to be an adult without carrying all this old stuff that doesn't belong to you?'

We follow the imaging, the photograph album. Starting from the present, we scroll back and pause; it may be at some current unhelpful reaction, a dysfunction in how the client is dealing with life now which goes back no further, and I may be able to help them on that. However, we may find the imaging pauses at an earlier stage, perhaps at adolescence; or it may take us back further still. I follow the person's images, working from where they take me, not where I think they ought to go, getting the feel of it. Though the seed is at the bottom of the map under many layers of silt, I don't have to say, 'Now, tell me about your childhood.' The person will tell me: 'I can't go into a four-ale bar – I get terrified because I think there's a black dog behind it'. Or: 'I can't stand on an underground station, I'm petrified when the train comes out of the tunnel'. We work downwards from where the image is now, not immediately trying to map it upwards. 'What's the feeling when you're standing on the platform, what's the impact on you of the train, what does your body feel?' They'll start marvellously undoing their images and taking you back to what that train coming out of the tunnel signifies *for them*.

Avoiding interpretation

Some people would tend to give the whole interpretative thing: 'Now, that is really phallic – out of the womb comes the emergent penis'. I say, 'My foot to that!' That may absolutely *not* be what the person means. All the theory in the world is valuable only so long as we keep it not in front of us, but behind.

So we're watching for the child's intervention in adult situations, helping the person take responsibility for its re-scripting and release. Holding the hand of the child, metaphorically if not actually, we re-live situations in the way they would like – not as it happened, but as they would like to be able to do it in future. We're reinforcing their ability to make choices, become responsible for their own lives, discover the difference between authority and authoritarianism – and to become their own authority. We help the child to grow, help the person unplait past from present, get the ground back under their feet so that there's not only soil for their roots to work in, but light around them. Then they can reconcile father and mother within themselves, take an individual stance, find their own voice. We help them look at the possibility of *meaning* behind their experience, affirming that at no stage is it too late to redeem the past, but it's only redeemable from the ground that's under their feet *now*. The future springs out of the present. We can't redeem it from the past, but the process of going back is itself redemptive, releasing our locked-up energy and bringing it into current life.

So at last they return, not to the original womb of Stage One (Fig. 3, p. 35), but to the essential seed and its own potential. The womb was after all only the container of the placenta that fed and nourished the person. It's the seed we're after. Stages Two, Three and Four are about the return to the individual Self, as a child of that Self, not of the original parents. (Jung called them our 'accidental' parents, and the Self our 'chosen' parent.) Stages Five and Six are a return to that Self. A lot of psychologists and therapists get lost there. As I say, the wise don't come in for counselling; yet occasionally, early or late, we find ourselves willy-nilly beginning to work with these final areas – and, my God, it brings out how far maturity and wisdom are even remotely anchored within ourselves!

Plate 8

Bringing down the Moon

CHAPTER FIVE

The Mother,
Her Image and Archetype
Barbara Somers

In the early years the mother stands in for the Self.
She is sun, moon and stars to the child; she is the universe;
she is meaning and purpose;
she is the arbiter of whether it lives or dies

Here we're probably talking about the whole matrix of consciousness itself. This is an exceedingly seminal subject and mother is obviously writ very large. We've looked at the seed; the mother is the container of that seed. Our language about her will be extreme. 'The Mother' isn't just our own personal mother, though it's her we talk about. Behind the personal mother is the mother *image*, and it's inevitably a collective as well as a personal image. Nobody truly sees their mother clearly; they cannot. It's quite impossible to be objective about this most subjective of all relationships. The mother always has to carry something of the image with her. And behind the image lies a major *archetype*: the Great Mother. Our myth, legend, and folklore have carried the archetype of the Great Mother forward for us for centuries. It's the Mother principle in all life, and it's part of the human psyche, of human experience.

The Mother archetype

I find the Jungian and Transpersonal and Psychosynthesis approaches valuable in recognising that mother is not just the person, she is also the image, and also the archetype.[14] I'll look at the Transpersonal, archetypal level first before going on to talk about the image, and then

---

[14] Frances Wickes was one of the earlier Jungians. She'd taught children and had her own too, and helped to bring the child forward in her books 'The Inner World of Childhood' and 'The Inner World of Choice', where she put together everything that Klein and Freud had to say about the Child. She brought out the hope that we've not only come from somewhere but may be going somewhere – that there's not only the original womb, but the later creative womb, the X-factor or spiritual impulse. Each area of psychology has something to say; if any one of them claims to have it all, they limit us and can kill out hope. This is true of religions, philosophies, psychologies... and everything else.

the personal mother. In a valuable book[15] Jung points out in how many aspects the mother archetype can appear. She may be found not only in the personal mother but in almost any woman with whom a relationship exists – the grandmother, the mother-in-law, the step-mother, the nurse or governess, even the remote ancestress. Then there are the images that come up in dream and fairy tale. Here are the goddess, Sophia, the Mother of God, the Virgin; they represent our longing for redemption, as do Paradise, the Heavenly Jerusalem, the Kingdom of God. Here are motifs that inspire devotion, feelings of awe – heaven, earth, the moon, the woods, the sea, still waters, the underworld. Here too are church, university, city or country. The mother archetype is in images – a ploughed field, a garden, the cornucopia – things of fertility and fruitfulness. We dream of a rock, a cave, a spring, a tree, a deep well. She is to be found in vessel-shaped flowers, in the baptismal font, in hollow objects such as ovens and cooking vessels.

Jolande Jacobi[16] writes about the many dragon myths in which a monster is dismembered. The 'devouring, terrible mother' must be overcome if we are to acquire an independent ego-personality. The 'mother' is the symbol of the dark unconscious, and the youth must destroy it before he can develop his own ego and consolidate it. The bright light of his consciousness is symbolised by the sun's rays or by the arrow, sword, or club with which he slays the dragon.

The emergence of the ego-centre out of the mother container is, in a very real sense, the dismemberment of a dragon or monster. Jacobi goes on to describe how, after destroying the death-dealing monster, the hero must descend into the dark unconscious. By bringing the strong light of consciousness into the depths he finds the Self, in the form of the 'pearl of great price', the 'treasure hard to attain', 'the precious hoard'. Now he must bring it back to the light of day. Thus he creates the world by the slaying of the maternal dragon, the archetypal task of the first stage of individuation; the second stage is where, devoured by it, he returns older, wiser, and reunited with the Self.

That's pretty wide-sweeping, wide-ranging language. The amount of legend, folklore and myth involving this symbolism points to the

---

[15]   See Jung, 1938-54, Para. 149-198, especially 156.
[16]   See Jacobi, 1965, Page 64-65.

fact that the Mother archetype is an important concept. However, I'll look less at the archetype and more at the personal mother, remembering that, as we've seen, behind the personal mother there lies the Mother Image, and behind the Mother Image the Mother Archetype, and behind the Mother Archetype the whole Collective Unconscious out of which our little points of consciousness have had to struggle into the light of day. Why does mother always get kicked in the teeth? Well, it isn't just poor old Mother; it's the battle of consciousness to emerge out of the great sea of the darkness of the unconscious that lies behind it all.

The personal mother

Looking with someone at their personal mother, one of the basic questions to bear in mind is, 'Who was Mother, who was Father?' It doesn't necessarily follow that it was the obvious way round; the father may carry the mothering nature and qualities, and the mother the fathering nature and qualities.

The child's first experience of the mother is the womb, but with the emergence from the womb the body-contact continues, the child sensing the mother through touch, smell, taste, feel, two arms that hold. I like this concept: *two arms that hold*. I will look at the personal mother in terms of this hold, taking it at three different levels: firstly, the good hold or *good enough hold* (in psychological terminology, 'positive bonding'); secondly the *too loose hold*; and thirdly the *too tight hold* (these two would be 'negative bonding').

I have a cassette titled, 'Asleep in the Womb'. It's the sound the child hears in the last three months of its inter-uterine life, a lovely, continuous pulsation – 'boom ... boom ... boom' – with a slight hiss-back, like the sea, waves coming in, waves going back. The hiss of the mother's bloodstream is the background to the child's life as it comes towards the threshold of its physical birthing. Some people hear in it a roar, with a beat of thunder in, but I hear it as a soft, gentle, beautiful sound – I see why the rhythmic and long-distance train journey is so cradling, why so many of us are drawn to the sound of the sea, why water has such an effect on us. That heartbeat sound of the blood provides a continuum for the child in the womb, and whether it's afterwards broken or not depends very much on the nature of the mother.

The mother's viewpoint

It's easy to forget that a woman becomes a mother neither by spontaneous combustion nor immaculate conception. She too has her origins. Yet after birth, her subjective life is still the placenta on which the born child feeds. She is a continuation. And generally, she has to learn to become a mother. Women have been told from time immemorial, 'Ah, your mother instinct will come out as soon as you have the baby!' but it's an old wives' tale; some go on waiting for ever. The girl who is a woman who becomes the mother is also a child of her times with her own restraints, guilts, expectations and the scripting of her own culture and social background. As a fallible human being, she will inevitably have to carry the mother *image* that she has inherited. Fraily human, she is also going to be seen as *archetypal*, the ideal haven, provider, solace. I came across a poem by Rilke – just read it!

> Mother, you made him small; it was you who began him.
> To you he was new, and over the young eyes you bent down
> a world that was friendly and staved off the strange.
> Where, oh where, are the years
> when you, simply by stepping in front of it,
> screened with your slender figure the seething abyss?
> Much you did hide from him thus: the room
> that was creepy at night you made harmless;
> and out of your heart full of refuge,
> you mingled a humaner space with his night-space.[17]

Follow that! It's beautiful, but it's also what the child *expects* of the mother. Becoming a mother may indeed be something of great joy for her, great sense of achievement, great fullness, a resolution of her nature, a mystery and a miracle, opening up reaches of her consciousness that she never thought possible. And a lot of women do have that experience. Yet most don't have an awful lot of preparation for being mothers (though many expect some transmogrification of the first order). She may equally validly have been struggling to handle the birth of the child, to meet her own expectations or her partner's, or to raise the child on her own. She may like only small babies and feel threatened by growing ones, loving kittens but not cats, lambs but not sheep. Or she may loathe the small baby stage and only begin to relate to the child when it gets 'interesting'.

---

17   Rainer Maria Rilke, Duino Elegies, from the Third Elegy.

She may not know how to handle children or young people at all. She may feel motherhood as an overwhelming responsibility, a threat to her own identity, a bondage on her freedom. So much depends on her own degree of openness and potential for growth.

We have to bear all this in mind when listening to someone talking about 'mother', remembering how suddenly she was projected into it. While fraily human, her children often have such a need for the archetype that she isn't *allowed* to be fallible. Though fighting perhaps to free herself from her own early conditioning (she too may never have left the nursery) she's suddenly expected by them to be ideal provider and haven, and by herself and others to be at the same time the ideal mate. A lot of children become carriers for the unrecognised conflict, the unlived, unrealised life and lack of personality development in the mother, or in both parents.

We need to see the mother as at least a person, a real woman, before we begin to look at the child's relationship to her. Hearing from them how she rejected and left them, how poorly she bonded with them, we ask whether she was ill herself, in hospital at a crucial early stage in her child's infancy, emotionally depressed or distressed, having marriage problems? 'Was she in hospital for the birth?' I ask. 'Did she have you at home? What was her emotional position at the time?' Was she traumatised by the birth, overwhelmed by external pressures or by other children in the family? So much depended on her own maturity and how free she was from *her* childhood and its blocks and problems. Sure enough, if there are too many unresolved childish hang-ups within herself, they'll be constellated in a really big way when she has her own child.

I'd remind you that there *is* such a thing as a positive mother! Listening, I sometimes wonder: 'Surely mothers can't all be as bad as that, such ravening monsters? Doesn't anybody ever have one worth having?' Well, of course they do. But children of the 'good enough' mother (and it's to be hoped there was also a father helping the child across the threshold) don't often come into counselling. Those who do have nearly always been given some sort of wounding in that primary relationship. So the over-emphasis on the demoniacal or absent mother comes out – and she is omnipresent.

Mother's place is in the wrong!

This is because of the subjective nature of the mother. She can never fulfil all she appears to stand for. Given good bonding, the child can afford to be disillusioned in its expectation, finding the reality even more acceptable; but if it has poor bonding the child is left with nothing but its

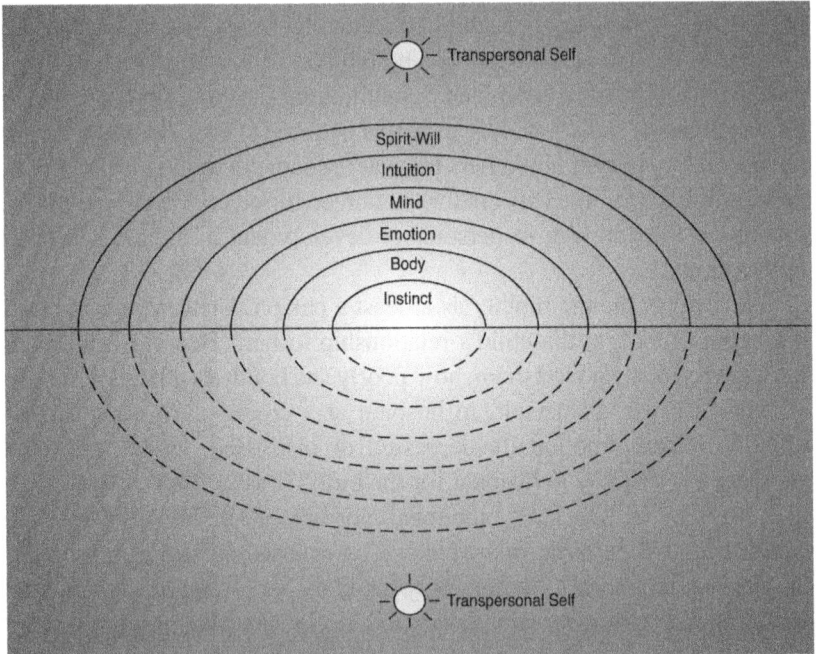

Figure 5   Levels of Consciousness

fantasy hopes, which are never met – can never be met. So the fantasy increases, and the person projects the longed for, perfect, adoring, embracing mother out to the world. (However, if they found it, that would give them the *too* good parent – and that wouldn't work either!)

The map at Figure 5, above (to be read from the bottom upwards) shows the levels of consciousness available to an individual. Classically, in the Eastern religions and in esoteric teaching, the instinctual, emotional and intuitive levels – the non-rational modes – have been related to the feminine, while the physical and mental levels are associated with the masculine. The spiritual is a conjunct of masculine and feminine, obviously including them but going far beyond.

So while, as we shall see, the father, the Father Image and the Father Archetype have a bearing on the physical, mental and spiritual aspects, mother as feminine mediates to the child those things which the Feminine Principle itself mediates. Crucially, she is the primary shaper of the non-rational side for the child. Her impact at the instinctual level has a lot of bearing on *gender identity* ('Am I a boy, am I a girl?'); at the emotional level it's about relationships and openness to the world; and at the intuitive level, about subjective *creativity*, and also the ability to make contact with the inner world and anchor it in the outer.

Apart from whatever happens within the womb itself, when the child emerges into the world, in the very first moments of its life, mother will be sensed as body – breast, nipple, hands, skin; as touch, taste, smell, feel; as ambiance, atmosphere. At no time is a human being aware of touch and taste with such animal sharpness as in its first months. We've seen how it's to be hoped that mother is experienced crucially as two arms that hold.[18] Because 'hold' is so crucial, we shall look at the mother and her interaction with the child in terms of that hold, which may be 'good enough', 'too loose' or 'too tight', and at its effect in each of the stages (see Figure 3, the Emergence Map, p. 35).

The good enough mother

We shall start with what in his enchanting phrase Winnicott called the good enough mother.[19] I love this! He said – and, goodness, one agrees with him! – that the mother really does not help the child by being too good. Supplying absolutely everything is not preparing a child for later life; this wicked world is notoriously under-populated with people willing to act as parents to wandering children. The too good mother is no preparation. Equally, of course, the disastrous mother is no preparation. The best mother for any child is good enough, getting it roughly right when she's not getting it too badly wrong, open enough, human enough to allow her humanity to pass over to the child.

At Stage One, from birth till five, and particularly till three, the child

---

[18] In ancient times, practically all cultures had rites of passage to ensure that if for some reason the child wasn't laid on the mother's breast it had an immediate touch of hands. The closeness of bodies was part of the birthing process. If there was a gap in the circuit, if the mother died or wasn't able, some woman-figure or wet-nurse stepped in and the gap was bridged. Nowadays, if the mother misses the first contact, it's difficult to set the process going. However, it's not impossible; even if the child has been in an incubator for days after the birth, psychologically the gap can be bridged.

[19] Winnicott's work on the maturational processes of the child is well worth reading.

shares the subjective life of the mother, as we've seen; indeed, in the first year it seems they share an ego identity. Like the white of an egg, the mother provides the nourishing background that allows the embryo in the yellow part to grow. By her touch, by her placing the child against her own flesh, by her breathing, her smell, her milk, she gives it a sense of outline, a spatial definition, so that it can begin to recognise itself as a subject. And it is not only subjective to the inner world of the mother; by degrees it becomes a subject in its own right, beginning to objectify and recognise itself as a little 'I', a 'me', a somebody in the world. Children who've hardly ever been touched (brought up in homes or fostered a great deal, perhaps) find it extremely difficult to have any sense of body, of spatial boundaries.

At about three months the thumb comes into action and the child begins to grip hold of things and retain them. Given the good enough mother, it will pick up a rattle, wave it around and, losing it, will look to see where it went, expecting that 'what vanishes can also come back'. It's notable that children who've *not* had that continuity – perhaps they've been put in hospital – will tend not to bother to look for things they've dropped. That continues into later life; given a good enough mother, the person can tolerate things going in the hope that they'll come back again. Those without good bonding in those very crucial early months and years expect that what goes probably won't come back, so isn't worth looking for.

So the regularity of the heartbeat, the continuum of 'what goes away can come back', are provided by the mother. She gives certain benign guidelines to kick against, to step over, to stay within. Given these, the roots in the child will go down into a good soil and begin to take hold. Without this benign and loving discipline, too much early responsibility may be put on the child, who has to make its own guidelines.

It's all very well to say 'all children should go to the breast', but it doesn't necessarily follow that it makes for better bonding. What sort of breast was it? Subjectively, the child picks up what's coming out with that milk. That's why I talk about 'hold', rather than about the breast. Some children would do a great deal better to be held by somebody loving and fed with a bottle, than against their own mother's rejecting breast. We know that not only Rhesus monkeys but children in orphanages and asylums just shrivel up and die if they don't have at least a degree of touching. However, certainly the laying of the child on the mother's breast would be the absolutely perfect thing and, if she's a good enough mother, that sense of bonding, the sheer physical sensation of skin contact, is a tremendously important matter.

Gradually, with the help of toys and pets as we've seen, the child can be weaned away from the totally symbiotic, subjective life shared with the mother and begin to experience a world 'out there' as well as a world 'in here'. The good enough mother, in helping the child to define its body outline, gives it enough imagined ego strength for its inner and outer worlds to begin to integrate together. She's required to be in the foreground in the years from nought to three; then by degrees she moves more into the background so that the child can go and explore the outer world, but always coming back to the safety of the inner.

It's the mother's action of touch and feel that gives the child the sense and enjoyment of the sensuous. We may seek it in later relationships, but never again can we share the same subjective life with someone as the child does with the mother. Have you ever seen a small baby held by its mother, and the look of total bliss on its face? When it's been fed and touched and held, and is warm and dry and comfortable through its entire body, it's blissed out!

If the ego is to emerge naturally and without damage, the primary requirement is that the child should feel safe to be itself. Good or naughty, it needs to feel it's still loved, and that the affirming background, the same heartbeat which was there in the womb, the regularity, the predictability, the sense that 'what goes away will come back', will continue.

At Stage Two, from five to twelve, the good enough mother will draw back and allow the emphasis of the father (or his substitute) to begin to affect the child. She encourages its forays into the outer world, standing behind it as a base from which it can go out to explore the world of the father and his otherness, of school, peers, siblings, other gods, other authorities. She supports its first relationships, backing up this little individual in enlarging its experience of its own gender away from her influence. So she helps it on its way towards its sexual identity (we'll see later what happens when the mother doesn't do that). She's a launching pad for exploration into outer space, but she still provides a safe haven, a secure place, a continuum to which the child's small space-capsule can return.

By adolescence, at Stage Three, the good enough mother supports but lets go. Her function now is to fall into the background, forming the matrix, the root base, the ground soil for future growth. She becomes the unconscious security from which to face the challenge of the unknown. Remember adolescence? It's lovely to have the smell of cooking coming from the kitchen, the sound of mother in the background, but you don't want her too much in the foreground. Adolescents say to their mothers, 'I wish you'd just keep your apron on and stay home – I don't like you looking pretty, going out for a job.' They don't always put it quite like that – though sometimes they do! The good enough mother knows when to retreat quietly, while still there as a presence.

If the good enough mother has begun to move from the foreground into the background, both boy and girl should have quite a sense of themselves, knowing, 'I am female', 'I am male', 'that is my mother, this is me'. She will have allowed, at any time from adolescence to adulthood, for the other sexual gender to appear. Someone will eventually take her child away from the nursery; the boy will meet his own woman, the girl her man. And the good enough mother allows that 'otherness', letting both of them move out and make their relationships in the world without too much sense of guilt. They don't have to keep looking over their shoulders – 'Is it all right with mother?' – because she has made it clear that it *is* all right with mother. By keeping in touch with her own womanhood she sets the ground base from which boy and girl become man and woman, and found their own families. And so it goes on through generation after generation.

The hope is that the adolescent will move into adulthood in Stage Four with a strong sense of space and boundaries and bodily outline, and of their own right to be in the world; also with some idea of their sexual gender however they may choose to use it. As the ego emerges, the young adult moves on to sociability, lovingness, openness to experience and change, the ability to be in company and equally to tolerate aloneness in a healthy way. The known is felt to be safe; it provides a basic security allowing for a flexible, open approach to life. The unknown is challenge; inner experience is seen as an area of adventure for the emergent individual, not of threat from some primary monstrous figure. Moving on to the fullness of adulthood, they can leave the parental authority figures behind, learning to relate to a new kind of authority within themselves.

Towards maturity at Stage Five, mother and all she represents have dropped back into the unconscious in direct proportion to the emergence of consciousness into the outer world. Then, if indeed she has been a good enough mother, background and foreground begin to take a different shape; mother, woman, unconscious, past, roots – all in later life are seen as helpful, not as threatening.

And somewhere in this stage between adulthood and maturity, if we're going on to individuate, we need again to come to the unknown, but with that background we can do it with confidence. Any hurts or wounds received in the first years will inevitably affect all these stages later on, but the good enough mother is the best guarantee for the future that any child can have. Given that, we can withstand most of the later knocks of life. Somewhere in this stage it's to be hoped we move on, coming to a different, a higher, creative womb mediated by the *anima*. And the *anima* again leads to the dark, the unknown, the apparently dangerous, out of which the whole thrust of consciousness has emerged. Without that good enough background, this can be very threatening and challenging.

So – the good enough mother: a very difficult thing to be. Most women do it willy-nilly, by fits and starts, trial and error. And most manage to get there; we may have the illusion that not many do, but a miraculous number manage it. The good enough hold gives the well-bonded child, and they are around – a lot more of them than we might think. I'm reminded enchantingly of my very deaf friend who, hearing for the first time the sounding of the sacred 'OM', said, 'Isn't it lovely that the sacred word is "MUM"'.

The too loose hold

Next I'll look at what happens if the mother's hold is too loose, and the child senses that it isn't held firmly. This is something it's extremely aware of. If a small baby is passed from hand to hand, it's amazing how firmness – a hold not too strong, not too tight, but firm – can stop it crying. Although in the early months and years the mother's hold is very primary (and the father can give that mothering hold too), someone else's will do as long as it's firm. With somebody whose touch is uncertain the child will start crying. Thus a child with poor bonding will often scream when the mother takes it in her arms, yet quieten down with a stranger with a different kind of hold.[20]

---

[20] It's possible to have successive mothers. One man had a mother who was pretty distant. Instead he remembers a whole series of motherly nannies. Each disappeared at the most unfortunate moment, to be replaced by another. His psychological history was dominated not by Mother or Father but by all these changing nannies. In some extended families, too, the aunts and grandmothers will have provided the mothering principle, being bulwarks against some of the worst events. Another woman learnt from a foster mother how to be a mother herself.

Think of the mother with the too loose hold. The roots will be in her own psychology but, while she holds the child, it will be psychologically and physically badly held, badly bonded. It's going to have a sense of being dropped, let go, 'let down'; later it may well feel rejected. Such a child is bound to have a raised anxiety level, tending to be ungrounded and with very little sense of roots, because touch and hold haven't established it well within its body. Its feeling of being in the world at all is tenuous. Psychologically, and often physically, it has a precarious grip on life, a tentativeness, an ambivalence, a loosely-knit image of itself and who it is. It hasn't had a firm soil in which to put down its roots, and tends to be unrelated to its own body and instincts. Rejecting its own 'rejected' body, it takes the road of self-rejection. We will look at how having too loose a hold in the first years affects individuals with firstly more passive, then more active temperaments:

The passive temperament

Let's take the more passive individual. Looking back wistfully to what might have been, or forward in fantasy to what they wish could be for the future, they have very little sense at all of the here and now. The bad is in the present, and the bad self-image, of course, comes quite naturally. They continuously seek to identify with somebody, longing eternally to establish that hold with anyone who'll be a mother-replacement, searching for a sense of outline, shape, grounding, rooting to be provided by someone else. There's an anxious, neurotic, self-punishing tendency; they'd do anything, pay any price to buy their space, to buy affection, love, affirmation, usually from somebody stronger than themselves who would give them a sense of outline and identity.

If a person wasn't held then they feel unworthy of being held; if they felt unloved, they feel unlovable; rejected, they feel rejectable; if criticised, they feel bad. Here is the familiar split between head and heart. The passive, anxious, timorously-held child tends to become the neurotic, self-punishing adult. Taken to extremes, they're in line with Freud's masochistic type, apologising for their very being. There can be a bottomless pit of need for reassurance. Longing for a re-establishment of the primary symbiotic commitment and fusion, they can't get enough of it; and this plays merry hell in relationships.

One man lost his mother when he was two and a half; he carried on his job extremely well but had every look of anxiety about him. A very thin little man, he had very thin little legs. Quite ungrounded, all up in his head, he was most typically a child of the too loose hold, over-idealising any relationship, longing to be overwhelmed, taken in, taken over. When it happened (he married a very dominant woman who was only too happy to do the overwhelming) he loathed it, feeling nearly suffocated. But he could never let go of this wife in case she failed him.

However, in addition he carried within him the image of an *anima* figure, a 'beautiful beloved', and when he found some beautiful beloved 'out there' (totally inappropriate as she usually was) for a while he would feel absolutely entire. He had the mother (in the relationship with his wife) and also the beautiful beloved of the image. He tried terribly hard. However, he just couldn't pull away from his retrospective search for the original relationship with mother. The inner drive of his own adulthood pulled him towards the beautiful beloved, but just as she came in he would cry off and go back to mother. And when he got back to mother, he would cry off and try to go forward again. That continuous pull back-wards and forwards is very typical of somebody with the too loose hold.

People with such passive temperaments feel they've no right to *have* any space or boundaries, let alone an understanding of that space, those boundaries. As adults, they're split not only between head and heart, but between head and body; they go up into their minds and walk around as though they didn't have a body, nor any relation to the present. Certain types of symptom may be linked with the too loose hold. This man had neck lesions; his thinness, his ungrounded look, his back problems, his weightlessness, all showed the split between body and head. A lot of depressing things can come out of this: being out of touch with feelings; 'nerves'; the loss of various senses, particularly smell and touch, which can take an hysterical form; and depression, of course. The person hasn't been held, hasn't been given an outline, hasn't been helped to root or to feel as if they've been born into life; hence their terrible self-image.

These are people who sit right on the edges of chairs, terribly, terribly willing to help all the time. We see them rushing old ladies across the road – the old ladies kicking and screaming. Their posture shows muscular and nervous signs, since their *being* has never in itself been sufficient; they've always had to *do* something in order to be, in order to be accepted. So they're busy-busy with nervous ticks and anxiety-rigid backs. They look as though, if touched, they'd just crumple, but they're gripping the ground with their feet, trying to get an anchor-hold in life, trying to grasp a space. You can feel the poetry of it.

In relationships they often choose stronger people, hoping they'll be helped to establish some sense of self-identity. They have an intense need to be needed. Longing to have someone around for continuous affirmation, they may have great trouble with being alone, often experiencing a total loss of self-identity. Depressed, they will say, 'I fear there's nothing inside – I feel empty'. They are searching for total commitment to a person or a cause to replace the symbiotic relationship found once in the womb, but never again; a lot of their life-search may be towards that symbiotic merging. And, of course, the other person may feel absolutely swamped by their insatiable demands, spoken or tacit. They nearly always end up by being hurt, dominated and rejected. Obviously all this is ruinous for them, such hurt human beings with such a real need for later cherishing and touching.

And behind this over-loving, needful, gentle person is something very strong. With such a person we may find ourselves in a hidden minefield of hypersensitivity and touchiness: they're so easily hurt! They manage to give an impression of silent suffering and martyrdom which leaves the stronger person feeling an absolute brute, an insensitive tyrant, not knowing what they did. All they know is that they wounded this wistful person, who says: 'But I never did a thing to harm you – how could you do that to me?' It's said, 'Whatever you do, be aware of the strength of the weak'; the strength of the strong can't begin to compare with it! They can be very, very demanding. Paradoxically, the too loosely held child is either fearful of bonding or longs very much to be bonded. Often you find the paradox within the same person, difficult both for them and for their partners. Either, when you come out to make a contact, they test you as to whether you are going to reject them after all, or they want you to fill up that bottomless pit with your affirmation, support, time and, in extreme cases, with your total attention.

Unable to anchor adequately in the outer world without help, these very passive people too loosely held tend to be trapped at the inner fantasy level (like Walter Mitty, all that heroic stuff in fantasy, and following his wife around like a pet dog.) They tend to over-value the feminine because they fantasise, searching everywhere for the original womb, for bonding, for primal mothering, for the lost, paradisaical world. They're often very good with animals. Unable to meet the challenge of mature, adult interaction, they look either for the very strong, or for the wounded. They have a nose for hurt, injured, damaged children of all ages. Thus they play child to the stronger or parent to the wounded, weaker person, or they go into boy and girl relationships. Confrontation at adult level is always difficult. They reject rough, mundane, earthy, nitty-gritty stuff that has to do with the body and the instinctual values, though they may be found on rarefied psychic, esoteric fringes.

So they bring in to counselling their head, heart, body splits. The major thrust of my work with them is to help them build in a more acceptable self image, to reinforce their own self-acceptance. It may mean *being* a good enough parent. With someone from such a very wounded background the major need is to accept them, to love them until they can begin by degrees to accept and love themselves. Perhaps it's simply to hold them out of suicide – naturally a very strong possibility for such a passive person trying to get back into the containing darkness of the original womb. Simply to be there with them, being the good enough mother, can help those with deep wounds to come out of their regressive backgrounds.

I have faith in the seed within them, that it will begin to break through. Though time may pass between this new holding and the growth of the seed (it may take many years), I feel very strongly about this. I would hope to be with them in a loving, nurturing, bonding way, till they can accept the transition. The very holding becomes the transition.

The active temperament

Children with a more active seed or temperament may respond to the sense of being dropped and rejected by coming out fighting. These are the rebels, protesting against the too loose hold. Later they probably take up causes, usually for ideas rather than for people.[21] The split between the body, the instincts and the head works somewhat differently; whereas the passive person tends to be fluid and without boundaries, here we have a tendency to become rigid, obsessive, even sadistic. Such people are self-punishing, punishing of others, rejecting their own rejected bodies, despising everything which has to do with the feminine, with the heart and its non-rational values and with inner subjective experience. They fight against the pull back to the unconscious, relating very strongly to external consciousness, gripping it to hold it tight.

---

[21] Judging from their characteristic approach to the world later on, Ghenghis Khan and Adolf Hitler, amongst others, may have had this kind of poor bonding.

In relationships there tends to be a fear or disregard of physical contact, of anything that is loving or soft, of heart value, of feeling; there is an avoidance of any kind of deep commitment. Symbiotic relationship they do not want. They reject other people as if unaware of them; they would find their deep feelings threatening if they knew of them. They fear commitment. Often in and out of relationships, they tend to take the parental role, becoming the authority, the super-ego. They major in dominance; dictatorial, authoritarian, perhaps with a strongly sadistic streak, they humiliate the other out there. Some wit said that a sadist is a masochist's best friend; I suppose it also works in reverse. The typical set-up has the masochist willing to receive pain in order to be loved, with the sadist giving pain, rejecting for fear of being rejected, saying, 'If I get in there first, *I* do the rejecting.'

There's an unconscious counterpoint to this struggle: because they are so rigid and authoritarian on the outside, they are inwardly attracted to, even if threatened by, people even stronger than themselves – authoritarian men, animus-ridden women. It's as if they have an un-conscious need to be overwhelmed, conquered, pervaded. With such continuous warfare and aggression, you'd think they were in love with the people they were fighting!

People of this type have to be driven right past their parameters to admit they need help. They come into counselling much less often, obviously, than the more passive, as a very last resort, because they don't know what else to do. Usually very close to breaking-point, they're brittle and internally vulnerable, and sometimes very difficult to work with. They need an extremely strong kind of loving, firmly helping them to recognise their own vulnerability, their own sensitivity, their own loneliness, their own needs. They need help to see that feeling and love aren't necessarily soft and weak, and to value these things in themselves and in others. The counsellor's work needs to be towards the healing of the split between head, heart and body. This isn't often much attempted; if it were, it would probably be more effective than is realised.

These more active people tend to go in for external activities: mountaineering, exploring, endurance sports. With the loneliness of the long-distance runner they major in areas of solitary challenge and testing. They can turn their aggression into creative drive of the very first order; instead of breaking away from mother, the past and the need to be included, they can become great pioneers into this higher womb.

Negatively they may seek and strive to become top in order to be one up, proving they can survive without people – 'I'm OK!' But, if this can be turned over to the creative mode, it brings in courage, leadership, a broad sweep, the ability to paint on the wide canvas. They can become innovative, breaking into new terrain both inwardly and outwardly, achieving great things. Many of the scientists opening up the link between physics and the nature of the subjective universe might well have had this kind of background.

Gender identity

Because of the too loose hold, there is always a blurring about what is sexual and what isn't. The lack of hold makes unclear the difference between the sexual and the sensuous. If we're healthy, all of us enjoy the combination, but here they tend to be put into clearly defined, watertight compartments and rarely do the two come together healthily. The person may merge them completely, or handle it by splitting them totally apart. It's very sad to miss years of sensuous cuddling! If the baby had very little touching, any approach is seen as quasi-sexual and the most acute embarrassment may arise: 'What the hell's going on?' They shrink away – the other form of rejection – 'Don't touch me!' People like this are unable to embrace or show any affection to others without a sexual connotation to it; the sensual fringes too far over into the sexual. Some, though not all, of the tendency to lesbianism or homosexuality may be based on the need for primary mothering; some women who say that they are lesbian may in fact be seeking for sensuousness – and I think a great number of men are too. Also, the need for some kind of off-beat, sensuous evocation, some fetish, in order to be able to perform sexually, very frequently goes back to this too loose hold. Hence, again, the offbeat approach in sadism and masochism.

With the too loose hold we don't clearly know our gender-identity – 'Am I a boy, am I a girl?' – because the Feminine Principle hasn't held us against itself long enough to make it clear. We don't know whether ours is the otherness of masculinity, or the similarity of femininity. Mother hasn't 'cared enough', given us time or attention enough, to help us define these things. Anyway, knowing nothing about our bodies, we can only guess at our gender; we have to learn it. Remember the small baby, blissed out by being fed and touched and held? Maturity of the psyche may mean being able to have that once more, but this time with a sexual partner. Some Freudians and Kleinians hold that this is the very test of maturity. In our kind of work it's hardly that, but at least the person makes a normal and happy transference to an adult partner, without any confusion as to whether they're 'doing it with mother'. The too loose hold gives no clarity about this.

One woman said she had been 'a walking nervous breakdown' for years and years. She'd been quite understandably taken into hospital in her mid fifties and given ECT (electro-convulsive therapy); then, in eight years of analysis, she thought she had worked over most things. But here she was. Despairingly she said to me, 'What can I do about it? I'm coming up to seventy-three, my mother died twenty-one years ago, there is no hope for me!'

Now for the very first time she could talk about her experiences. She had never before felt able to mention her pretty horrendous culture and background. Mother had taken a lover when she was pregnant with my client. Leaving four other children behind, she'd left home and lived in hotels in Europe with the lover, whom she later married. For the first three years after the baby was born she was left on her own in hotel rooms; perhaps a porter was paid to go up to her if she cried. She had no sense of roots at all. Unable to remember in detail, she sensed that she must have experienced what Freud endearingly called the Primal Scene – love-making in the room. At least, she'd heard it through the wall. Certainly she always associated sexuality with pain.

Because she had never been held, but always passed around among nannies, she was very much out of touch with her body, which produced sporadic skin rashes. She could say 'that is a beautiful table', putting her hand on it, but she couldn't put her hand on her own skin and feel it; she was completely out of touch with it. She'd never had any sort of orgasm, induced by herself or by any of her husbands, though she'd had three children. She just couldn't put together touch and feel, her flesh and her sexuality. We worked to bring her back in touch with her own skin.

On holiday a year before I met her, she'd been fascinated by hearing from her hotel room in Italy the sound of a pair making love. The room was over a well, up which came orgasmic moanings and groanings. At one level, she was very amused to hear it. She was also surprised to find herself in quite a depression. We worked on it together, sensing the atmosphere of what it was about, and she realised how much it triggered for her the sense of being left out of everything, of having no roots and no foundations.

Her lifelong terror that she had lesbian tendencies also came out. She'd been married three times (to men!) but a woman colleague had once started to kiss her, not in a fully sexual way but 'tending in that direction'. She was appalled; as she said, every part of her body responded and, to her horror, she felt a tremendous reaching out to this woman. I was able to say how remarkably like the blissed-out feeling of the very tiny baby this is. Through working with the image and the archetype we discovered that there *was* hope for her, that relationship could be redeemed within her, because mother was alive within her. Healing and redemption can take place at any moment through the 'naturing' of the Earth Mother archetype, the *naturing* quality of the earth.

People who had too loose a hold may have a very active inner imaginal or fantasy life, but have great difficulty in anchoring it, giving form and expression to it. They are handicapped when it comes to verbalising, vocalising, externalising, informing outwardly that rich, subjective side. There's a division not only between head and body, but between inner and outer. However, some people simply outlive all that; their creativity goes right through it. Despite all, people both active and passive can make something tremendously creative of this.

If their ego-strength can hold or be strengthened, the more passive, receptive, inturned individual can, through the very nature of their own need and their own lack, develop a hypersensitivity which can become an exquisite sensitivity to the needs of others (I choose deliberately the word 'exquisite', so aware, so vibrant, so resonant). Martyrdom can become sympathetic rapport with the hurt, the lost, the damaged, and an ability to strengthen them. The search for the symbiotic relationship can become an ability to stand alone against – anything. Placating and buying space can become tact and insight in handling different people in different situations, lovability and diplomacy of a very high order. They may become artists in life and artists in relationship. Rejection of the body and of earth and instincts can become a real understanding of how ecological and aesthetic sensibility can be given form in the external world, as they learn to affirm and value love, tenderness and sensitivity. Very often, people who had none of these in their beginnings mediate them to others as no-one else can, because of the nature of their quest. They talk the language of the lost and the unredeemed, able to speak in a most extraordinary way of being *found*, of redemption.

That's the too loose hold.[22] Myth, legend and folklore richly encapsulate human experience. However, ours is a young science, only a hundred and fifty years old. We're guessing, making rough maps. Meeting many people who have been deprived of the good enough hold, we can begin to formulate what may be the expectations of the human being. The important thing is to work back through their imaging from what the person is now, to how as a child they saw their world. So we begin to understand what the original seed might have been, what their expectations were and how far they were met. If they had a good background, then in the face of current reality they can let go expectations which are purely fantasy, becoming more and more related to the here and now. If they aren't related to the here and now, there are probably a lot of fantasies which together we can map. The more we work with people, the more we find that we have in common collective expectations of the mother image and archetype. Certainly, we only have to say the word 'mother' and follow the images to gain a good idea of what the person hoped of her.

The too tight hold

Here the mother holds the child tightly because of her own unfulfilled emotional needs. The possessive, too tight-a-grip mother is nearly always an insecure mother. For any of a million reasons she will have put too much emphasis on to her mothering role; if she loses her child, she will of course lose that role, so consciously or unconsciously she has a heavy vested interest in holding it close to her.

Too tight a grip doesn't allow for the child's ego to emerge (whereas the too loose hold wasn't reinforcing enough for it to emerge). Here the ego, struggling to develop, is held back to Stages One and Two. The tight grip keeps it at an infant level, continuously retarding or preventing growth to psychological and emotional maturity. Somebody who's been held too tightly will go on into adult life willy-nilly; the ego-Self axis will have to extend in the developing ego by the sheer passage of time. But if

---

22 Mother may have been inconsistent in her hold – too loose at one level, too tight at another; maybe too loose at the instinctual level, and too tight at the emotional or mental, because she was basically insecure herself. Moods change and these variations can be very great. Also, one would think that all the children of one mother would have pretty much the same experience. However, it doesn't follow; a whole series of new dynamics comes in with each child; body-contact is a two-way thing and chemistry is important. Some parents just don't like particular children, though very few of them would admit to it. It's quite possible for the same woman to be a good enough mother to one child, hold another too tightly and a third too loosely, affecting sibling rivalry. No human being can be absolutely impartial to three people; there are bound to be certain temperamental factors.

mother holds on, then at every one of the stages there's going to be a twea-king back to her. She has the child on an elastic cord, belly-button to belly-button. And how difficult it is for the child to break away! The tweaking may be done very, very gently and subtly or it may be much more overt – 'Don't you dare do that, my girl/my boy!' Just as the person is getting some sense of self-identity, beginning to succeed in something – tweak! comes the pull on the umbilicus and back they go to mother again.

This is the too tight hold. It's suffocating, enwombing, entombing, smothering. The child hasn't been set free. The mother didn't drop back enough at the right stages; she stayed too prominent, too much in the fore-ground. The child has no background except through her; it's still in the nursery, held in a silken web of love, duty, guilt, resentment, all muddled up together. A child so held from the early stages is very unsure who it is or what it is. It may have to fight and wrestle, as with a dragon, for any kind of ego-strength. No impetus to leave home will ever be given from outside; it has to generate the courage somehow off its own bootstraps!

What of the very dominating mother herself? It's only in her mothering role that she has behind the scenes the power she wants. She may have a natural strength that she's never been able to express, or be driven by an ambition that she hasn't used elsewhere. But her very sense of who she is, of being in the world, is now wrapped up in the mothering role. As we've seen, if she lets her children grow up, grow away, she loses not only her role but her identity. Thus, while it can be about power, it may also be a great need, a weakness of ego structure, ego strength and self-identity.

What does it feel like to be too tightly held, physically and psycho-logically? The mother's own sense of insecurity pushes either herself or her child into centre stage. If the mother is the centrifugal force around which everything swings, if the child has been thoroughly, totally overshadowed by her, then later it will find it almost impossible to be the centre of *anyone's* attention, having always been peripheral to mother's centrality. On the other hand, children who were themselves always pushed forward into the limelight may grow up expecting to be the centre of attention, and find it very difficult later when they aren't.

Ask someone, 'What do you feel like when I say the word *mother*?' and they will tell you! 'Ahhh – get off me, let me breathe, I'm being crushed down!' Take asthma. Various pressures lead to asthma, yet it is a likely physical manifestation of the too tight hold. One woman who had it felt great velvety-black vampire wings coming over her and suffocating her absolutely. On the other hand, a man who also had asthma responded to the word 'mother' with the feeling of standing on a mountain top in a very brisk wind. He was so used to having his mother always with him that the sense of standing on a mountain breathing God's free air was very threatening. These two could hardly have been more different, yet they were both too tightly held and they both suffered from this difficulty in breathing. I look for the degree of suffocation, airlessness, not enough space being allowed; the psychological background may well show the too tight hold.

Many young people too tightly held don't, as they get older, manage to leave Stages One and Two. Mother is always the line of least resistance. Even as they mature physically, they're still psychologically at home. If the outer world becomes too dangerous, then back they go to mother; if relationships become too demanding – back to mother; if inner creativity is too taxing or if the light of understanding reveals too much – back to mother; if the demands of adulthood and maturity are too rigorous – back to mother. It's very, very difficult to break that pattern.

One effect of the too tight hold is that the child's gender identity is blurred. Again, we can see it in terms of the active and the passive temperament; the boy or the girl caught back in this way either gives up passively, going with the mother, or tries actively to fight against her suffocating hold. The 'smothering' mother may be less mature than the growing child itself. I've known people 'breaking up to break through' who were, as children, almost (but not fully) conscious of having flipped roles, taking responsibility for a childish mother or father, becoming parents to their own parents.

A passive girl may have great difficulty in unplaiting herself from the symbiotic, overshadowing femininity of the mother; she becomes what Jung called the negative puella, the girl-child who never really grows out from under the shadow of her mother to establish her own femininity. The girl with a more fighting temperament, more positively active, will be pushed over to the masculine side, denying and fighting against the feminine, led by her own *animus*. Aggressive towards the mother, she will consequently be aggressive towards her own femininity, majoring as a partial man to the detriment of everything feminine within her, denying the feminine in all life.

The boy too, ungrounded in his own masculine nature because of the foreground hold of the mother, may passively become a 'mother's boy', a negative *puer* who never wants to grow up. If he manages to make relationships, he may tend to homosexuality simply because he hasn't had any positive opportunity to relate to his own masculinity. He may have a strong draw towards the mothering kind of boy or man, unable to take the risk of meeting the otherness represented by the feminine – except in the mother. He's trapped. On the other hand, a boy with a more active temperament may become too assertively masculine, but not with the healthy, balanced masculinity that the good enough father mediates; he disregards that. And it's not his own masculinity. It's stereotyped: it doesn't fight for, it fights always against. He may become very aggressive towards the feminine and full of denial of it.

Either way, the too tight hold is obviously ruinous to mature relationships. Once again there is the split between the head and the feeling heart, the head and the body, and it's a very strong split. These people are almost too well-identified with the body, having had too heavy an outline put on them; but it's somebody else's outline.

We've seen that if the mother has too tight a hold, it ruins the possibility of gender identity at the instinctual level and messes up open relationships at the emotional level. It can also deeply affect the child's subjective creativity. The moment they're about to create something, they're tweaked back again. Where there is a very strong dominance of the mother, the child may have an early flaring, tender, insecure talent; but do they have the persistence to hold it? It often dies when put to the test of common day. There is a tendency never to get down to it, to be *dilettante*, to make a thrust and then be hauled back. They need the extra push which the masculine principle could give; but the mother, with her very strong commitment to mothering – over-protective, grabbing, smothering – keeps them with her, at home, in the nursery, however old they are. There's often an early death in a case like that.[23]

Someone held in this way may be very creative, but always as an offering to mother – to the Great Mother. In myth, it's an offering to the Great Earth Mother, the libation of the earth; it's Dionysus, it's wine. Very frequently people with that very tight hold get drawn over into drink and drugs. Talk with them, and you find which way they're going. Some

---

23   See 'Puer Aeternus', where Marie Louise von Franz uses the story of 'The Little Prince' by Antoine de Saint Exupéry to do a marvellous mapping of the negative *puer* tied back to the mother. It's sub-titled 'A Psychological Study of the Adult Struggle with the Paradise of Childhood'. (von Franz 1970. See also 'The Puer Papers', Hillman 1971.) Ed.

of them are trying to get stoned back into the original symbiotic loss of identity (for them the ocean of perfect rest and security). Completely unable any longer to go on fighting to establish an ego, these are giving up and letting themselves be overwhelmed by that original womb. They simply can't fight, they're too tired, too unmanned in every way; they just give up and try to do it all as unconsciously as possible. However, others may be searching for a different kind of Spirit through the bottom of an alcohol glass. A drug can be an attempted movement towards opening up a new kind of consciousness. These are not being dragged back, they are pulling towards the first apprehension of, and meeting with, the *higher* womb.

The creative area is that of the mother, but the pull of the truly creative person – and this is true of everyone, not just of creative artists – is towards the *higher* womb, towards the meeting with their own contra-sexual nature. That meeting and marriage would enable the person to become a creative being in their own right. But the overwhelming mother doesn't permit this; by her hold she can prevent her son or daughter coming to their creativity, tweaking them back instead to the original womb. The umbilicus may stretch, but it's still attached at the navel. Mother's still holding her end very, very tight and no matter how far the person may struggle over to adulthood, there's going to be the pull back again.

I knew a highly creative choreographer very much caught by the too strong hold of the mother. He led a dance team, taught students, fathered five children, travelled all over the world. He was constantly trying to write a play of his own but, though he worked at it, there was always a bit of scenery to fix, an excuse never quite to achieve. He frequently fell in love – and he did it thoroughly! He'd see his *anima* in someone out there, she would draw him on and then he'd become creative. He said (not realising how important it was), 'I can only create when I'm in love'. Thus the counter-pull from outside would draw him on towards the higher creative womb – for a time. But he didn't quite make it. From the navel, a pull of great strength drew him back. The new relationship would fall flat (and it always did) when the inspiring woman found she was dealing with a man who hadn't yet come out of the nursery. Every such relationship broke up; he'd had about thirty of them by the time he was fifty-four, so he'd been trying for a long time. And each time, he went back into a deep depression. He didn't literally go back to his mother (she had died sixteen years before I met him) but psychologically that's where he went.

It is extraordinary how many human beings manage to emerge heroically from poor bonding. For certain temperaments, the inadequate hold even seems to be needed. Their histories show how few great artists had a good enough hold; emerging becomes a life-and-death necessity, making them infinitely creative, and often they are able to go on to light, fire and meaning. It's as though that fire by friction, which gives such a very bad grounding, seems to engender in some people a life-thrust, an absolutely essential need to find the higher womb. They have to; otherwise they will die.

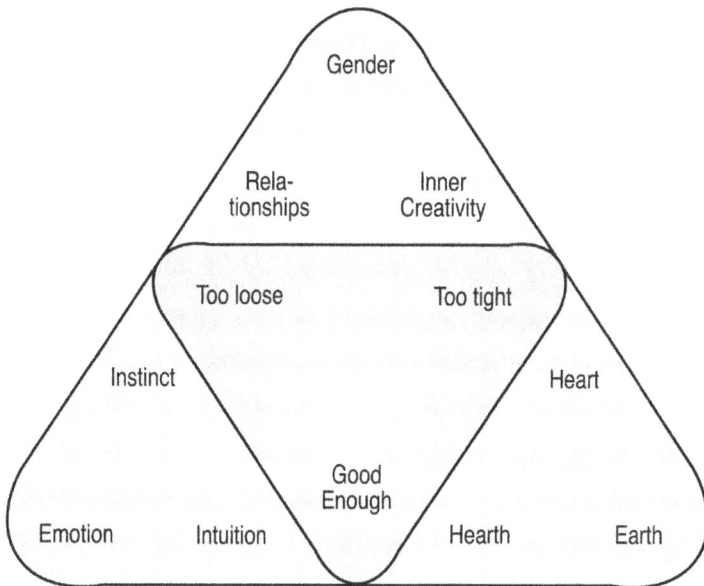

Figure 6 The Mother Principle

Working with the mother image

Counselling can come in at any point to counteract these negative pulls. As I've said, the mother's place is always in the wrong. She can't get it totally right, because of the entwined nature of this most subjective of two-way relationships. Here again are the major points:

By 'the mother' we mean the *Personal Mother*, the *Mother Image* and the *Mother Archetype*. Mother touches all those areas affected by the *feminine principle*; she reaches the inner, subjective heart side of us, the emotional and intuitional; she has a great deal to do with roots, the sense of inner and outer; and with the instinctual level, which affects gender identity. At the emotional level she inevitably affects *relationships*; relationships to other people, to our inner world and to the world at large, to nature, to the earth and to water. She very much affects our subjective *creativity*, our courage not only to have an inner world, but to be brave enough to explore it.

If someone is caught at the stage between nursery and adolescence, the counsellor needs to act as a transitional object; if between adolescence and adulthood (the bit that most often needs exploring), to act as a good parental figure; and if between adulthood and maturity, it is necessary to be able to act as *anima* or *animus*, the creative inspirer. Psychologically we all leave mother at different stages, and many people won't have done it at all. If other priorities and values haven't come into the foreground, the person won't have moved from adolescence to adulthood, where the ego-Self axis is clear of the whole background, let alone to the maturity of Stage 5. They'll still be struggling to bridge that first gap.

What are the person's expectations? Working on the mother, I help bring her down to size. It's to be hoped that they'll come to see her as a child of her own parents, of her times, of her social and cultural setting, with her own restraints, guilts, expectations and *mores*. No longer this Great Mother image, she begins to be seen as an ordinary, vulnerable human being; perhaps they begin to relate to her humanity as a woman, and gain the strength to let go of her.

Also, it may be because the child itself hasn't been able to break away from the symbiotic relationship with mother that she remains too predominant. Just as the good enough mother in time ceases to be foreground, so it is for the *child* at a psychological level to get mother into the background. This is where the father comes in. He helps the child to drop the mother into the background at the appropriate stage, and move out to explore the space around. If that bridge isn't taken, if he is absent physically, psychologically or emotionally, then the chances are that the person will be unsure, and want to go back to the security of mother; internal space will be a threat, and outer space a challenge of the very first order.

A number of men find that they have taken on the mother role, the mother image, without realising it. They've been nurturing, caring, nourishing people and, though it's been kept down inside them, it may have come out in unusual ways. Asking 'What is Man? What is Woman?'

is really asking, 'Who was mother? Who was father ?' They may find contrary impulses: a slightly older child within them may be desperately trying to kick mother and fighting bitterly *against* her, while a younger inner child desperately *wants* mother and her attention. It's a battle! At the unconscious level, two inner 'children' are pulling in different directions, accounting for a great deal of the push and pull and confusion.

Having somebody *wanting* to explore the mother with us, homing in on her perhaps in the middle of something totally different, can in itself be tremendously valuable. It's not, 'Ah ha, we will explore the mother now!' – boom, just like that. But just to focus on her for as long as it's needed may help to re-constellate a good enough mother, to give a nurturing, nourishing affirmation of identity at the general level, give a sense of roots. A launching pad for our inner and outer space craft, such a person will help us explore our inner nature and begin to move into the reality of the outer world with a greater sense of having some background behind us.

Plate 9

An Equal Music

CHAPTER SIX

The Father: His Image and Principle
Ian Gordon-Brown

While mother is for heart, father is for head.
Where mother is for the life ethic, for sympathy,
father holds to the work ethic and to reason

So – mother comes first. We came out of her body, we fed at her breast, she was most likely to have given us the bottle, she provided the first world in which we lived. But the environment presents us with a magnetic polarity: after mother we naturally come to – father. Positive or negative, by his presence or absence he critically affects the dynamics of the home and has a tremendous effect upon the development of the child (and thus upon the adult that the child becomes). As we've seen, it's essential that father or his substitute come in to represent for the child the 'otherness' of the world outside. He is a bridge to the outer world, and his counterpoint helps both boy and girl to break away from the primacy of mother.

The Father principle

Where the feminine principle is primarily about relationship, the masculine principle concerns our identity. Figure 5 showed the levels of consciousness; now in Figure 7 (overleaf) we map how these levels carry the feminine and masculine principles. The feminine principle, and thus the mother, affects the child particularly on the levels of instinct and emotion; also in the subjective internalised creativity of intuition and the feminine side of spirit. Now we see how the father's effect is at the level of the body, of the mind, of the masculine side of spirit. We've seen how emergence from the womb, the nursery, the school, depends on mother. Now father affects its further emergence – from the world of the mother and on into life.

The two great principles, *logos* and *eros*, are represented by father and mother. Since she's to do with *eros*, mother is primarily concerned with relating. As Jung said, the Father principle is the *logos*, the Word. Father is chiefly concerned with identity, affecting it at every level

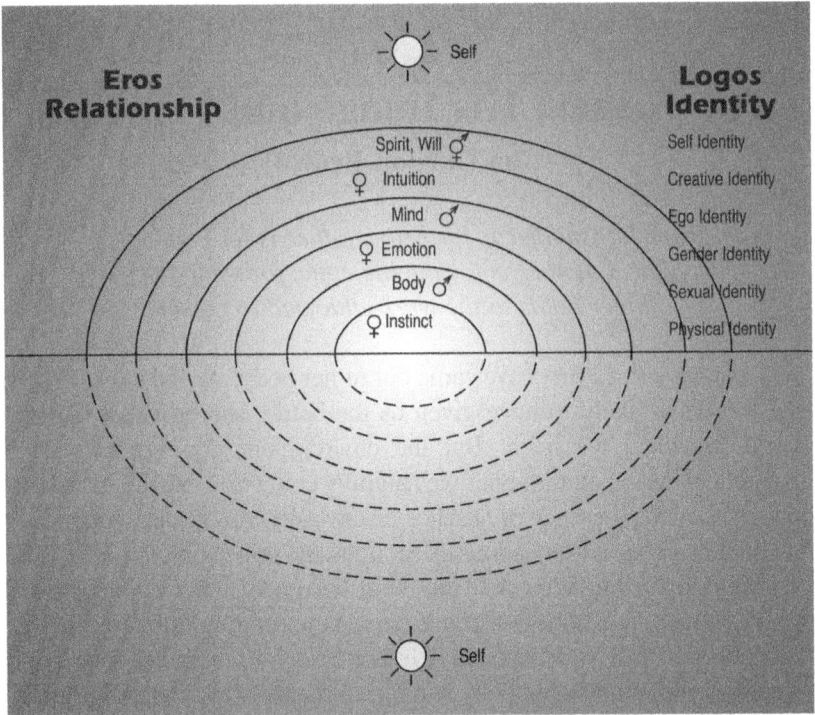

Eros
Relationship

Logos
Identity

Spirit, Will ♂	Self Identity
Intuition ♀	Creative Identity
Mind ♂	Ego Identity
Emotion ♀	Gender Identity
Body ♂	Sexual Identity
Instinct ♀	Physical Identity

Figure 7   Levels of Identity

(including those under the aegis of the feminine). The *eros* principle has to do with instinctive knowing, with feeling, with the soul, with quality rather than quantity, the dark, unconscious side of things. *Logos* is about vocation, knowledge, higher creativity, the light; it's about consciousness. While *eros* is for heart, *logos* is for head. Where *eros* is for the life ethic, for sympathy, *logos* holds to the work ethic and to reason. It's *eros* that looks to the past; *logos* looks to the present and leans towards the future. *Eros* is to be found in the kitchen (and we remember always that it may be the man who is 'mother' and is carrying the *eros* principle); *logos* will more likely be found in the lab.

While *eros* asks, 'Who am I?' *logos* aims to bring some of the answers. At the level of *physical identity*, while the mother's hold gives a sense of being *in* the body, the father shows us how we can act through and *out of* the body. Father also affects our *sexual identity*. Though the emotional level is mainly feminine, yet it is father who truly affects our *gender identity.* While the mother can say to her daughter, 'Yes, you're a woman', it's only the father who can acknowledge that and make it real. On the mental level, father helps us establish our *ego identity* and our personal authority, saying, or failing to say, 'Be who you are.' At the intuitive level (again, broadly under the aegis of the feminine) he affects our *creative identity*, the higher creativity in form and meaning that comes out of the light. And at the level of spirit our very *Self-identity*, with its inner impulse and drive, is affected by him.

Behind mother lies the feminine principle, with its elements of earth and water, moonlit and starlit rather than sunlit. Instinctive, emotional, intuitive, perceptive, she is about the spaces between things, about flow and movement. Her tendency is towards identification; she will merge with the other – 'thou'. She is at home in the common ground of instinctual response, the roots and beginnings of things. She holds within her a river of feelings flowing to an ancient, primitive ocean. While mother holds *being* values, asking 'Who are you?' rather than 'What have you achieved?' Father is about *doing*. He affects our externalised, rational functions. Though he is about identity, he's not about identification.

While her awareness is diffuse, unclear, his is a focused awareness. His areas of primary influence being physical, sexual and mental, he's about authority and externalised creativity, majoring in objective reasoning rather than in subjective feeling. Coming out of the masculine principle, his elements are Air and Fire. Unlike the feminine, which is always there and has a circularity, the masculine is about progression and growth; it develops in an upward movement, through stages, journeying towards a goal. There's an analogy here with the development of an embryo. As Jung said, masculinity means to know one's goal and to do what is necessary to achieve it. Reading Figure 8 (overleaf) from the bottom upwards:

At the first level the Father principle is concerned with doing, making actual. For the child, the father is concerned with the values of *action* and achievement. The next level is about *security*. The masculine principle asks, 'How can you have a society without order?' Then comes *responsibility*. Since it represents purpose, the Father principle needs discipline. Too much, and you lose touch with spontaneity and the lovely flow of the feminine; yet if there isn't enough, the order of society falls apart. When this balance can be approached and taken forward, the next level, that of *vocation*, is reached. This is about initiation, learning not to be dominated by time, making new beginnings, knowing how to make effective changes in the outer world. The *logos* is the Word lived out in vocation. The energy it calls forth from us depends on our innate nature; there are 'hard professions' and 'soft professions', and we may be in the wrong one and need a fundamental shift. Beyond that is the level of *consciousness*, represented by Abraham Maslow [24] as Self-actualisation. Finally there is *spirit*, the Word, the logos itself. Carl Jung calls it Self-realisation. I can't say much about this level.

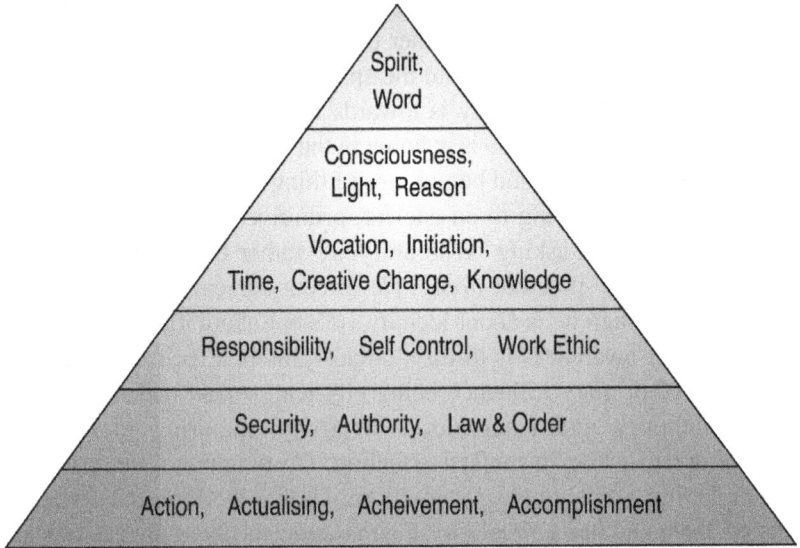

```
                    Spirit,
                    Word
              Consciousness,
              Light, Reason
          Vocation, Initiation,
      Time, Creative Change, Knowledge
    Responsibility,  Self Control,  Work Ethic
    Security,   Authority,   Law & Order
  Action,  Actualising,  Acheivement,  Accomplishment
```

Figure 8 The Father Principle

As with the feminine, the expression of the masculine may be positive or negative. It's about the focusing of energy, but this can be done in ways that are less than democratic. It's also about managing; but is the management by consensus and consultation, or is the manager a 'god-father'? Positively, the masculine can stand back, be analytical, seek

---

24   from Maslow's Diagram of the Hierarchy of Needs, with Self-Realisation added to it:
      Self Actualisation, Self Realisation
      Self Esteem
      The Esteem of Others
      Need to Belong (with friends, partner, lover; for human contact)
      Need for Security – may fight with the need to belong
      Physiological needs
    See Abraham H. Maslow. 1954.

clarity. Negatively, it is autocratic.

Someone with such a father may tend towards a life that has no centre, no identity. Lacking *logos*, they may instead live out only *eros* in the area affected by mother – which is relationship. In the latter part of the twentieth century there has been a considerable devaluation of the father's role in Western society. Welfare States have taken over many fatherly functions, providing to a considerable extent for the children. The personal father who then leaves their upbringing largely to the mother will strengthen her influence and further weaken his own.

In areas traditionally belonging to the Father principle (the Law, the Church, Government, Politics, the Military) the very concept of organisation has been devalued and authority much weakened, even rendered non-existent. However, as yet there is very little self-authority to replace it; hence the lamented decline in collective 'standards'. The lack of positive father has a lot to do with hooliganism and crime, making for the erosion of personal responsibility and initiative. Making things soft for people (through affluence, through the 'perfect environment', through 'ideal' all-providing schools) in practice destroys the Father principle. There are certainly many invalid arguments for not making things too soft for people, but here is the valid argument: feather-bedding, if it succeed, is bad for the masculine principle. For a man to grow from the child, friction and difficulties are needed. In one way, the Welfare State is a psychological disaster. It may have arisen in part out of a lack of masculine principle in its mature form. At the extreme, that lack saps our society and undoes the very nature of creative tension.

The Personal Father

Now we shall look at the influence of different kinds of human father, the actual person, whether positive, authoritarian, weak or absent, substituted for by another man, or by a woman; seeing what effect he has had on us. Look again at Figure 3, p. 35, the Stages of Emergence, showing how the ego and the Self emerge into consciousness. In the nursery, at school and into adolescence, the ego has had to emerge from mother, from the parents together, and finally even from the parental images. (During the final three stages, adulthood, maturity and wisdom, the ego's task is less to do with getting free of the parents and more to do with individuation and the coming together with the Self.) During the first three years in the nursery the child sees father as an extension of mother. The father is mediated by mother, and while the mother represents the womb, the Paradise Garden, the father is God. And God in the Garden of Eden is the voice that says 'THOU SHALT NOT! – and if you do, then out you go!' The child has to learn, not so much to obey, as to *disobey without a sense of guilt*; to strike out and establish its own gods. Though to eat of the fruit of the tree is to be expelled from Paradise, yet, to be mature, the child must disobey the God who says 'NO!' Only then can he or she meet the God who says 'THOU SHALT'.

Between three and five, the child is beginning to differentiate father from mother, and the father or his substitute is becoming increasingly important. It can initially be very threatening for both boy and girl to be left to father, especially if he's authoritarian; and the oldest child, because of having had an exclusive relationship with mother, has a particular problem here.

But father is fascinating. For one thing, he has a special relationship with the loved and desired mother. According to Freud, although the Oedipal father threatens the child's special relation to the mother, the child's task, without being overwhelmed by the loss of specialness to her, is to discover the otherness of father. Indeed, the father is another law, another authority, helping the child to *disidentify* from mother.[25] As initiator, he aids emergence into the world, widening the child's contact with it. The boy is initiated by him into the outer world away from the nursery, finding at first a huge excitement in new things. Alas, school soon scotches all that, and irritation may well come to inhibit the father's own very real enjoyment of the child. But the boy needs to identify with father; he needs to project the hero on to him, thus establishing his own masculine identity and breaking the excessive power of mother. If he stays under her power, as we have seen, he will be ambivalent about his own masculinity.

The girl needs to grow *with* mother, but not to *be* mother. She begins to play coquette with her father; he is a love object, mother a love subject. With the father the girl has her first experience of objective loving. In practice, a lot of women are brought up as men in this regard. But the girl needs the father's otherness as a counterpoint, enabling her to establish her own femininity, different from that of her mother. The danger is she will identify with mother and never become a woman in her own right.

The father and the mother may be warring within a person but the aim

---

[25] There is emphasis in Psychosynthesis on this dis-identification

is wholeness: that *logos* shall be related to *eros* within each one of us, the Sun to the Moon. To come fully to the Self, to be in the process of consummating the Inner Marriage, we need to have come to terms with both mother and father. For this, the good enough parents prepare the way.

The good enough father

As with the mother, the perfect father is not to be desired. But what positive experience will be gained if the father is good enough? We've seen how the child between about three and five begins to discover through father its sexual identity, its gender identity and its ego identity. Eventually the person will begin to discover their creative identity, and finally their Self identity. This all leads to a great confidence in the Self.

At first, the good enough father holds the lifeline for the mother while the baby needs a lot of time and attention. But as the months go on, he begins to haul mother back, reclaiming her from the baby, helping its separation from her by first reclaiming her for himself. Then, as the baby's next source of love and support, he's uniquely qualified to help it to explore.[26] This is a less cosy relationship than the one with the mother; more robust, vigorous and stimulating. It makes leaving Mum seem rather attractive! Father acts as bridge between her and the outside world, helping the toddler to build up confidence for his explorations so he can start to make the map he needs of how society works. The boy learns to kick against his mother. He is proud to be involved in 'man's work'. He is also forced to begin to share; Dad becomes a rival.

As time goes on, the good enough father demonstrates to his children how they can take the initiative and face problems creatively. He unfolds for them how to think for themselves. He shows by example how to be in a business or vocation: he's in the world, he works; thus he helps them discover what their real goal may be, their function. Is the girl or boy at heart a teacher? A born organiser? What kind of student can each become, what kind of person? Is it their vocation to be craftsman, priest, workhorse, gardener, nurse? Fatherly virtues have been a bit out of fashion since the 1960's, but by setting standards the father helps the children value achievement and sense the worthwhileness and pleasure of doing things well. He helps them stand on their own feet, reinforcing their ability to say Yes and No, maintain boundaries, claim their own ground

---

[26] See Skynner & Cleese, 1983, Page 190-191.

and the space around it, their place in the sun.

From late adolescence into the twenties, as ego identity is being developed, father provides for both young man and woman a support structure, available but unobtrusive. By precept and example he helps them consciously to own their own mind and thoughts, as distinct from their less conscious values. As *logos*, father shows hope for the future. He helps his children to discover a personal meaning in relation to the whole, finding out who they are and how to fit into society. Of course, worries and fears may well come from real events –disappointments, accidents, crises. But if we are discovering who we really are, the worries frequently fall away.

If this sense of our own identity has not been built in, we are more likely as adults to be off-centre; we have a distorted field all around us. If we can get back 'on centre', these distortions just cease to exist. Learning who we are, we will be able to act in ways that further the Self. There are times, for instance, when it would be right to say No to promotion; if our real love is for doing the job itself, then it's to be hoped we would have the clarity and courage to refuse to be promoted above that level. (The Peter Principle holds that everyone gets promoted to the rank just above the one at which they are most competent! This state of affairs is fuelled by those who do not know themselves well.)

The good enough father helps with all this, supporting his son at the apprentice stage and sharing with him as friend and elder colleague. While the feminine principle is competitive on the subjective side and in relationship, the competitiveness and ambition gained through the positive father aids his daughter too to do what she must and follow her own calling. He doesn't say, 'Reach the top', he says, 'Be yourself'. Achievement is very important, but it needn't mean fighting your way up the ladder. Many fathers set a poor example, continuing in work that kills them instead of having the courage to walk out. Redundancy can help here!

So the on-going, goal-directed, purposive nature of the good enough father helps both his son and his daughter to grow up, each becoming their own person. And he mediates spirit, purpose, direction to them, so that as they move through adulthood they can find their own God. They have the confidence to go beyond the security of the past and, accepting the present, to allow the future to come in. This is when their identity becomes God-identity. Finding their own myth and meaning, their life-task, their journey, the Self and the ego come together – and then a note sounds.

The authoritarian father

Less than good enough fathers have a considerable effect. The authoritarian father is on the whole weak, especially at the emotional level; this is why he needs to be authoritarian. In both the boy and the girl he inhibits change, ego development and transformation, replacing self-control with control by fear. The child's consciousness is fixated in the old order and in traditional ways, and the adult who emerges is tied to the past.

The effect this has on his sons differs from that on his daughters. The boy is trapped in the past, growing into an increasingly rigid man run by tradition and security and outside pressure. If the son is of acquiescent temperament, it can prevent him from discovering his self-identity. In a Walter Mitty-type daydream, he looks to father and is caught in his authority. He lives always in the tension between the innate possibilities of his own nature, and what he's forced to do by Dad. He's on the horns of a dilemma: it's painful if he doesn't obey, but then there's the buried pain of not doing what he really wants to do.

On the other hand, the boy may rebel. Perhaps he rebels to be different. Then he may well be broken by outside pressures. This can happen at the sexual level; a twist of the masculine may take place, so that for the rest of his life fantasy is better than reality, masturbation than real sex. Under the aegis of the authoritarian father guilt correlates with sexual identity. The son's identity as a man is in fantasy only; feeling a boy among men, he starts well and then gives up. He needs to take personal responsibility, establish his sexual identity without guilt, and move on. He too needs to become father and initiator, whether the line he founds be children, tasks, or ideas. His authoritarian father has stood in the way of his self-discovery; now he must escape father's scripts, make up his own mind and find his own vocation, his creativity in action.

A girl with an authoritarian father projects his image on the men she relates to. Picking someone like her father, she seeks endlessly to work out the relationship and redeem it. Alternatively, she chooses someone who is the very opposite, and attempts to push him into father shape; for instance, she may try her hardest to make her partner into a bully. Frigidity is common in her reaction to sex; she may in fact be searching not for sex but for a guru, a nice holy father unlike her own. Her task is to develop self-awareness, to begin to think for herself and explore the meaning of her life. She needs to examine her feeling that relationships with all men must be incestuous. She too needs to establish sexual identity without guilt.

Again, a woman may be deeply in love with her authoritarian father, finding her weak husband quite unlike him. Always she is more incestuously married to father than to the man. The father may have turned to his daughter with the message, implicit or explicit, 'You're a whore if you have any man but me. You are my woman, only mine!' And, seeing her father in all men, she closes up her womb – just like that! The womb is like a money-bag: if mother isn't holding the string, father will be. 'You can't make love to your father, can you? That's incest.' Hence, once more, frigidity. The daughter needs to develop her own mind, rather than churning out such a father's predigested views, and come to her own calling, vocation, meaning, given by her own ego-identity – and it's not necessarily about earning money. She needs her own inner creative link with Spirit, her own God, her own true identity. Otherwise, falling in love with priests, analysts, doctors, gurus, her God will be the mirror of her own father.

In the family, the authoritarian father may crush the wife, who then says to the girl, 'Go on then, don't *you* be crushed too. Do what you need to do, not what I've done.' So the daughter comes out fighting. This leads to the ganging up of women against men.

The absent father

Another way in which the father is less than good enough is when he is not there. It may be that he's physically absent; or he may be weak, and therefore present but useless. Again, the father who acts as another little boy, a brother to his children, anxious to be 'chums only', is actually absent. Lack of the influence of father, whether through weakness or literal absence, leads to the uprising and re-emergence of the feminine principle, and so to the devaluation of the masculine. General inertia follows; needs are projected out on to society as continuous demands for provision, or continuous rebellion against society. The children of absent fathers need guidelines, but very often they refuse to listen to or accept them.

If someone's father was absent, the effect is likely to be anxiety, impotence, fear of failure and lack of energy at work. There may be a feeble ego-identity, and thus a difficulty in developing adequate struc-tures. The person tends to be watery, over-dominated by the feminine (back in tears they go to mother). Thus the sons of absent fathers may be very timid about commitment. As adults, they daren't stop; they may be addicted to work and prone to heart attacks. There may be a tendency towards a homosexuality that comes not from their own nature, but from the strong influence of mother with father absent and no-one to counteract it.

Yet, if mother and father are both 'good enough', the child will often be merely 'good enough' too. How then is a person to break through to a higher type of creativity? It is by testing itself that the masculine gains strength; challenging the competition, fighting to achieve and overcome difficulties. The struggle with father and the father image is necessary if we are to become ourselves. 'Kill the father!' Even with the not-so-good father, the reaction can be benign if the child will struggle. What truly creative person does not have some wound?

The gentler daughter of an absent father may tend to be over-feminine; becoming soft, she can't anchor any animus strength. On the other hand, girls of an aggressive temperament may themselves try to replace their fathers. In families where the father is acting as mother, the mother may be playing father. Angry and vengeful herself towards men, such a mother may be giving a 'negative animus' to her daughter. This doesn't only happen with authoritarian fathers; it's the shadow that lies between consciousness and unconsciousness. That which is not present is not absent, it is unconscious! The mother may be carrying the father's compensatory side and projecting it on to the girl. If father was weak, ask what was in the unconscious? The answer is, violence and anger.

The dead or vanished father

He also has his effect. If the children don't remember their father, or didn't know him at all, they may well tend to idealise him, mixing stereotyped bits from films, from books, from fantasies. The picture is over-coloured, but, suffering from his absence, the child does need an ideal. The boy will tend to seek lost hero-figures everywhere; he has to be on the heroic quest, his phallus the seeking sword. He may not outgrow this – which can be difficult for relationships! The girl may grow into a woman seeking the ghostly lover, the valiant knight on his great horse; this stops her from relating to any real man, warts and all.

If the father dies during a person's childhood or adolescence, the account is closed at that point and it generally leaves unfinished business. While the mother image is eternal, the father image holds past, present and future apart. It's very odd: by dying, the father jeopardises the present, and he also puts a taboo on both past and future. He says in effect, 'If you want the future, you must fight me for it.' When he dies there's an intake of breath, an intake of time; the Sleeping Beauty has pricked her finger. Time stops. The child becomes frozen: 'I can't go on, I need father's permission to move.' Mother can stop time too. If she does, we're mummified. With father's death it's as if we were 'daddified' in time, with all growth and development arrested. Our inability to live in the present means there is a lack of identity, perhaps none at all; the centre is off-centre.

In some people, however, depending on the degree to which his hold has already been loosened, the father's death can itself have a remarkably releasing effect, signalling the son to become himself for the first time, and the daughter to see men in their own right. At last the person feels, 'I have a future, because the present is OK, and the past is redeemed'.

The father image

We have looked at the Father principle, the archetypal father common to all humankind. And we have looked at the influence of different kinds of personal father. We now come to the father image, the idea we all hold of the father.

It is particularly this *image* of the father that I usually find myself exploring with people. Though when his children are in midlife poor old Dad himself usually has little actual power, his image can still have a huge effect. I ask again: 'Who was father, who was mother?' – who wore the trousers, who made the decisions? It may be that roles were reversed, and father was in practice representative of house and home while mother chiefly held the career in the world. In one-parent families the parent had to be both. Was there a father substitute? If so, provided he turned up before the child was about seven, he was probably a benign influence, as good as father. However, if he arrived later than that, some damage to the child may have followed.

I say: 'Tell me about your father; what was the atmosphere around him?' Mother is a nuance, qualitative, a presence in the air. Father is quantitative; you can weigh and measure father. 'Do you feel he was in, or not in, the house? Was he a presence, or an absence? Was he secure, or insecure; heavyweight, or lightweight? Did he seem real, or was he a stereotype?' Find out too: 'Did father inhibit or encourage personal growth? Could you discuss things with him? Are you still being supported financially by him? What were your father's attitudes to work, ambition, competition, achievement, vocation? What was the *strength* of his view and opinion and discipline?' So, as we let the images go back and forward, our work together begins. It's wise also to check out the current situation; might an overt change in this adult person threaten their relationship with the actual parent?

I aim to find out from the man, what were father's views on sex, morality, rights and wrongs. Did he allow, permit or express any show of affection? Or was it lack of affection that was demonstrated? What about touching; father to mother, as well as father to child? We examine the taboos – 'Thou Shalt Not!' and 'Thou Shalt!' – which always stem from him. Scripts from the authoritarian father may have included: 'Sex is for procreative purposes only!' 'Sex outside marriage is not permissible.' 'Marriage is simply to legalise sex.' 'Sex is OK with "inferior" women, never with "superior".' And what of homosexuality? Do father's scripts affect the person today, in body, in sexual performance, in action? Is the adult still reacting for, or against, the father?

With the woman, we find out if she is still living by her father's views and opinions, or is she set against them? Her task is to develop her own ideas, rather than adopting those of her partner, who often stands for her father. In helping her to get out from under, we look at father's attitude to responsibility and the primacy of work. She may need to arrest the pattern of overdrive and obsession – or its opposite, an 'underdrive', an inertia. Is she rebelling against an authoritarian father, or identifying with a weak one? And what was the girl's reading of the parents' sexual life? Are her memories of abuse real memories? If a woman is sure she was being raped, indeed she may have been. But was it perhaps more a matter of atmosphere and feeling than of fact? 'Is father over the bed? Under the bed? In the bed?' She is certainly in trouble with relationships if her very *animus* is her father, taken on board; if she is under the drive of father, she will persist and over-persist, even unto death.[27]

Working with the father image

It's a valuable skill to be able to hold a line with people. While allowing them freedom, we say, 'Just to bring you back to your father again…' We keep to the road, though well aware of the scenery on either side. I watch

---

[27] See Ted Hughes, 'Birthday Letters'. 1998. Ed.

for tension, flushing, denial; if they're 'resistant' I make a silent note – 'watch the block there' – and move around the scenery a bit. Very often, what's known as 'resistance' is the person's reaction to our getting it wrong! I might say, 'Do you find it difficult to talk about that?' – bringing the block to their attention, which is in itself very valuable. And it can be appropriate to set them the task of doing things that were forbidden by father.

It's extremely important to help them see that all relationships are psychologically redeemable. The aim is to release them from the parents, whether positive or negative, present or absent, alive or dead; to unplait the image and help them take back into themselves what is valid for them, so that the image can go back to the proper place. We're helping them come to terms with both parent and parent-image and, standing free of their script, be born out of them. Then they can begin to parent their own inner child.[28]

Self identity at the spiritual level comes in here; the beginnings of confidence in the Self. We have seen that, through father, the children began to discover their sexual identity on the physical level, have their gender identity confirmed on the emotional level and their ego identity affirmed on the mental level; and by now their creative identity is probably establishing itself on the level of intuition. When mapping someone's *spiritual* identity, ask, 'What do you identify with?' Is it depth? Or do they identify with height? Mother is about depth (as Jung pointed out), about relationship, empathy, identification *with*; the emphasis is on quietness, stillness. Father is about height, movement and direction, about identity itself, about detachment, about dis-identification *from*.

People who come into counselling with an early wound certainly do need to explore father as well as mother. To discover the father's face, I ask the person, 'What is God like?' Someone who is truly religious (as opposed to someone who is only a supporter of a church) often has a weak father and a mother who was the authority. We've seen that the future depends on father. Those great Teachers who say, and really mean it, 'Take no thought for the morrow', have overcome the father and his scripts. They live, really live, here and now.

So father, by his presence or absence (positive and negative) critically affects the dynamics of the home environment. He mediates the masculine principle or energy. He provides us, or should provide us, with a

---

28   See James Hillman, 1996, on 'The Parental Fallacy'. Ed.

fundamental pattern of what masculine energy is, the levels at which it operates and the part it plays in the development of consciousness and self-awareness. We can then become aware of the Father principle in the family group, in social groups, in work groups, educational groups; in the community, the nation and the world.

In conclusion, I offer a map of the development of the masculine principle from childhood to old age. It is evident how the father affects each stage. Again, the map needs to be read upwards:

Story & Myth	History
Wise Old Man	The Androgyne
The Old Father	The Patriach
The Young Father	The Master Craftsman
The Hero	The Journeyman
The Youth	The Apprentice
The Boy, or Puer	The Child

Figure 9 The Development Of The Masculine

The Boy

We start with the *puer* of story and myth. At first the boy child is happy and free, spontaneous, playful, open, fearless, full of wonder, with a real need to join in the 'excitement' of what men do. This aspect in us all never dies. But, soon, the happy child is bound to be replaced by the wounded child. At best, he has to realise that the world does not revolve around him. And he withdraws. And so he may freeze in time, unhappy, frightened, lost, angry, manipulative. (Many adult men are stuck here, still searching for unconditional love, refusing to come out and play till they get it.) And then, at school, innate or family or social scripting teaches the boy to be competitive in pursuit of excellence. This leads on to the next stage:

The Youth

At one time, adolescents were typically apprenticed to a trade. Now, the teenager can be seen as an apprentice to the masculine principle. This is a period of powerful polarities; does he conform or not conform, obey or leave the nest? Whether the experience is positive or negative, he is struggling to be male with father as model. And the young person just out of childhood often has a dull and arid picture of what adulthood will be. Perhaps he has experienced it as sensible, rational, boring, practical, weighted down with responsibilities. 'If I join them, here's an end to fun, freedom, spontaneity, laughter and joy.' No wonder he may well be reluctant to grow up! Instead, he fantasizes about his hidden genius without doing anything about it. Seeking total control, he longs to be perfectly understood without having to explain himself. He will grow up only if life is just as he wants it; otherwise, no deal! Many adult men remain just such youths who have always refused to grow up. Allowing no room for debate, complexity, the possibility of being wrong, they play to the crowd, but underneath they are lonely, miserable and frightened.

The Hero

Historically, the apprentice would have moved on to become a journey-man within his trade, though now, alas, there are few journeys left! This is the time for the young man to discover his kingdom, his authority, his responsibility. He projects the heroic out to sportsmen, pop stars, explo-rers. It's a major time for the development of his sexuality, the emphasis being on *contrast*. This stage of the journeyman goes wrong because of the lack of a personal goal. What is the journey? Often the only answer can be a violent one. Those who get stuck at this level and never move on may not demonstrate that violence physically, being calm and patronising in the face of opposition. Yet this young man 'knows'. He will turn into an older person who doesn't change his views in twenty years. Simplistic, avoiding, seeing everything as either this or that, he is never swayed by other people's ideas, but is able to stand firm and ignore them.

The Young Father

No man is a hero to his own family. The heroic journeyman has ideally moved on to become master craftsman, the father of his family. This is the stage of responsibility. As with the hero, his personal need may be in conflict with changes in society; but this is a real adult, wholeheartedly taking responsibility for his own life and for his family. He does not blame, he is full of honesty and integrity. However, if it goes wrong, this is the stage where men turn to the suppression of the young. He may become a nervous parent, repressing his son by planting self-doubt in him. Or, jealous of younger men, he may prevent the youth or the hero from achieving anything. Here you have the autocratic father; perhaps he has become a schoolteacher, policeman, prison warder who abuses his power over the boy, dimming the shining of the young.

The Old Father

The Patriarch is the teller of tales, the keeper of the myth. In the business world, the move may be from executive action to a more paternal role. Flexible and fluid, he has clarified his own values, principles, ideals and goals. And they are never imposed on others, but open to scrutiny and change. If this stage goes wrong, he turns into the poor old *senex*, the old but not so wise man, doddering about as he always has, his age the most obvious thing about him. Backward-looking, complaining about the ills of the world, he has become an irascible petty tyrant, not wanting to go anywhere or do anything and scornful of those who do.

The Wise Old Man

This is a conjunct figure, where masculine and feminine have come together in a living androgyny. He is in balance, a psychological androgyne. The negative side here is the Wicked Wizard; the positive is Gandalf, the Laughing Buddha, the Zen master, tricky, funny and loving. He is immensely wise. Completely spontaneous, he enjoys life, has fun; he loves children and animals and simple things. He is ageless, focusing not upon the ills of body or of society but on life itself. He eats when he eats, sleeps when he sleeps, laughs when he laughs; in him the masculine and the feminine have come together in glorious interplay. This is the marriage of Heaven and Earth.

Plate 10

The Ark

CHAPTER SEVEN

Brothers and Sisters and the Family
Barbara Somers

Here's a highly instinctual small being
with a passionate nature thinking,
'If they love Billy then they don't love me'

What effect do our brothers and sisters have on our lives? We certainly haven't discovered everything about someone's earliest years until we have also explored their relationships with any brothers and sisters – or the lack of them. It's another very formative area for the child, yet it's amazing how its importance has been ignored and overlooked in general therapeutic work.[29]

It's our brothers and sisters who first introduce us to the 'otherness' within the peer group, as father originally did in relation to mother. Experience with brothers and sisters affects every adult relationship, leading to friendships within our own age-group, ease in social contact among peers and co-workers, to grouping and pairing, often to introductions to courtship and marriage. They teach us how to share love, possessions, secrets, inner and outer space, and it's with them that we spend time in creative play, so tremendously important to a child, allowing for natural competition with equals. Then we can go creatively into the modern world without feeling threatened by those on a level with us.

Or not. We may in fact *be* threatened, if that's what life with our sisters and brothers was like. Without them, we tend later to relate only at a parent-to-child or child-to-parent level. Unless we had replacement cousins and friends, we may grow up unsure of peers and equals. Without the close intimacy of family life a whole dimension is left out, and it has to be learnt later.

During the latter part of the twentieth century, many young people tended naturally to relate to each other like brothers and sisters. They became their own family, forming their own support-structure against 'them' – the parental, authoritative, authoritarian world. They gained strength and support from each other, rather than turning to the adults,

---

[29] At one time there were hardly any good books on the relationships with siblings – the subject came more to the fore as dynamics were explored in Family Therapy.

their elders, as they might once have done. Their relationships were very often interchangeable, with lots of experimental pairing. Permanent pairing (and marriage, if it happened at all) often came quite a bit later, whereas for their parents or grandparents, marriage and permanent pairing came first and the experimental kind afterwards.

If two young people met, they might become an intimate pair, switch around with their mates and friends and perhaps eventually come to relate to each other again. Sometimes, having lived together in a sexual relationship, alone or within a community, they were able to move back from that to relating with each other as brother and sister, while pairing off again in other directions. In earlier ages this would have called for a very considerable maturity; for these young people, it seemed almost to be the point from which they started in their exploration of relationships. History has yet to relate what will be the long term effects of this, but, exploring with people born then, we must bear in mind this attitude, unusual to earlier generations, that arose spontaneously among them.

Our place in the family – Family Triangles

We need to know where a person came within the family hierarchy. Were they an only child? If not, where did they come in the chronological history of the family? How many brothers and sisters were there above them? How many below? How many boys, how many girls? We shall look at the only child who then becomes the elder child, at the second child, the third child and the younger child, and see how different triangles are formed.[30]

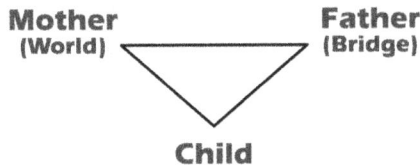

Figure 10 The Single Child

Starting with the *first child,* I map the family as a triangle. The man and the woman come together and the child is born. At that moment, a

---

30 Through my therapeutic work I have discovered the absolutely essential quality of these triangles. I realised I was opening up a very important area with a simple technique which has become very valuable to me.

fundamental triangle is set up: mother and father and child. The parents, still the same people, are suddenly thrust into it. Having gone through the experience of having the child, they now have to take on the images and archetypes of mother and father, as we've seen, and become stepping-stones for the child from the womb towards interaction with things and people outside.

The only child

Every first child is for a period the only child. Its parents are likely to be quite young, in the early years of their relationship with each other; they've probably not yet resolved their own movement away from comparative freedom or individuality, and they're still getting to know each other. So it very often happens that the child is born to a pair of relative strangers. A lot may be put on this first and only child in the early years. It takes the full weight of the parents, good, bad or good enough. It's their experimental guinea-pig. Every child requires itself to be special to its parents, particularly its mother; it's quite natural for a child developing an ego structure to be the centre of its own universe. However, should no other children, or their replacements, appear on the scene, two things can happen.

Firstly, the continuing only child may be over-indulged, treated as extra special; it is after all the centre of the parents' affection, attention and expectations. Depending on its temperament and individual nature, this can make for trouble in later life. Feeling itself specially loved (and it doesn't take much for a child to feel itself at the central hub of things) it can go on into later life still looking for special treatment. Growing self-centred, self-oriented and jealous of rivals, such people can be heard requesting, even demanding to be treated with that degree of specialness which was the unbroken pattern of childhood. With the family triangle in mind, given a later issue with two peers, two friends, two colleagues, we can sense how the person is trying to push in, become involved, be specially placed.

However, being 'special' can also mean carrying the parents' unlived subjective life and their expectations, becoming small piggie-in-the-middle in the unresolved relationship between that man and that woman who are the mother and the father.

Secondly, and conversely, the child may be *under*-indulged. Aware that this is an only child, the parents may be over-strict, treating it as a small adult and expecting it to behave as one. Spontaneity is inhibited in favour of being 'nice', clean, well-behaved, reflecting well on the parents. This very often applies when the parents are older, or are particularly stereotyped, tied, confined within their own scripts. Such children may lack confidence; shy, introverted, they're on the outside looking in through a window at a group, or out of a window towards a group. They defer to others, finding competitive situations difficult. There is the threat that both parents can descend like gods and bang them, whereas in a larger family a bit of naughtiness can, with some skill, get hidden and lost in the network. And there's nobody else with whom to compare notes about the gods, or about anything. Later they may go on trying to make all others into indulgent parents whose special children they can be. Also there may be a very strong inward search for replacement brothers and sisters; they are extremely careful to maintain friendship and very possessive of their special friends.

Only children tend to be over-serious, relating well to adults because they've had most practice there. However, unless they had plenty of contact with other children (effectual brothers and sisters), they may remain unsure with their fellows and out of touch with play and what they call 'childish' activity. Hyper-critical, they don't suffer fools gladly, and may grow up indulgent and permissive at best, judgemental at worst. With very little tolerance when, conversely, special treatment is demanded of *them*, they may respond by becoming boorish, insensitive, tyrannical, overbearing. Indeed, they may be pushy, controlling, 'must be first', as early as play-school.

Over-responsible, perhaps somewhat precocious, very often highly intelligent, an only child (or an elder child) is frequently given educational benefit. Often talented, creative, artistic or scientific, the exploration of the mind is very important to them. Research indicates that elder children tend to do better at school than the younger ones. This isn't only pressure of expectation, the parents' anxiety they should do well. It's a wider thing; being talked to early on, having a lot of attention, will have helped them become verbal much more quickly. Mother has more time to communicate with a single child than when she has one hanging on each breast.

Most children will have fantasy friends; even if they do have brothers and sisters they may not like them, building in a whole 'pretend' family with whom they *can* live. But, lacking outside relationships, the only child is particularly likely to be strong on fantasy ones. It often has a very rich, intense inner life and an ability to be alone without feeling lonely. With a close affiliation to nature, it makes friends from inner space. Toys too; I check what kind of toys the person had. We saw how there's something in the quality of the subjective life which the child identifies with the toy. It goes with our small person into the world and helps make the connection between inner and outer.

It's possible for the only child to be both over- and under-indulged at the same time: materially they're given everything, but that's not what they really need. People who were only children often feel that they were not understood. I ask, 'As an only child, what were your feelings about love and friendship, power and control? How did your special relationship with your parents, the dominant figures, affect you?' (With nothing as counterpoint, they were particularly vulnerable here.) 'Did you develop a submissive, placating attitude, or an ability to manipulate the triangle in your own favour? Or did you become isolated, self-absorbed, self-reliant?'

If the person had not known how to handle the ordinary interchange of the world out there, which can seem like an attack, even a penetration, I'd ask, 'Did you tend to withdraw, hole up, go it alone? Are you touchy, easily suspecting rejection? Do you now feel that other people are demanding of *you*, trying to take your possessions?' After all, you don't *share* your teddy bear with mum or dad – or not for too long, and not in the same way that you can share or refuse to share it with another child. 'Did you have to learn to share later?'

The elder child

Of course as soon as the next child appears, the only child becomes the elder child. The triangle changes – a reversed triangle and a different dynamic. And now, here's this newcomer on the scene ! However well-handled by the parents, and at whatever age the only child becomes the elder child, it's probably impossible not to feel a sudden fall from grace, from the centre of attention, a loss of specialness; though good-enough parents will include the first child in the second pregnancy and help it not to feel left out. It's much easier for the child to deal with this in its first three years than later. After three, when the ego-identity of the elder child is being established in relation to both parents, it may very well feel ousted by the new baby and betrayed by the gods.

Often and often, people will tell me exactly how they did feel ousted and betrayed. That secure triangle, two parents each concentrating on *this* one, suddenly became – those two together concentrating on *another* one! Even if hitherto the child had had the total concentration of 'bad' parents, at least that had given it a special function. Young children have a very

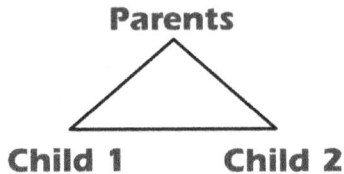

Parents

Child 1   Child 2

Figure 11 The Second Child

labile emotional colour-range and can run the gamut from tragedy to joy, love to hate, within a few seconds. Here's a highly instinctual small being with a passionate nature, thinking in the very black-and-white terms quite natural to a child, and now – *QED*, straightforward, uncomplicated and instinctual – 'If they love Billy then they don't love me.'

And a lot of us grow up still feeling that. It's only through the experience of love that we learn that any number of others can come in and everybody gets a free share of it; a very sophisticated experience of life which not too many people have. The art is to accept that for every *pro* emotion we are bound to have its *contra*. We can't love deeply until we hate passionately; it's an almost exact measure. To accept both ends of the stick and then to act from choice is part of growth and adulthood.

To pretend the feeling of jealousy isn't there is highly dangerous. It's very passionate stuff, full of strength and vibrancy. If it isn't expressed and handled there's all the doubt, guilt and ambivalence that go with having to repress or smother a strong emotion. Jealousy is a very positive energy, often involving hatred of the people we love for betraying us, and certainly of this little swine that's come in and changed everything! It's not in the least unknown for the elder to keep trying to kill the younger from the moment it's born. The child may well have absolutely murderous feelings, which do have to be put under and handled. There may be some strongly loving feelings as well towards 'this new little one'; but still the wretched new little one is bound to be a threat. There's the need to be comforted and held, and frequently the child regresses into tantrums in the effort to be itself babied again.

Children of school age are often very mature, having the development to hide, manipulate and handle jealousy which a three-year-old would not. The elder may act as pseudo-adult, disguising its feelings behind caring for the new baby (being particularly loving to it, over-conscientious with it, very good about it) and all to win parental approval: 'I'll grow up and parent this thing myself, and get some sort of control here!' And it can be all the worse if the younger is born when it's as old as six, seven or more; if it's been the special and only child for several years, its instinctual jealousy may be all the stronger. One person commented:

'I wanted to kick and hit my little brother, and my parents too. Twice I got quite paralysed; my arms and legs were stuck and I couldn't move them till I let this energy out. And my feet and hands have always been cold. I'm sure it's because I pushed down my feelings so, at that very early age'.

A lot of research has been done into birthing, but effects put down to birth-experience often don't go back as far as that. An energy may well have been trapped at a later stage. This is the value of the imaging, which takes us to where it wants us to go – and not necessarily into the womb. I check out: 'When did your next sister or brother appear on the scene?' Were they felt as an interloper come to take mum's or dad's love? And just watch what happens in such an adult's current relationships when a third comes in! 'Now I'll be betrayed!' – ousted by this other arriving on the scene. This repetition of similar patternings can be very, very painful. Only the trust in the Self, the belief that in some measure we choose our environment, makes it acceptable. I would personally try to tear heaven and hell apart if I thought that no one had a chance in the face of all this.

The elder one may remember being sent away while mother went into hospital for the next baby. No child is really going to understand this, however much it is explained to them. As far as they're concerned, they 'must have done something naughty'; the sense of abandonment is very often counteracted by an enormous sense of guilt. Here is another colleague's experience:

'My first memory of my brother was of being sent back to my little nursery school while my mother had him. My father came to visit me there, but he went back home. I very soon found myself looking after – this baby! I must have been jealous of 'this baby' from the start, and probably chose to become a mini-adult in order to handle it. I remember a story – how it impinged! – about a little girl with straight hair like me. And the reason she had straight hair was because she had let the rain fall on her baby brother. She'd had to walk around with an umbrella over this baby. I remember reading and re-reading that story.' It may be that the elder boy has a fairly tough time with the father. Sometimes there is awful enmity between them, a feeling of 'The king is dead, long live the king!' Equally, the elder girl can have a rough time with mother. Look at it from the parents' point of view: the father will, generally speaking, be much more threatened by the appearance on the scene of another man, a boy vying for his wife's love, than the mother will be; and the mother will be more threatened by a girl, also vying for love. A great deal depends on the relationship between the parents, and their maturity.

Certainly the first child does seem more often than not to have a greater degree of *in*security than the others. It is the experimental one. No mother of a first child is absolutely confident about what to do; it will have soaked up mother's uncertainty about how to handle it and still as an adult carry all the expectations that go with that uncertainty.

If, as elder child, we are several years ahead of the younger, we may *welcome* the second child's arrival, especially if there hasn't been a particularly close bond with the parents. The younger may fill a gap, help take the strain of 'them' and be the ally we've waited for. 'There are two of us now; we can gang up against "them", share secrets, plot together.' Here's a comrade against authority. My own brother was six years older than me, and my mother did a very good lead-up to my appearance, along the lines of 'This baby's a birthday present for you'. It goes down in family history that he was allowed home from school and told that Mummy had a new little sister for him. He looked at me for a long time, turned up his nose and said, 'I don't like it, can we send it back?' And that was his general attitude for quite a while. We had a very good relationship, but that was mainly because I so patently adored and worshipped him that I won him over, albeit unconsciously.

The second child

So the next child has come in to this triangle (see Figure 11). The debit of being a second child is that it often takes the brunt of the elder's jealousy, not in public, but behind the scenes. If it comes quite a few years behind, the first one is likely to be elder brother, big sister, young parent to the smaller, who often finds itself lumbered with three 'parents' all ganging up against it. Though it closes later there's a vast age-gap between a child of fifteen months and one of say five years; often too young to play, the new one is nothing but a nuisance. The younger may feel the elder to be more privileged in every way. It may have the elder held up as an example, positive or negative, very often academically. Many times I have heard people complain that they were given the older ones' hand-me-downs, from love to ideas to clothes. And who really likes having somebody else's cast-offs – big sister's dress, big brother's trousers, boots, old trainers – dumped on them?

Among the credits of being the second child is that the parents are usually more relaxed. After all, they've already practised! The first child has probably borne the full weight of their experiments and expectations, and perhaps they are now busy with a third one. It varies with the background, but very often the second is more sunny and less intense than the first, feels freer, is not so clamped into having to be over-responsible. When I meet a second child as adult, I watch what happens when they come in as third to a pair, the outsider who has to be integrated. If they are having trouble with being third, I ask myself, 'What was the original triangle?'

These triangles are terribly important. In our adult relationships we may be seeking a re-enactment of the actual or fantasy relationship, not with the mother or father, but with a brother or sister. Perhaps that important fact has been overlooked. Our relationship to the other children, our placing within the pecking order, is likely to be triggered when for example our own children are born. We might then suddenly find ourselves in a state of 'sibling rivalry', wondering what on earth it's all about, totally overlooking the fact that we may be re-enacting the coming of a newborn baby into our own young lives.

The third child

When the third child arrives the dynamic changes again, and another triangle is added to the map.

In Alchemy, the third comes in as catalyst, and Child Three is inevitably a catalyst – all odd-numbered children are catalysts because they break up the even, realigning the triangle into a diamond. Humans naturally form pairs rather than threes, so the third one will always add another factor, leading to change and maybe to problems. 'Two's company, three's a crowd.'

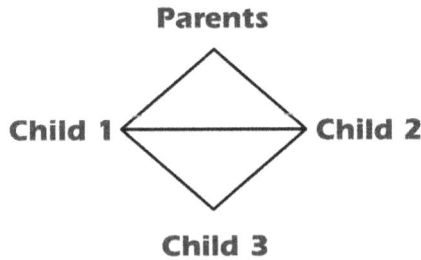

Parents

Child 1 ⟷ Child 2

Child 3

Figure 12 The Third Child

What happens depends very much on how Child One and Child Two have interacted with each other. If it's been a sticky relationship, then it can be a marvellous relief to the two to have a third walk in. 'Ho ho, here's the relief-troops come up over the hill!' and they immediately gang up with the newcomer against each other. However, if the two of them have liked each other fairly well, just as they have settled the *status quo* in comes this unknown scout from outside. This they will not like. The parents will almost certainly be giving quite a bit of attention to the new child, so *two* others are displaced and put out of paradise. They'll have to sort it out between themselves. They may gang up, excluding the third.

As time goes on, three children may play the parents off against each other. Or one or other may take sides with the parents against the other two; one may assume a parental role with the others or tell tales in order to be 'in' with either side. One child may become a Mercurius figure, messenger of the gods, speaking for the parents, trying to hold the bridge; or interpreting the other children back to the parents, becoming go-between, the carrier of the message. One may be the scapegoat, and another the fool. Whichever child is left out becomes outsider, the pariah or rebel: 'I don't really care!' They may put themselves out from choice – or always be struggling to get in. Either way, they have difficulty with one-to-one relationships.

The middle child

This one can grow into adulthood utterly confused, feeling that most of these things apply. One said, 'I feel like an only child, and I feel like an eldest child – *and* I feel like the youngest as well!' Sensing she had to placate everyone (whereas the others, by being the first and the last, had a natural permission not to), she would take it out on her dolls.

This is where mapping the family history can help, working out where we were placed and how the dynamic changed at the key points when our sisters or brothers went off. By the very nature of change, the child isn't always in the same position; the pecking order shifts. I ask, 'Where were you at the points which suddenly altered the whole dynamic? When your sister was in hospital – left home – when your brother hit father in the eye – was in trouble with the police for stealing?' Draw the map, and we see quite a bit of the history not only of the person's setting among all those people, but of where they were at *that* moment within the dynamic. As time went on, perhaps first the two eldest formed a pair, then the two youngest, then later the two boys, the two girls and so on. I explore any jealousies between the elder and the younger son or daughter. Nobody's jealous of the one in the middle; it's the middle one who's jealous of the others!

When people set up triangles for themselves in adult relationships, it can sometimes be brought straight back to this. One man told me there must be something very odd about him:

'Whenever I formed a good relationship with a woman, I'd be drawn to a second woman at the same time, naturally fouling up the first relationship. The second woman was always a bitch! I'd come between a "good" sister whom I liked and an "absolute bitch" sister I didn't like at all. Whenever I was with the good one, I expected the bitch to turn up. So I'd fetch her in anyway, so that I wouldn't be taken by surprise! I now realise it was better the devil you know than the one who is waiting to jump in on you. Conversely, if I met a woman like the bitch sister, I'd immediately start looking for the good sister.' This pattern had gone on for years.

In the multiple families of today it's possible to be, say, the second child with regard to father, but the fourth with regard to mother. The half-brothers and sisters may vary greatly in age and, when it arrives on the scene, the child may have perhaps six parents!

Child Four evens things out, allowing two lots of two. Then if Child Five comes in, there's another set of three, and so on. Equilateral triangles, isosceles triangles, every kind of fascinating and interacting triangle – it's well worth mapping with someone how and where they stood in all these. The way people go into and act in later groups and organisations is anchored here: love, hate, rivalry, companionship, the playing of roles, the protection of one's own boundaries – it's all being richly lived through in the jostling of the family.

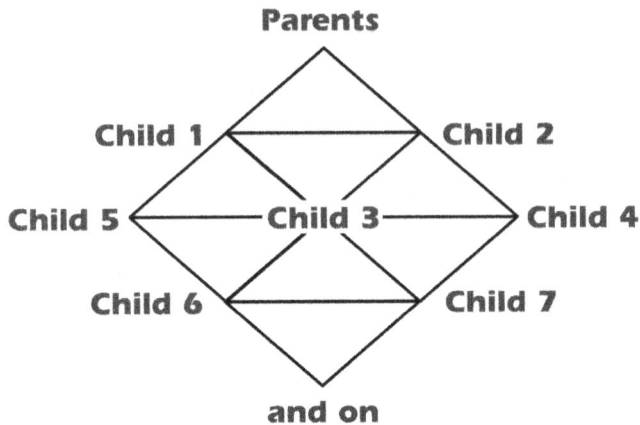

Figure 13   Many Children

The youngest child

And sooner or later the parents are presumably going to give up! This brings us to the youngest child, the one who remains the 'baby' of the family. This one may be laughed at as the butt of the others, and, although that laughter isn't always malicious, it can certainly be taken as such by a sensitive child. 'Baby's fun, baby's the buffoon!' The child who is the youngest, whatever age they are, whatever age everybody else is, is always at the bottom of the heap. At any given stage, everyone else is by definition older, more advanced, more privileged, more capable than they; always able to stand up just ahead of them, walk a bit faster, catch the ball more easily. It's very difficult not to feel fairly inadequate.

The youngest child may be pretty well ignored. It may have arrived as a surprise just when the parents were really wanting to be clear of the family and do their own thing. So it's in everybody's way, always under the feet of pounding brothers and sisters. On the other hand, the youngest may be kept young, babied by the parents; perhaps, now this lovely new little stranger has arrived, they are reliving their lost youth. One or both of them may have an emotional investment in holding on to the 'lovely new little stranger', not wanting *all* the children to vanish from the scene since they would then have to face each other.

So, this poor little blighter has quite a lot to carry. Ignored and seen as a nuisance, or babied and made special again like a first child, it may well be thoroughly and heartily loathed by every other child. Whether it remain the butt of the rest or whether the older ones mother it, the dynamic will have changed again. One baby didn't bother to talk at all until he was over three, because his brother and sister would translate for him. He didn't make sense, but they would seem to understand: 'He says he wants to go to the park.' Their mother wondered who was dominating whom? Were they trying to teach the baby? Or was it just that *they* wanted to go to the park?

The youngest is bound to be witness of a changing scene and shifting inter-relationships. The others reach adolescence, each taking their different approaches; this one will witness the conflicts, perhaps the coming together in a new way, of the parents with the adolescents. As the eldest moves towards adulthood and leaves, there will be a change-round in the dynamic of those remaining. The pecking order alters. And although everyone else is ahead, the youngest may be the most perceptive; the observer, with the best view in the family. Having seen the others rebel, the adults face crisis, the teenagers go out, they've learnt how to do and how not to do many things.

The youngest may get out very fast, even ahead of time, determined not to be the one left behind. Alternatively, they may well be left to care for ageing parents (this applies even today, and it's a lot to take aboard). They may not have been expected to live a life of their own. The others could get up and leave and go, but they had to stay around, the only child at home – until such time as they *did* get up and go. And so the circle is rounded, the youngest is the only one left, and we're back to the only child.

Twins

While identical twins are obviously two, they're very often treated as *one*. This makes it difficult for them to establish separate identities. A doctor colleague described twins she'd treated, one of whom was a young mother. She came into the clinic with her identical sister and her child, and it was as if there were two mothers. First one twin was holding the child, then the other, and the doctor couldn't tell them apart. Their behaviour was identical in terms of caring and nurturing, discussing the baby as though they themselves were one single child; an odd experience for these 'children' who hadn't separated, to have this unified infant between them. It can obviously be an extraordinarily difficult and complex thing –though it could probably be great fun!

Stories are often broadcast about twins. One man and his twin brother – not identical – had been brought up in an orphanage and then separated, one going to foster parents in Canada and the other staying in England. When he was about thirty-six, the one in England went looking for his lost twin. On meeting and comparing notes they discovered extraordinary likenesses; they had the same tastes, the same books on their shelves, even used the same kind of shaving lotion. They'd married, on the same day, women who could almost have been twins themselves. Such stories are quite usual.

I knew someone with identical twin daughters. Very much pushed together till they were about fifteen, they menstruated on exactly the same day; if one varied in the cycle, so did the other. As each began to seek her own identity, struggling to get away from the other, one of them came in to counselling, and it was then that their menstrual cycle first split.[31] Another pair of twin girls had separate bedrooms, but when they were about sixteen if one of them went to bed early she would come back down saying, 'For goodness sake come to bed, I'm tired!' This symbiosis makes for difficulty; almost you could end up with one person instead of two.

There may be something compensatory in their twin-ness; sometimes, one carries for the other either the light or the shadow, moving into the distinctly opposite role, compensating almost *pro rata* for something in the other. It can be that that's just how they are, but, more deeply, it's likely to be the struggle between them to establish their separate identities. They may assume those roles in order to *part*.

The death of a brother or sister

The early death of any sister or brother can lead to a sense of continuous grieving. Particularly the death of a twin at birth may leave a person as if mourning 'the other half'. They're often unconscious of it to start with, but the story comes out and it is a story of grief. If this has happened, I suggest that we conduct a ritual – we may need to go through a number

---

31 In the same way a whole dormitory of girls, if they stay together long enough, will tend to menstruate on the same day. The moon obviously has an effect, but women coming in with all the different variations of rate over the twenty-eight days begin to move towards each other when they live together, adapting mysteriously off their own cycle.

of them – of burial or cremation of the baby in order to make a termination to the grieving; otherwise there's still a missing link, an end that has not been rounded.

If it was later that the other twin died, there's the danger of an extra onus being put on to the survivor, with resultant guilt and rebellion. Over and over, those who have lost a twin feel that they ought to be living for two. The weight of the *two*, the grief and the loss and the expectation that once would have been shared between them, passes over to the one left, however well the parents may handle it. And no matter what the parents do, there may be that movement in the survivor so often found in people after wars: the one who lives feels they were 'too bad to die'. Their comrades died, they survived, and they carry guilt for a very long time afterwards, punishing themselves to expiate it. A writer I knew, highly successful in her own field, went through her life apologizing and placating. It turned out that her twin had died at birth and very early on she had heard her mother saying, 'It should have been you that died!' Here is a colleague's story:

'I'm the third of three children, but there are ghosts. My sister is eight years older than me, my brother six. About two years after he was born my mother had an abortion, probably because of financial problems. A year later she was pregnant again and the baby died an hour after birth. It was a boy. She felt it was her punishment for the abortion. And then, two years after that, I came along, a son! I lived. I was her proof she'd been forgiven for it. So a whole mythology was put on me already and as the younger one I had to live up to it. Mother's fantasy dominated us all. Father was pretty much out of it really, at the time of the growing up. My brother, the middle child, became a juvenile delinquent, the bad boy, very hostile, really evil to me. My sister played a funny role: she teamed up with my brother and supported him, and she teamed up with my father because they looked the most alike. So she was the closest to my father and to my brother; she was the closest to me; and also to my mother. She became the go-between and was very motherly towards me.'

'However, my sister and brother were separate from me because I was so much younger. So I became precocious. When I was about six and they were twelve, fifteen, my brother and his friends would get together with dirty magazines, baby-sitting for me. So I knew what teenagers were doing! I was appreciated among them for being cute, but couldn't quite be a part of it; I had to grow up fast so as to join them. I knew that when

I was older I could be equal to them – my life was ahead of me – but I felt left out at the time.'

A different but very human tendency is for the rest of the family to put the one who is dead into a kind of holy aspic, which can be very trying for the survivor. One man had a sister known as Angel Annie. He was only ten months younger – an extremely close conception. Angel Annie died. And he was dressed in little Annie's clothes. He was actually called 'Little Annie' until he was about three, when his own nature began to come through. For the first years he didn't know whether he was a boy or a girl, and although apparently an entire male, married and raising his own lineage, he still freely admits to a problem with gender-identity. And he still feels terribly guilty, crossing his t's, dotting his i's, doubling up on everything, still holding up holy little Aspic Annie as a saint. And there's nobody there! It's very difficult for him to contend with someone who isn't there. How can he compare with somebody who's gone? Annie's not around to prove what a little horror she might have grown up to be.

Sometimes the very reason for the birth of a particular child is the death of another. It's commonly put out by the doctor and the social worker and the priest, really meaning to be helpful: 'You must have another child as soon as possible! That'll take your mind off this one that's dead.' The child is then a replacement. I know of two who were even given the same name. It's horrendous; it comes into the same category as: 'Come on now, don't worry, have a baby and your marriage will hold together'! It makes the child into a carrier for something else; it's inappropriate and it's very difficult to handle. It doesn't allow the vitally necessary ritual of mourning to take place, nature's time for grieving. There is a time in a healthy life when grieving will pass over naturally to relief, and then the next child is ready to be born.

Adopted and fostered children

The question: 'Who was mother, who was father?' is particularly important for the adopted child, and also for the foster child, who had maybe a whole series of parents. Were they really mothered by one of their sisters? Was it a brother who was father to them? There are many complicated questions: Why was the child adopted? Was it adopted after years of strain and stress caused by the parents trying to have a child of their own? What was it like for the adopted child to come in at the end of all that, and have to carry so much hope, so many dreams? Did the adopted child come in to a ready-made family (which is also the step-child's condition)? If there were natural children in the family, did they always feel second best?

As adults, if we were adopted we are now allowed by law to try to find our real parents. We may have a very powerful need to return to our roots. Who were our own parents? We may have a sudden yearning to find out. A colleague working in an adoption agency saw how people come in at particular crisis points; perhaps when they're about to get married or have their own children. Up till then, they've been happy with knowing they were adopted and with their adoptive parents. But suddenly they need to go back, seek their mother or their father, trace brothers and sisters, see the house or children's home where they were brought up.

There's a need for great respect and reverence for the moment when somebody suddenly says they want to go back and look. They are too often told, 'Well, it's too late now, you won't be able to find them. Come along, let's think about the future!' Seeking them is a very necessary rounding-off of one stage of history before moving to another. If I come across this, and especially if I know that the person isn't going to be able to find the parents but will remain lost, with that yearning, grieving, that lamentation, that unfilled empty hole, I aim to go into the much deeper need to return to the parental soil. They may need to return to the place they think they came from, going through some kind of ritual, before they can bring themselves forward.

Step-children

The step-child obviously has difficult things to deal with. On remarrying, the parent may have brought a whole step-family into the child's natural home. Or the child may have been brought away and into a new place full of step-brothers and sisters. Here is one step-child's story:

'My brother and I were very close, because we shared the loss of our first mother – *our* mother. At first, my father was very close to both of us and mothered us. And then my stepmother came along! She produced her first when I was three years old. I don't remember my step-sister's birth, though I have memories earlier than that – she was blacked out by me. So was my stepmother. She was a big intrusion. Because I was a girl, I was asked to look after my step-sister. And when I was six, another step-sister arrived.

'My brother and I clung together so closely we hardly had two identities: we were one person. But when those two came, they seemed to be just babies. I still tend very readily to mother and look after younger women, jumping up to close windows if they're cold, the old pattern! The over-responsible bit of me comes out. I think it was compensation for a tremendous jealousy. My stepmother was a very powerful woman, and I had no way of getting at her, and since I didn't dare get at my younger sisters, I looked after them. But I resented it very much.

'When my brother rebelled – he left school with tremendous upset – my father moved in very strongly, taking me as his great hope of becoming 'the degree person'. That caused tremendous tension between my brother and me, since he wasn't academic while I'd become the bluestocking. He rejected the family, and he felt rejected by them. My sisters were terrific rivals; they were very beautiful, and as they grew up they caught up in height. That was terrible. I remember how I hated tall women. The only thing I could hold on to was that I was cleverest! As soon as I could make friendships I moved out of this family; my friends became more important than any of them. I had no close relationships with them – the negative things were too strong – except for this bond between my brother and me.'

Thus we choose our own friends, re-patterning the family. Jung spoke about the 'accidental family' we're born to, and the 'chosen family'. We often find we've replaced with friends the key figures in that original triangle or diamond or whatever, feeling they'll allow us to climb out of our stereotyped script into a different formation. However, if it's an unconscious choice, we may reconstellate the old family pattern all over again, with the new friends producing all the old family problems. I ask couples, 'How many members of the family, chosen and accidental, are sharing the marriage bed with the two of you?' And they wonder why they're impotent with each other!

Refugees and children who were evacuated

Since the Second World War, thousands of children have been displaced and made refugees all over the world. It's well worth watching out for them, and also, among those born before or during that war, for the evacuated child. Many of them will consciously have forgotten all about it, but it may have been a huge trauma. Lots of children went away *with* their parents and were uprooted for a while, or perhaps didn't see their father or whoever for a long period. But others were evacuated into another family, and had no idea why. Too young to understand the nature of war or displacement, all they knew was that they had been thrown out from their own home and put in with, fostered on to, somebody else. The fairy-tale of Cinderella, the myth of Little Boy Lost, may strike chords with those who were evacuated, pushed out from home willy-nilly in a collective move immensely more powerful than themselves. With their gas masks and their labels put on them they were sent off, landing with a bunch of substitute parents, maybe substitute sisters and brothers. They just may have preferred these new 'parents' to their own, and then had to face coming back home. There were all sorts of shocks to the system for these young children. Some, sorted for selection at the local railway station, were chosen off the train as if at a cattle market by prospective 'parents'. What about the poor little things who were left till last? Like picking up sides for games at school – not being picked for the rounders team! One man said:

'I was fourteen, and I can remember very clearly that for at least the first week I was put in the room of a son of the family. I had never before shared a bed with a strange child; it was particularly traumatic as I'd just been separated from my parents and all my brothers and sisters. It was a different cultural set-up altogether, a great tearing-up of the roots. Very many people of my generation went through this in one form or another.'

It was all accompanied by tremendous uncertainty, and perhaps the fear that the parents would be blown up in the dangerous place the child had been sent away from. It's easy to overlook this. The person often doesn't remember: 'Well, I was only two at the time.' But a child of two picks up the atmosphere in the environment. The shock may have been even more tremendous for those who came from overseas (Britain took children under sixteen). One man had been put on a train at the age of fifteen, leaving Europe, knowing his parents had been in a pogrom. He came here, parents dead behind him, no relation in the world. Many people carry this vast wound in the psyche. A friend and colleague came out of her country when she was two, carried across three nations and over the sea. She didn't remember it until we started working through the imaging, when up came, with vast clarity, the memory of everyone saying, 'Ssh! Be quiet! THEY are out there!'

I know that my deep love of having a room and a place of my own is innate and natural to me, but I also know it was affected by my being evacuated. One morning very early I was picked up out of my bed by my mother. In tears, grief-stricken, she had no explanation that I could possibly understand. A little cardboard box with my gas mask in it was wrapped round my neck and a little label fixed on me with my name. I hated this label and kept pulling it off. That was the worst thing, being labelled like that! I was shunted away to Northampton, of all places, where the bombing must have been almost as bad as the London blitz, shoved into a house which was totally strange and alien, with people I didn't like, and put in a room with a girl about four years older than me. She chose me, wanting some other little girl in with her. Every night she told me all about her view of sex. She was an absolute little beast! She really rough-housed me, and it was a huge shock. My mother would come every weekend, and cry all the time until I was dragged away from her.

So finally I went to Northampton station and climbed on the first train that came in. I thought any train would be going to London. However, it was heading north, to Edinburgh. At some unknown point the guard put me off into the arms of a huge policeman. I was taken to the police station and given cocoa and buns. I discovered then that cocoa and buns is what policemen eat. So I was taken back to Northampton. A week later, I did exactly the same thing. I don't know where I was heading this time, but once again I was led off and put into the arms of another big policeman – different policeman, different station but same cocoa and buns. Back in Northampton I stopped eating, and when I started to starve they had to bring me home to London – where I loved every minute of the blitz. But I have not forgotten the trauma of being evacuated. It reminds me to remember it with other people.

The scapegoat

Practically all families have a tendency for one person to be held up as the shining example. The greatest conformists of all, they fit in exactly with the required attitudes of the family – and pretty boring they can be! Another child will be made the 'bad' one. This is the one who simply cannot conform, who rebels against all norms and expectations; yet maybe in the end this is the one who will go out and away and found their own New World. From among these comes the fascinating Scapegoat, required to take the family's collective neurosis or resentment or anger or repressed emotion.

Scapegoats are useful; they carry everything for everybody. Family therapy shows how, in a number if not in all families, one person will become known as the 'ill one' or the 'weak one', the 'difficult one' or the 'stupid one'. Anything which cannot be accepted consciously by the family will be shipped over at an unconscious level to this carrier, the scapegoat of the family. If they're taken into care somewhere else, or perhaps if they go into counselling, the entire dynamic changes. The carrier for all has been removed and the family pushed into a position of having to own their own difficulty, silliness, illness, weakness or whatever. They can no longer put it over to Little Johnny or Our Lulu.

However, when this child is rehabilitated, there's an immediate move from the entire family to reinstate it as scapegoat. It's required, so that the others don't have to admit in consciousness that they too are in trouble. A great deal of pressure is put on to the person to go under again, sink, become neurotic or psychotic or ill, be handicapped in some way once more. If that person doesn't return to the family, or won't take it, then another scapegoat will do; if one escapes the net, another is taken on to become a necessary carrier of material which the family is not prepared to face. A lot of what in the past was considered genetic neurosis or psychosis may be the emergence of this pattern. And maybe there's a 'good' scapegoat who carries all the best values of the family; an awful lot to carry. We need to look at the scapegoat role that the person may have played or have forced somebody else to play, and it may all arise out of these original triangles.

How children born with physical or mental difficulties fare in families varies enormously. They aren't always scapegoated, by any means. I've known children in a family with such a child who have become the most remarkable people in terms of the caring, the love, the taking-up and the understanding that they have for this one – the protection that goes on. Families can be the most marvellous things. Some fight like hell amongst each other, but the moment a shock comes from outside, the whole family rallies. However, a very difficult child may well become the carrier of the shadow for everybody.

Doctor Thomas Weiss, who has worked most of his life exploring with such children, claims that they are not *damaged* children, they are a very special breed – little reminders from somewhere else of what love and laughter and joy and fun are like. He said they come in from a different place, like sunlight – they just talk a different language – and they have something very real to teach us about simplicity and love. A man of about thirty-six told how his mother and father made terrific sacrifices for his elder brother, who had such difficulties. At forty he would wander about, but his mother still always kept an eye out. A friend he was visiting said, 'Don't you think you should let your mother know where you are?' 'What, me? At forty!' He obviously understood the joke of it.

Exploring the family

To explore with somebody the family and its effects, I might begin with the time from birth to five years. 'Where do you come in the family? What are your memories of the birth of the child below? What was your experience of jealousy in relation to your parents and the other children? How well did you fit into the general expectation of the family pattern?' Most families have certain definite expectations. Temperamental differences among the sisters and the brothers can often bring them into rebellious confrontation, or leave one of them feeling like an outsider because they don't happen to conform to the norm of that particular family. Was this an introverted, sensitive child who went to the wall in a boisterous family? Or an extraverted one who became repressed within an introverted group?

We can map together questions involving memories of school, from five to puberty. I ask, 'Do you have traumatic memories of having to go to school, the first leaving of mother? How did you relate to peers, to teachers, to friends? And was it OK to be a boy, was it OK to be a girl? What were the family attitudes to this?' It used to be that only boys were acceptable. There may have been quite a lot of sex-play of the 'mothers and fathers, doctors and nurses' kind, all part of the experimentation of that particular stage of development. What are your memories of this? Did it occur with brothers and sisters, or with school friends, or with both? A woman whose parents were running a boarding school lived with her older brother within the boys' area and was used like a prostitute by those young boys. Her brother never defended her. It made a fine old mess of her later experience of life. That is perhaps unusual, but even in the smallest way something of that nature can fundamentally affect a girl's whole attitude to sex later on. The same applies to boys.

I may ask too, 'What was the pattern of competition with brothers and sisters as you began to jostle for your own space among the family, and for the favour or otherwise of your parents? What was the pecking order at particular stages within the family ? Were readjustments made as you all developed? Were there different rates of growth?' If the child parented another one, was there a reversal of that at a later stage? What about favouritism, the parents towards the children and the children towards each other? How far does that affect adult relationships now?

When exploring together their life from puberty to early adulthood, I check out growing relationships with brothers and sisters; likenesses and differences between children become more clearly defined during these stages. How did they affect the person? 'How far, in adolescence, did you rely on your brothers and sisters to make the first friendships and bring outsiders into the house?' I check out the changes in the pairs and triangles, and how the children's attitudes to each other changed as the various characters began to develop in their own particular ways. How much freedom of talk was there amongst them, and between them and their parents, about sexual matters? For the boys, how were masturbation and nocturnal emissions regarded? And menstruation – how was this treated with the girls?

During puberty and early adulthood there's an increasing need for *space and boundaries*, as we shall see. As they grow, there is a wider magnetic energy-field to each individual. It may suddenly become an issue if they are sharing bedrooms or find that younger children's fingers are always prying into their secrets. 'What was the attitude towards privacy among your brothers and sisters? Were they able to share and keep quiet about secrets, or was there tale-bearing to your parents?'

Then, what about the 'courting' stage? What was the whole family's attitude to the period leading up to partnership, marriage? 'How did it affect you when the older ones began to pair up with the opposite sex?' Could they bring their partners home, would they be accepted? Then, later, what were the inter-relations between brothers-in-law and sisters-in-law?

I check out also periods in hospital, departures of the parents to work or on holidays or wherever, and of brothers and sisters to school and away. 'Did you experience any traumatic moments? Were there deaths in the family? How far did divorce, separation and change bring about a re-balancing between the parents as you all began to grow up?' These breaks, these moments of departure, particularly when it was a permanent departure, will have thrown the weight of the emotions of the parents and the other children back on to each other, so that a smaller unit had to carry what was once shared between a larger number. These can be very important crises of adaptation in a person's life. Although not 'remembered', having mapped them through we may find them to be major keys to later attitudes. An adult's reactions to matters of bereavement, or death, or separation, or absence, may well have been pre-patterned in the time of the family among their brothers and sisters.

Plate 11

Overview

CHAPTER EIGHT

Space and Boundaries
Barbara Somers and Ian Gordon-Brown

DIFFERENT TYPES OF PERSONAL SPACE
Barbara Somers

Good enough parents have children who expect space by right

Sometimes certain people seem able to 'loom' in our lives. The fear of their coming in on top of us can be reduced, their looming presence diminished, if we can learn to manage our *space* and the *boundaries* around it. If we can control space, then we can control people's apparent size. The idea is to learn to change our physical posture, remaining vertical and holding our space; then we ourselves can move in physically on someone who's trying to be invasive. The secret is to move *towards* them, rather than shrinking away which sends the non-verbal message, 'I am available for invasion'.

Our need for space, and for boundaries, varies between times, and between people. There may be a fear of having not too little but too much space. We tend to set up four types of personal space:

Intimate Space is up to six inches away. Into this we allow only lovers, the very closest friends, near relatives. To have it invaded without permission is a real affront; it feels like a threat, an attack, a psychological rape; we are very vulnerable here. It can be funny to watch (although it is very real) how, packed together in queues, in rush-hour buses or trains, we avoid eye contact, we don't see each other; looking into space, we treat each other like objects, because if all these people were subjects, they'd be quite intolerably close. Indeed, if the powers that be have a man marked for execution, they will avoid looking at him, or at any one, and this is a danger sign. Intimate space is an area for exploring; we need to map how we're handling it and what impact very close relations have on us.

Personal Space, six to eighteen inches away, is the distance we naturally take to talk with friends and intimate family; we adopt it at parties, for instance. Strangers who break into it cause a reaction. In third-degree questioning, the interrogator will invade the personal space of the victim with a leg between the knees and a sudden hit. This knocks most people off centre extremely quickly, causing breakdown. It is *people-poisoning*, the overstepping of personal boundaries. So this second level of our personal, family space needs exploring.

Social, impersonal space is from about eighteen inches to four feet away. It's the distance we adopt for interviewing, for business transactions, for 'getting to know you' encounters. This is small-group distance, rather than public address distance, and as we move into a deeper kind of relating, so we come physically closer. This is where any variations in height between people show up. We sit down if we want to be submissive; however, to gain control we stand up. Note how, if there is a desk between, the boss will stand and invite the employee to sit. If there's no desk, the boss will sit down and the employee will be left standing! Either way, the employee is discomfited.

Finally, *public space*, anything over four feet, is the distance adopted for the stage performance. We have to project ourselves across a space like this. Small groups cosy in as they get warmer and the space between members becomes closer.

It's worth noting people's body language, their expression, their stance. We open and close, like flowers – or like man-traps! If we want to be intimate, we fold towards the other. If it's: 'I'll keep my options open here', we fold away; we raise a shoulder, fold our arms, smile. The body often shows a completely different feeling from that being expressed in the conversation; though we smile, our eyes and eyebrows may be giving other signals. Someone used to reading the language will listen to the words merely to fill the gaps in what people's bodies are saying.

In working with people, it can be well to address space and boundaries from the start. I have my own chair, but then try to give the other person a choice. I check out: 'Did you have problems with space and boundaries? What was your role and function in the parental home? And in the present home? Do you have your own space *by right*? What about your own time?' A small bit of God's earth does belong to each one of us, and each one of us needs to know it.

The way we handle all this is affected by whether we had too loose or too tight a hold. While well-bonded children can later define and take their own space, other children, those either under- or over-protected, will have little sense of anchorage. Those held too tightly may fight to win and defend their distance, groping for space and stance, gasping for room. People given too loose a hold may, by placating, try to buy their space. Feeling about to be dropped, they have a very precarious hold on life anyway, are uncertain about the ground of their being, their own identity, life itself. Lacking roots, they may be habitually anxious, watchful, tense, placating: 'Don't leave me! I'm sorry!' Let us consider some people and the space around them:

Figure 14 People and Space

The Bully. This person challenges others' spaces. Small and sad inside, they daren't let you close; it mustn't be found out that they're really not very big.

The Doormat. 'Do come and walk all over me!' is their stance. Then, in astonishment, 'Why is it they all wipe their feet on me?'

Creeping Ivy. Here is a small person clinging, with creeping tendrils, saying, 'But I am so little!' They get round other people's space, demonstrating the power of the weak.

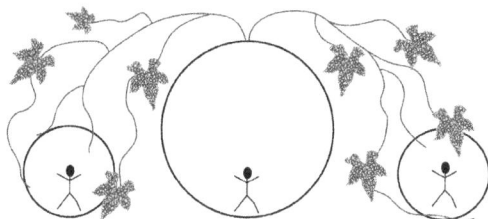

The Sapper. Moaning, 'Just poor li'l ole me here, with my terrible problems,' they feed on the people around, sapping all our energy into a bottomless whirlpool.

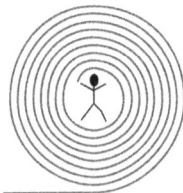

Atlas. 'How is it I always end with everyone's problems on me ?' Dead counsellors have this on their tombstones. They aren't in their own space, so everyone feels free to off-load on them.

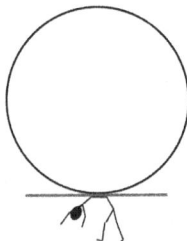

The Sucker cries, 'Let me into your space, I haven't got one of my own!'

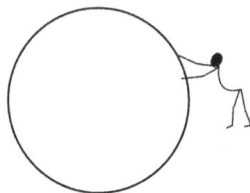

Dreamboat is feeling and intuitive, but ungrounded. Dented, broken eggs, they need to be turned the right way up and mended; and also to be commended for their sensitivity.

Ration-all. Here is the head/heart split, and the belief that all can be done by head. Though the person can often handle the objective world well, the heart is dried up, split, cut off.

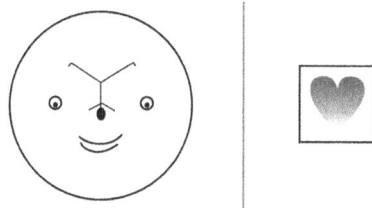

Prickly Pear. A shout is heard from afar : 'Nobody *loves* me! *Nobody* loves me! Nobody loves *me!*' Hard to get near, yet this person is very sensitive and vulnerable, and really has been hurt.

Handling crisis

None of us can altogether avoid crisis, and stress too is by no means all self-induced; *unavoidable* stress is certainly sometimes present, for example during war. Everyone at some point experiences change and loss – bereavement, redundancy, loneliness, illness – though by learning to handle space and boundaries we can manage it better. Good enough parents have children who expect space by right. They expect to be liked – it's only normal! The ground under these people's feet is firm. Their crises are unavoidable, but passing. Taking a natural stance, flexible and open to change, they bounce back. While 'crisis' for all of us spells both 'danger' and 'opportunity', these people see it as opportunity.

However, there are also a vast number of *avoidable* crises, caused by contradictions between bits of ourselves, by an 'either this or that' stance. And avoidable stress occurs whenever there's a tension between who I am inside and how I act outside; when my lifestyle is inappropriate to my nature; when mind and heart pull in different directions; when I try to live by other people's values and expectations and not my own. And this is often the case! 'I can't be me, or people won't still love me.' But I can learn to replace that with, 'It's possible to say what I really feel and yet be loved.' 'If I'm not busy, I'm wasting time' can be replaced with 'I need both to do and to be.' 'Either it's real or it's all imagination', and I learn to say instead, 'There is both an outer and an inner reality.' For, 'Either they stay with me and understand me, or I can't be me', I say, 'If I take full responsibility for myself and express it, then they may stay longer and understand better.' Instead of 'I'm terrified to say it, so I won't', I can say to myself, 'I know what I'd like to say, and yet just now I'm deciding not to say it.'

Here are three major steps to becoming anything like a rounded out person: I am me.

I accept me.

I take responsibility for me.

Like Mind, Emotion and Body, these can be seen as a three-pin plug; all in together, and the light comes on.

We need the ground under our feet; we need the space around us. Imaging can be extremely valuable here, and it's often the adolescent period that needs exploring. Though by puberty our space was beginning to be anchored, yet we hadn't fully escaped the nursery and its stereotypes; indeed, habits set up earlier on may have been underlined and driven in deeper at adolescence. As we've seen, our adult images may take us back via adolescence to childhood, or from childhood, exploring upwards through the stages to the present. Either way, the images can show us how we're caught in old confining habits that need to be released. We need to claim the ground under us *here*, the space around us *now*. The more we're helped to anchor the present around us, the more chance that these stereotypes will drop off.

I ask people about the images they hold of themselves: 'When you're *down*, really down, what's it like, how does it feel? How much space do you take up; what are your boundaries like?' They'll curl up, or come out raging. Again, I ask, 'When you're feeling really "uppish", really good, what's the ground beneath you then? How is the space around you?' If they can be persuaded to act it out, we can both see it. Asking: 'How would you like to appear to others?' will give them a very good idea of what they're trying to put over, which may not bear more than a partial relationship to how they're feeling inside. I find out other people's expectations of them: 'How are you expected to act, to be, to fill your space, to claim your boundaries? How do people try to mould you?' A person's response to this question can tell them a lot.

Afterwards I open all the doors and windows: 'Come on, shake all this stuff off, now! Claim your own ground, your own space. How does that feel? How would it be if you could work outwards from that place? Let's have a real and realistic place to work from, now!' Sometimes, just asking these straight questions without any imaging, perhaps getting them to act out their responses, can be most revealing to them. The feeling of the body helps them to anchor these things extremely well.

There's something very odd about time. It's a strange mystery. If time, big and overwhelming and enormous, can throw us off our centre, then it will come and claim us. But if we can handle space and boundaries then time drops into place, becomes plastic, and we can get it off us, off our centre – we're in control of it. Then it stops so pressuring us. We return to our centre. If people have difficulty coming to their centre, then relaxation and dance, exploring the space around them, their own ground under them, can be very effective. Or they may prefer centring from a sitting position: 'Just feel around you. What's it like ?' If they can't work from the inside outwards, then working from the outside inwards may help. Remember the cushion.[32] One of its values lies in what it can *be*: it can be the child; it can be the person you want to beat up and remove out of your space; it can be the person you long to hold closest to yourself. The cushion is one of the happiest ways of exploring both 'in-space' and 'out-space'.

In terms of in-space, people curl in on themselves in moments of grief, bereavement, loss, anguish, pain, loneliness, isolation – the things that make them feel lost and alone and unwanted. To bring the cushion into their space gives them something to hold on to. All that anguish of theirs, that introverted, in-turned agony, can be passed out of the gut where it's being held and maintained and put over to the cushion. It gives a bit of psychological space; by degrees the cushion *becomes* their pain and leaves them freer to work. I use it in cases of divorce, rejection, redundancy – anything that leaves someone with an empty space that was once filled by a person or an animal, a job or a place. It's very, very valuable.

---

[32] See Page 63ff, Chapter Four.

It's the same for the out-space: to externalise things locked in to the body (the anger that needs to come out, the aggression, the fire, the creativity, the extraverting energies) this cushion out here can be punched and bashed and wrung out. A lot can be done with the cushion in depression, and a lot in aggression. One woman had problems with a man in her life. Holding the cushion, I stood up and invited her to see him 'out here' and give me some of his qualities:

'What do you see?' 'A Walter Mitty figure who changes all the time.' I move in to stand about four feet away from her, in her Social Space: 'How do you feel towards this person when he's standing roughly here, where I'm standing now?' 'A very big question-mark as to how to cope. I'm making an attempt to see him more as an object.' Now I move in to her Personal Space. 'I feel warmer, more compassionate, more sympathetic.' 'We won't explore it any further! But observe your body.' 'An absurd feeling!' She laughs. 'How does your *heart* feel?' 'I think it's thumping hard,' she responds, feeling her wrist. 'You don't have to discover if your heart is thumping hard by holding your pulse! The heart's *here*! You can always put your hand on it – you needn't ask your head to count how your heart's beating!'

It's the quality of the change in distance that makes the difference. Pick the moment – there has to be trust before we ourselves can carry the cushion into someone's intimate space. A tiny thing like a cushion can tell us and, infinitely more importantly, tell the person, what they need to know.

And always we need an *inner sanctuary*. Because she could see a tree, which reminded her of home, Odette Churchill could withstand even being tortured. If we have somewhere to go, we can hold on. Working from our own inner space, we can help the other person all the way through to have theirs. I ask, 'Is there a *place* you feel at peace in?' I keep building that in, suggesting that if they're stressed and hassled they can at least act *as if* they were in that place. Thus they can be helped to build an inner sanctuary of safety.

FIELDS OF ENERGY
Ian Gordon-Brown

Many mystical and esoteric groups have known for multitudes of centuries the importance of the subtle interconnections between energy fields.

These fields of energy are generated by us as individuals, by groups and collectives, and by the planet itself. Increasingly, they are being explored by modern science; some radical breakthroughs must be due in the next few decades. They form a very important aspect of the absolutely fundamental theme of space and boundaries.

Individuals, groups, communities, families, nations, races – different aspects of the Collective – all have their own characteristic qualities of energy. These are reflected in style and in attitude, and are experienced through the feeling tone. Individuals carry an atmosphere around with them. It's a matter of chemistry. The tone colour of some people is frankly too energetic for us; they grate up the spine, while there are others with a different tone towards whom we have a particularly warm and friendly feeling.

Spirit of Place

Places have their own spirit. For instance, New York: certain people find it impossible to be there for more than a couple of days. Their psyche feels shattered by the energy field of the place. Others find it exhilarating, exciting, stimulating; they eat less, sleep less, they go there to be 'charged up'. Cities affect us. A person may be grey and depressed, not because of their parents, nor their job, nor their relationship, but because they're living in the wrong place, the wrong psychic atmosphere. Perhaps they shouldn't be where they are, perhaps they need to move?

Again, in Britain, someone may sense a line across the country, and their depression starts south, or alternatively north, of it. They may have struggled for years, but in the end it came down to the very simple fact that they were living in the wrong place. One woman in the helping professions lived and worked in the South East of England for twenty-five years and absolutely hated it. She felt half dead – until she went somewhere north of Manchester, when suddenly she entered a totally new energy field, and came alive. 'Why on earth do you stay down here, then?' It turned out she had traded one problem for another ('My parents live up there!') but for her there was a fundamental and real difference in the feel of the country. Other people feel that they enter another psychic space when they move past Salisbury and into the West Country; softer, more gentle, quite different. Some love it, some hate it. Within London too the districts have distinct energy-patterns. It's worth asking, is the feel of an area appropriate for us? And the energy may change, making a district less fitting than it once was.

So people's illnesses or psychological problems may arise out of an imbalance in energy. These are very subtly important factors. It's said that certain underlying rocks, the particular mineral we're on (limestone, sand, chalk) may draw our energy down and out of us – as may concrete floors! However, others find a particular mineral, rock, soil, even concrete, is what makes them grow. New York is on very firm granite. What is suitable for one is not necessarily right for the other. Just as the Celts don't always get on with the Saxons, just as there are characteristic differences between Latins and Anglo-Saxons (and characteristic *similarities* between the Americans and the Russians), so we can talk of 'mountain people' and 'plains people', 'deep sea people' who are quite different from those who fuss around the coast in small boats, 'river people' and 'lake people' who are different again.

Certain professions will attract those of a particular temperament or feeling. It's not just the colour of the Old School Tie; what matters is the characteristic tone and attitude, the style. Employers asking, 'What kind of people do we take into our company?' will know very well that though this person may on paper be quite the best for the job, they will never fit. What matters is whether the energy is complementary or supplementary, whether there's going to be a dissonance, and if there is a dissonance, whether it's going to be creative or destructive. A personnel manager may spend more time judging whether someone will be right for the company than anything else. If not, excellent as they may be, they just won't be happy.

Power in organisations

There are tremendous pressures associated with this. On the one hand, in groups based on the ethos and attitude of love, those concerned with caring, the power-struggle is terrific, and it's always unconscious. On the other, in industrial organisations, where the power-struggles are all overt, everybody knows who's on a power-trip; people joke about it, pull the person's leg, it's all open and above board, and it's something else that's unconscious. Jung talked of the polarity not of love and hate so much as of love and power. Where there is power, love can't exist and vice versa.[33] People in the first kind of organisation, those where the power-struggle is unconscious and the love aspect conscious, would flatly deny that there

---

[33] See Adolf Guggenbühl-Craig, 1971.

was a power-struggle at all. Ever more meek and more 'human', the power creeps out all over. It's dreadful! They know they're right, they know they're virtuous and good, and they're devastating.

Though we may work individually, we are also all members of groups. We tune in to the atmospheres of the different networks, and carry different functions and modes within their collective life. It may not be the prominent person at the top who's pulling an organisation together; a heart-centred person with quite a modest job or function may be the one holding the creative matrix of that group. And someone with that kind of responsibility or authority may on some occasions become a focal point for very considerable criticism. At other times, they may draw a smothering love and adoration; in certain types of religious group everybody pours their emotions on to one or two focal people.

We may know someone in such a position. Is there a particular and unusual psychic pressure coming to them, of which they may be quite unconscious? It's the heart that keeps the life-blood flowing, and a lot of people in big organisations have heart trouble. Taking other people's energies aboard without clearing them in a creative way can impair energy, and give a predisposition to such physical dysfunctions.[34] Subtle pressures may be imposed, not by the requirements of job or family, but by other people's expectations and demands. Watch to what extent everybody has their psychic hooks into them. How far are they protected?

Encroachment into our space can have extraordinary psychological effects. People who put themselves in key positions as directors, healers, teachers, priests have to realise that one of the requirements of the job is to receive all the inevitable projections, both for good and ill. They have to be willing and able to bear people's fantastic expectations, and also people's fantastic hostility. They could bear it given the right sort of energy field in the organisation, but is the chemistry synchronous with their own, or is it dissonant in a destructive way? It may be that erosion of someone's space has crept up slowly over the years without their realising it. Those with stress and pre-coronary trouble, though not setting out to be the head of something, may by degrees have been placed in that position. Slow creep-up, slow erosion; it's very, very important.

---

[34] There is a book called 'Body/Mind' by Ken Dytchtwald, very good on the interaction between Psyche and Soma. See also 'Mind as Healer, Mind as Slayer', Pelleier, 1977.

Working with people

Those of us who work individually with other people also have our own energy fields, and we need to take them into account if we're to remain alive long enough to deal with them! There's evidence that the rate of both neurotic and physical breakdown is rather high amongst therapists, psychiatrists, counsellors. That's why it's so valuable for us to check out our own space and boundaries, and we need to consider when we're with someone this collective background of tone-colour, attitude and style, exploring in the initial meeting the way the chemistry goes together. It's hazardous; there are many problems and hidden minefields.

Do we find this person in front of us heavy, oppressive, sapping, and if so, what is the fit between our energy field and theirs? If there are differences, are they likely to be creative? Do we like or dislike the person? And which is the better? Are we beginning to get too close? Or feeling that *they* are getting too close to *us*, that we're invaded or overwhelmed, that we'd like to distance them? Do we find ourselves feeling inadequate, we don't quite know why? Equally, are we bored with them? With some (and not just the 'sappers') we have to fight to keep awake; is just the time of day for resting, or is it something about *us*, our relationship with them?

Because we don't like feeling overtired or inadequate, because we feel we shouldn't be bored with people, because being pressured may not be part of our philosophy, we tuck it away. That's why we need to be constantly aware and sensitive, and to listen to how we are interacting; not pulling ourselves up by the roots all the time, but noticing the patterns that develop. In a very real sense we are inside the other person's psychic space, and they in ours. All this is intimately bound up with *projection*. Perhaps there are hooks in us, and projections are being hung on them. Or are we ourselves doing the projecting? One of the fundamental characteristics of those of us naturally drawn to this work is the need to be defined by other people; their needs give us a spatial outline. We need to be needed. We say 'Yes' too much, and 'No' too little. 'I'm so excited,

---

35   Certain jobs have built-in hazards. For example, where silicosis is a coalminer's hazard, sinusitis is said to be 'a typical analyst's problem'. Blocked sinuses may go with intuition, and in the very nature of analytical or therapeutic work lies the possible opening up of the intuitive function. Flaring sinuses are often spoken of as frozen tears, blocked tear ducts. Could sinusitis in an individual be a refusal to accept flowing emotions? Sometimes the very thought of a flowing activity like yoga makes a person angry: 'No I won't!' they declare, 'my disease is finite, it's limited; the *doctor* has to cure it.' Feeling and mind are split; at some point the flowing side of their nature has been cut off. Frightened of what might come out, what they might do if it were touched, they resist anything that causes them to flow.

so uplifted by my work!' But ask how we *feel*, now, and often we know we're hooked by it. There's all the difference in the world between loving our work and needing it for our very shape, which makes saying No almost impossible.[35] We certainly need somebody else to supervise and monitor us, helping us continue to grow, to extend our space and avoid getting too involved in some of these traps.

So we explore our own space and boundaries; we open up our diaries and sense our own body-language as we look at our case-load. What happens inside us when we read the names each morning? We watch the effect of the person who carries a draining, grey, depressed energy, and clear it out of our own system; otherwise this kind of invasion of our psychic space is likely to be a primary problem. And we need to 'listen' to what nourishment we're providing for different levels of our nature. It's highly valuable. Who's shaping us? How are we shaping up?

To what extent do we both work and live in the same space? This is a difficult and subtle matter. Some people, provided there is enough physical space around them, can do it; there are others for whom it is absolutely essential that they don't. Anyway, is it good for the client? What else goes on in that particular room; what sort of psychic space is it, what atmosphere builds up there? Ideally, it's better to have a separate room, though for many people the ideal is unattainable. It might be possible to use the room for congenial and appropriate types of activity at other times – reading, writing, painting – not mixing up the energy with too much heavy entertaining. If it's a largish room, curtaining part of it off for the work with people, even with no wall between, might well do the trick. It's as well not to sleep in that space; it may be almost better to sleep on the bathroom floor than in the room we work in.

When deeply affective (and effective) work is being done, a positive energy field seems to be constellated in the room itself. On the other hand, when we have had certain people in it, we may need to clear the atmosphere. We can clean the room, psychically and physically, simply by letting the fresh air through, by having certain kinds of incense, music, meditation. Green plants do seem to cleanse, purify, take some of the negatives. Having a water jug in the room can clear it. We can use water to refresh our own system by splashing our faces, holding our hands in running (not static) water; a shower at the end of the day has a positive and energy-giving effect.

One colleague used to run groups in her home. The family would clear the living room, taking their stuff into the bedrooms and the dining room.

A fairly heavy emotional discharge or catharsis went on in those groups, and it took several days for the family to come back and start to use the living room again. Noticing this, they set up a specific system of clearing and subjectively recharging the room afterwards: they burnt incense, played a certain type of music, cleaned and washed things, had plants around the place.

I find it helpful to set the chairs at an angle, so that the person and I don't have to stare at each other. When we focus intensely with someone, there is an energy-loss through the eyes – all those messages coming in and going out. (Whereas if people do things with their eyes closed, as in Yoga, their energy level tends to come up.) It's wise to break the focus; to look to the side of the person, to their ear, not between their eyebrows; to have flowers, or something attractive, as a focal point to which we can both keep deflecting. I use my glasses as a reason for looking down and moving around. Without being irritating to the person, that breaking of eye-contact is critical and very essential. I pretty soon know if I'm not doing it. I find myself *watching* them without *seeing* them; I've leapt across and am inside their space without knowing it. I check myself out: they cross their legs, I do the same; I move my hands, they move their hands; they put their leg down, and my leg has gone down too. I'm hooked! And the eye contact – I'm riveted by them! Equally, if I see them doing the same, I quite consciously arrest it ('Oh, look at that bird out of the window!'), deflecting, where it seems appropriate, breaking the pattern, but without drawing too much attention.

The shapes and proportions of rooms are important too. It's very interesting to see what sort of effect badly-proportioned rooms can have on the psyche over a period of time. A room may be small but, if it's rightly proportioned and well looked after, it doesn't invade or intrude. Watch the colour; if it's not satisfactorily painted and decorated, a room can impose a fairly heavy psychic pressure.

Watch what the other person is wearing. One man said he felt depressed in brown; his most enlivening colour was blue. 'Why then do you go on always wearing brown?' It wasn't as if he couldn't afford to change; he was hooked, 'used to that colour'. Just as some people change their name when they're going through a change of consciousness, others need to take account of their dress. I watch these things, because of the subtle effect colour and tone have on the psychic space. Working from the outside inwards by changing what we're wearing can be sheer magic, giving a tremendous lift.

CHAPTER NINE

The Meaning of Illness
An introduction to
Symptom as Symbol
Barbara Somers

There was a time not all that far away when to be hit by illness
was seen as a visitation from a god, a goddess, a divinity

This is a challenging and gristly theme: 'The Meaning of Illness'. I feel very small in the face of such a theme, thinking of all the millions of men and women through the centuries who, through their souls and their bodies, have wrestled with its problems. And their answers have been only partial. There's an encouraging story about a Little Priest, so small that he couldn't be seen over the lectern. One Sunday morning he began, 'Brethren, my theme today is the Light of the World.' With which a voice at the back piped up, 'Well then, you'd better turn up the wick!'

What is the meaning of illness?

There are as many different answers as there are people. What we share in common is that when illness hits us, personally, we see it as a threat, an affront, an invasion of our individual identity. We have to be pretty balanced not to. 'Why should it happen to *me*? What did I do to deserve this?' In youth, surging with energy, rushing forward into life, we can very happily ignore illness; but in the middle years – if not in ourselves then in our ageing parents or our contemporaries – the moment inevitably comes when someone is laid on their back. Then we are reminded of our own mortality.

Ageing

Growing old itself tends to be viewed as a disease to be averted, denied, dreaded. We deal with it cosmetically; many people fear it.

Programming, in middle age, goes badly wrong:
Inside, the personality,
Richer (with luck), more rewarding,

Feeling a mature twenty-one at last:

But outside, one incredulously sees
The flesh convexing and relaxing;
The skin, like an ageing suitcase,
Recording much exposure and a few knocks;
The pigment perversely leaving the hair
And turning up in blotches on the face.

But the hormones still ebb and flow
With tiresome incongruity.

Wrong again, God.
You should have given us glands with built-in obsolescence,
Or better quality bodywork.[36]

Ageing brings crisis in its wake: loss, failure, redundancy, bereavement, separation, loneliness, rejection, poverty. A lot of these crises come from outside, and if we lived in a sane society, a lot of them would be remedied from outside. But illness, whether or not we pick it up by contagion, always seems to come from inside; an attacker, a disturber of our internal peace, an invader from our own inner space. It's much too close for comfort.

Crisis

For the moment let's look, not at illness, but at what happens when a person is hit by an external crisis: divorce perhaps, or redundancy. The crisis hits us with impact in the present, and the natural response is to regress, go back on ourselves, recoil. We hope it's a recoil in order to advance. But now we find that, together with the present crisis, we've picked up a whole back-memory, a photograph-album of other times when we failed, felt lost, rejected, defeated. And on that back foot we catch the full impact, not just of the present but of the past, and of fear for the future. This is very natural; rather as, when we go back to the parental home, we may regress and feel small in exact ratio to the time we spend there.

If the crisis doesn't knock us totally flat, we come from the place of recoil to the place of gathering. We 'pull ourselves together', we get on the move. 'It's going to be all right!' we tell ourselves. And the time-lag

---

[36] Connie Bensley, 1981.

from recoil to gathering, as well as the time spent in the gathering itself, does give us the chance to move on. Crisis gives the opportunity to do so with a changed view, an understanding that we can't be exactly as we were before. But a lot of us go on unchanged by the experience and, within the following six to eighteen months, we very frequently pick up an illness.

Illness

And what when illness strikes? Again, we're hit in the present, and in the recoil we very often search for help. The mechanistic approach of allo-pathic medicine steps in very boldly and largely here; somebody who already feels fairly regressed and on a back foot may now also be infantilized. *Infans* means 'unable to speak'. 'Me doctor, you patient' too often becomes Me God, you infant. Leave your body to me, don't ask awkward questions, don't discuss your illness – even your dying – with anyone but me or the hospital staff. Some patients are able to accept this – in fact, they want it; thank God it's there for them. But many more find it an affront to their personal identity and integrity. As someone cogently put it: 'So doctors pour drugs of which they know little, to treat diseases of which they know less, into human beings of whom they know nothing.' Knife-happy surgery may follow: 'If in doubt, cut it out – just in case.' One woman who'd lost a womb, one and a half breasts and a lymph gland said, 'I'm not simply a surgical case, I'm a just-in-case.' 'Cured to death' is too often the result.

The best of doctors also rage. Thank God there are many around; truly healing, therapeutic, physician-type doctors... but they are raging too. It's saddening that many of the best of these are leaving their profession, looking for alternatives which take them away from the very vocation and calling which most needs them. If they do stay, they remain stressed and prey to fatigue, disenchantment, drink, drugs, suicide, things of which the statistics too hideously inform us.

The alternative approach

This is why many doctors and patients and healthy people turn to more holistic and imaginative ways of looking at things. The holistic approach is so exciting that I would like to sound a cautionary note: we must be very careful of polarizing or we'll go too far in the other direction. In moving towards alternatives, away from the allopathic, mechanistic approach, there is the chance that we become over-enthusiastic and, as alternative practitioners, try to make our holism too whole, too complete, too healthy. As a psychotherapist, I see a disturbing number of people who, deciding against allopathic approaches, have gone instead towards alternatives. They've had all sorts of treatments and diets. Yet their symptoms are either unchanged, or have moved somewhere else in their body or system. Not only do they still have their original illness, but now they carry an extra burden of inadequacy, shame, failure and guilt. We have to watch lest we simply move the symptom around.

As alternative practitioners, it's dangerously easy to be as thrilled by our patients and clients as proud parents are of their adolescents; we see them growing, becoming more creative, moving on, and we get so glad about it that we start denigrating all the allopathic approaches. Then 'Me God, you infant' becomes 'Me proud parent, you my child'. In Japan or China a craftsman or artist who made something too perfect always put a flaw in it – to make it more real, more human, more usable. If our holism, our wholeness, is too perfect, too complete, it has nowhere to grow to. We need not the complete circle but the broken circle, the little gap still to leap, and something may come of it – even, one day, a spiral.

Chronic illness

What about the stubborn illness, the unshiftable, recalcitrant symptom that we carry around and can't move? Importantly, it may be telling us that we live in an imperfect state of being, an imperfect world, a world in process of becoming. We may even be under the loving eye, or whatever, of a *god* who is also growing and in process of becoming. These questions have been asked from the beginning of time. They're still worth asking.

Men and women loved Jim, a very special kind of guy. Aged fifty-seven, he was a successful lawyer, an ace skier, a good mountaineer and an absolute charmer. He vastly enjoyed all aspects of his life and all the things he did. And he had stomach cancer; when I saw him he'd been told he might have six weeks to live. He'd tried diet, acupuncture, homoeopathy, autogenic training, he'd been given potions, diets, exercises, massage, meditation, he'd put off smoking, drinking and sex. And still he had cancer.

In the course of all this he'd been told that he was 'not a typical cancer case' – he didn't have 'the right psychology'; this must be a stress reaction to his very busy, very much-enjoyed life. And he was told, 'It's that you must be afraid of death.' By now he felt fairly inadequate, and increasingly guilty and frustrated. So he came and talked. We discussed this 'fear of death' he was supposed to have. And he went inwardly to a place of gathering, the place of quietening, of going within, a place where there's the possibility of absorbing and assimilating the impact of life. And there, quietly, with his eyes closed, he came to be a bit more in touch with what he felt this 'fear of death' to be. At first, pictures came up, mediaeval mind-images: Old Father Time, Dante's 'Inferno', corruption, worms, Hieronymous Bosch's nightmare characters. None of it felt right. And so, in that place of gathering, he began to let go his mental assumptions; he went deeper, quieter still and allowed to come to him pictures that had to do with what he *really* feared.

And the first thing he saw was his wife's face; then his children playing in the garden; a dog from his childhood; his stereo-deck; his skis.

He was surprised by the experience. Through discussion, he realised his fear was not of death, it was of *life* – of love and commitment. Death he'd been playing with for quite a long time, taking all sorts of risks. Life, love and commitment were his major fears.

And life gave him time. The provisional six weeks became eleven months, during which he began the process of relating, talking with his wife and his children. Most of all, he began to commit to himself, which led him to commit more to the family, and finally a little more to his illness. At last his wife telephoned me : 'He died with a smile on his face, and his precious paper in his hand.' He'd shown me the 'precious paper' some time before: a translation from an ancient Egyptian papyrus, very old, but for him very new. He was excited about it. This is what he was holding in his hand:

Death is before me today, like the recovery of a sick man,
    like going forth into a garden after sickness.
Death is before me today like the odour of myrrh,
    like sitting under the sail on a windy day.
Death is before me today like the odour of lotus flowers,
    like sitting on the floor of drunkenness.
Death is before me today like the course of the freshet,
    like the return of a man from the war galley to his home
    when he has spent years in captivity.

Did he find the poem, or did the poem find him? Do we have symptoms – or do our curing symptoms have us?

This *gathering*; we come to it when the present has hit us with illness, when we have recoiled, when we have tried many things and still have to address our sickness. At this place of gathering we are held in linear time, unable to go forward or backward, having only the choice of addressing our illness, our dis-ease. And it is here that we most need to pay attention to the language of symptom.

Symptom as symbol

People are marvellously symbol-creating creatures, and have been from the beginning of time. It's there in our art and our poetry, our painting and dance and literature, and in our dreams. And I believe this wonderful symbolic language that a human being can create is here in our symptoms of illness. By listening and attending, here at this gathering-place, we can see how the symptoms had been building up for quite a long time before surfacing into the body. They're an early-warning system signalling a disturbed homeostasis, an imbalance between who the person really is – or who they need to become – and their own chosen lifestyle, or the environment in which they find themselves.

A great deal of the time – not always – it's when the symptom's preliminary signalling system is ignored that disorders and stress-responses become either acute or chronic. And if the symptom is masked – whether allopathically *or* homoeopathically, alternatively – it's liable to displace itself and manifest somewhere else. For example asthma cases are often treated in a way appropriate for allergy, and in some of those cases I've seen the symptom move away and then recreate itself. With one person it came back as claustrophobia, and the exploration of the claustrophobia led back to what originally set up the asthma. (Asthma, as we've seen, tends to have to do with too tight early holding, with invasive hands that don't allow for identity; not loving hands that touch and give a body outline.)

I knew somebody who went to an osteopath and was cured of a frozen shoulder. Now, osteopaths are very brilliant people – don't mistake me, this is in no way putting down the treatment; but I'm suggesting that we perhaps treat too hard, too quickly, before we've listened to the symptom. When the shoulder was better, this person developed a very serious sinus problem. Working with the sinus problem, we reached her tears, which took us round again to the frozen shoulder! And that led right back to the small child. She was standing outside the room where mother was feeding the new baby. Her face was buried in her arm. Already, at three, this child had a pre-history of feeling locked out from mother and father. At school she always felt the outsider. She used to comfort herself by crying and sobbing into her arm. And now her husband had set up another relationship. Once more her face was in her arm. And it became a frozen shoulder – but that was cured. And so it became a sinus problem – and *then* she could attend to the tears.

Addiction

We must listen to the signals or we work against the body and not with it. At this place of gathering I have heard many fascinating dialogues between the person who has the symptom, and the symptom itself. Take addiction to smoking: let's try now to go with what the smoking may represent, with the action of it. Yes, it can be the desire to remain oral, to be at the breast, to replace the dummy; not in all cases, but in quite a lot of them. But it can also, or alternatively, be a way for somebody to desensitise themselves, to play for time, to centre – to steady the flickering world.

Different people do the same thing for different reasons. Some people drink to blot out, regress, be non-responsible, return to the original womb. But many do it because they have a thirst for meaning; in pursuit of a new vision, they're seeking a new spirit – and they do it through the bottom of a glass of spirits. Over-eating may well be to pad out against life, to muffle, to act as a buffer, to hide. But for many people it has more to do with adding weight, substance, dignity. If we treat someone in a way that takes even more dignity from them, we collude with the original problem.

The language of the symptom

My experience is that *some* cancers may come from the demand of the internal psyche to grow. It's sometimes said that cancer is about 'fear of growth, fear of self-expression, bitterness; the strong, powerful feeling of anger in-turned'. Yet, in many people, it may not be that; it may be the demand to expand, to be recognised, to emerge. And perhaps the person inside the body needs to know about that possibility.

During one year I worked with three different people suffering from arthritic feet; all were in line for surgery – three pairs of feet attached to three very interesting human beings. We explored what was for each of them the image for their feet, what the problem was linked with, and what the exploration of the symptom led to.

The first person's image for the action of his feet was: 'I'm groping to find my way'. It was linked with eye problems: 'And I can't see, either'. The exploration led us to look at direction, purpose, motivation, and his need to get on the move.

The second person had as image, 'I don't want to budge; I'm gripping the earth'. The link was with hypertension, a secondary if not primary, symptom: 'I'm too rushed, I can't get a breather.' The exploration was of the need to steady and stay still, reassess, be much more alone.

The image of the person attached to the third pair of feet was: 'Trying to belong somewhere'. It was linked with problems of the inner ear and with vertigo; that too was about trying to belong, after early fostering. The feet were now beginning to act out the need. The exploration had to do with her relationships, her housing situation and the deep need for connecting.

Three pairs of arthritic feet, three totally different people; all the feet in some way in touch with their own solution. I also know three people with heart problems, likely to go for treatment, if not for surgery.

For the first, the image the heart threw up was 'a soggy sponge'. This was linked with 'taking in too much', with greed and eliminatory problems. The exploration had to do with the tendency in every relationship to keep on taking in like a soggy sponge, and then – cut!

The second had similar symptoms, but the image was of 'Parmesan cheese, hard as marble, won't give'. It was linked by the patient with his own personal boundaries and space. And the exploration had to be of what he called his 'bloody-mindedness'.

Number Three saw the heart as 'a leaky bucket'. The link: 'I can't say No – I'm always placating.' Here too the exploration was of space and boundaries, and the *right* to say No instead of being a leaky bucket.

Three hearts, three individuals, three very different solutions, and they might all have had the same type of surgery or treatment. I find three a good, shapely number, so here are three clinical depressions, all of which were going to need drug treatment.

For the first, the image is of 'coming over the abyss of hell'. This woman linked it with 'boredom; wanting as a child to be an actress; needing colour'. Nobody would have guessed it from the look of her – as grey and grim as it's possible to be, and a dark wash over that – but the exploration here was the expression of her colour-range, her emotional palette. Depression was masking the very vital emotional colours that she needed to express. She said she'd rather go into depression: 'At least hanging over the abyss of hell makes me feel alive.' There was something dramatic in that; not just being bored out of her mind.

The next gave as image for her 'clinical' depression 'a blue-grey mohair shawl'. It was linked with warmth, the need to be held. 'I don't want to let it go.' She knew this was not the moment; she was not yet ready to get rid of the depression. She had to go into it, stay with the nature of it; somehow it was giving her the chance to explore the depths. Like a seed in the ground, she could allow that she wasn't yet quite ready to touch the surface. She needed a little more time to stay with it, work with it. Later, looking at it more, she came to see ways of dealing with it other than depression.

The third person's image was of 'being rocked in a new moon under all the stars in the sky.' It was the dreaming child, the story-telling child who, ashamed of being different in a highly intellectual family, had since university been in all the 'wrong' jobs. 'Rocked in the new moon under all the stars in the sky'! And this was 'depression'?

Might not individuals who can create such striking, rich, varied symptoms and imaging also have a deep sense of their own feeling requirements? The internal knower, the internal healer – not in everyone, but in many more than we think – knows more about the person's life than anyone else can. Many people have never been asked the questions, but at this place of gathering, given the right quality of evocation, people will come out with suggestions over and over – for themselves, to themselves – as to what they need and how they might set about it.

Listening

People are coming from all directions with this fantastically alive, rich material to be worked with. We need practitioners multi-skilled and flexible enough to be able to help them. We need to put the symbol-creating, richly diverse patient back into the centre again. Individuals often know more than they themselves can recognise about their own processes of sicknesses and health. Never know first and never know better is Jung's principle for dreamwork, and it applies for our first – and for every – meeting with another person. We have to remind ourselves that we need to work with the power of love, and be cautious about the love of power. It's so easy to drift, forget, and set up a new polarisation exactly like the old but with different terminology. To put patients back in the centre, acknowledging the artistic nature of what their symptoms may be bringing, is to help them return to self-authority and self-respect, help them back into life. It's not only listening, but *hearing*. We practitioners should then, but only then, apply our multi-disciplinary skills – in response to what they need, not to what we assume.

The place of gathering

Our gods have become diseases. Was Jung right in this ? If so, perhaps we need to dialogue with the gods and the goddesses – with the divinity. And that would take us to the remembrance of a time not all that far away when to be hit by illness was seen as a visitation from a god or goddess. Then, the place of gathering was seen as the place where one taught and listened, parleyed and dialogued with that divinity, so bringing in a different dimension. We try to handle things in linear time; but maybe, for the visitation of the god, we need also to work on the vertical dimension, allowing the opportunity, even in our lives, for eternity to intersect time. Then we may begin to see illness as the place of gathering, place of healing – an internal Epidaurus [37] for ourselves.

The illusion of the one-time Noble Savage in a state of total health is perennial, though it seems particularly marked in this century. 'If we ate the right diet, just as our ancestors did, we'd all be healthy.' I'm sure there's a great truth in that, but it can't be the whole answer. Each generation, as far back as one can read, believed the one before it had better ways of dealing with health and illness. Yet disease and deformity have been found in the remains of bodies from earth-burials and ancient tomb-burials. The plagues of the Middle Ages became the consumption of the last century, and have become this century's cancer and heart trouble. Perhaps we should attend and listen more, treating illness less as the arch-enemy, the arch-betrayer. While not wanting to hang on to it, at least we can explore its implications in our lives before we treat it out of ourselves and others.

It has been said that it is possible to look upon every illness as a

---

[37] That love is the greatest therapy was recognised in Epidaurus, a sanctuary for people in trouble. There, sleep was induced and the healing of the soul led to the healing of the body. Dreamers were apparently put into a small, deep place over running water and there left to dream. Then when they awakened from this incubation, this lonely vigil, the priest-healer was there waiting for them, listening to them, and the speaking of the dream is what healed them. The *Therapeutes* gave them time to go into their inner landscape and talk with the figures they met there; so they came out to greater wholeness, seeking it in the world.

measure of protection against a worse fate – such as an inappropriate life? Carl Jung said that when we submit to our fate we are more likely to call it the will of God; if we put up a hopeless and exhausting fight it seems more like Devil's work. The seminal work of James Hillman reminds us that we have always had imperfect gods, sages and heroes: Chiron, wounded, unhealing, yet wise; Aesculapius, god and patron of healers, so successful at raising the dead that Zeus struck him dead; Hephaestus, divine smith and artisan, skew-footed and broken-legged, yet supreme craftsman of Olympus; Achilles, Trojan hero, strong in war but vulnerable; Homer, poet and story-teller; Teiresias, blind yet insightful, the powerful blind seer, blinded person (and eye problems, often backed up by our dreams, may have to do with a change of vision; just as the initiates were blindfolded before they took the challenge of passing over a threshold of new consciousness). And Prometheus, fire-bringer, with his perennial liver problem!

I would add here the Goddess: raped, traumatised, having to forgive or take revenge, carrying the dark face of Olympus; dark-faced Hecate; Sophia, so hated, so feared; the dark face of the moon; witchcraft and evil things. Yet originally it was the goddess who taught mankind how to find herbs and heal with them.

The wise woman

My favourite character from fairy-tale and life, from the villages and the slums, is that unassuming elderly woman who mysteriously appears at just the right moment, both to midwife the babies and to lay out the dead. She is earthly-wise, and bread-making, and healing. Not quite universal aunt, she is universal presence, turned to when people have nowhere else to go. This wise woman would say, 'Dig a hole in the earth; tell it your problems.' She's not fussed, but where she walks things start to happen and people begin strangely to grow. She reminds us of touch and caring and nurturing; of the seasons and the way of the heart; of the times to take up and the times to let go, the times to be born and the times to die, the times to give and the times to receive. She is re-membering us.

In the fairy stories, and in reality, certainly in dreams, she often comes out as a rheumaticky old crone, but also she may be very round, almost circular, distinctly overweight. What would happen to her now, given the usual treatment for rheumatics, or the current attitude to that sort of roundness?

The journey

Listening to people dialogue with their symptoms, I am struck by the sense of a journey: that we come from somewhere and we go to somewhere, and illness is but part of the process. Light and shadow belong together, and pain and joy. Do illness and health – perhaps – belong together also? Privileged as I've been to sit in on the telling of many lives, I'd say that the crisis – perhaps the serious illness – that hits in the present has its value; it blows our assumptions and our expectations, showing how very ill-equipped we usually are for life's experience, and also how appropriately – or inappropriately – we are living. The place of recoil lets us protest and rage, try to placate, buy our way out of the situation, avert it, seek help from others, anywhere, everywhere, to make it not happen to us. We seek cures from our present and we fear for our future. This is not necessarily regressing; it may be a very necessary first step towards becoming child-like instead of childish, being vulnerable and open, not knowing the answer to everything nor neatly putting life into boxes.

The place of gathering is unquestionably the place to *remember* ourselves; to re-member, to gather in those disparate parts of ourselves that have been scattered everywhere. Every moment of insight, every 'Aha!', every sudden realisation which seems to be new, feels like the remembering of something old, something we'd only just forgotten. So lest we forget who we truly are, or live without the experience of being alive, I believe we should attend to this gathering-place where linear time intersects – or is intersected by – the timeless. If we are made in the image of gods who are the true background to human life, then our sickness is divine in origin. It's not merely sent by the gods, but is the foreground and background we all conform to. As James Hillman said, we can only do in time what the gods do in archetypal eternity. If this is the place where the god appears, where one speaks with the god, then this is also the point at which the god withdraws. And the one who has come through that process is allowed to move on from the gathering place, perhaps more fully into life, perhaps more fully into death; and it's to be hoped that we see these as one and the same reality, doing gladly that which we must.

Our symptoms and illnesses have been seen for a very long time as our sharing of the pain of the suffering God hanging, loveless, on a cross of grief and despair. But are they really that? Do we necessarily have to follow that, in the imitation of the dead god? Or are we, in our sickness and our health, participating in some profound mystery, the very blood and breath of our bodies being transformed into living spirit and fire? In health and in illness, are we taking part, through life, death and rebirth, in the celebration of a divinity already active in the human body, the human life? In our tension and struggle with our personal illness and disease, are we taking part in a major redemptive process? Are we helping, as the alchemists tried to do, to release the living gold that's already in the *prima materia* – to release the divinity which is already within matter? Are we, through the process of our struggle and our tension, helping that collective and vast process of raising earth to heaven, and bringing heaven down to earth? Is it that the uncompleted wholeness – staying with the gap to be left in the circle, with everywhere to go – is a new earth in the making? I very profoundly believe that this is exactly so.

As we look at psyche and soma we realise that the 'psychosomatic' lies in the interaction of mind and body, spirit and matter. The psyche speaks in symbols, and the art of Transpersonal counselling is to help the other and ourselves listen to the *symptoms* and hear what the *symbols* are saying. By degrees we learn the language, and can understand what is being said. Jung made a very important comment when he said that in attempting to understand symbols we come up against the wholeness of the symbol-producing individual, as well as the symbol itself. In studying the client's cultural background we learn a lot. I have made it a rule to consider every person as completely new to me. Like Jung, I don't even know the ABC about them. Dealing with the surface, routine responses may be fine, but given the vital problems, life itself takes over, and even the most brilliant theories are seen to be ineffectual words.

So here is a symbol-producing individual. Either explicitly or implicitly, I believe that the ego, the personality, the everyday self in the outside world may be a symptom of the Self, and the very Self is probably a symbol of something greater still. I'm positing the microcosm as symbol of the macrocosm. We listen and attend, letting the symbols and images of the symbol-making person speak, trying increasingly to *hear* what is being said; and there's quite a difference between listening, and actually being able to hear.

The Inner and the Outer meet at the Interface, and a vital pattern is created. We are consciously exploring their interaction, there where the total nature of the psyche, Inner and Outer, is seeking to rebalance under the impulse of the Self. This rebalancing of Psyche and Soma shows itself physically in a person's expression, their musculature; the way somebody stands is also their psychological stance, a very exact demonstration of their inward posture. Their physical actions are reactions to some inner impulse. Physical and psychological functions tend to run very much in parallel; by exploring one you are inevitably taken to the other.

The body

Jung said that no deep experience in life, no breakthrough in consciousness, no enlightenment is complete except that the body is involved in it. The body is the carrier, the grounding, the outward act of the internal Self. If any 'enlightenment' leaves the body behind, then it's only a partial enlightenment. 'I am an enlightened master!' 'And what have you done with it?' asks the Zen Master.

Body, mind and emotions make a trilogy. In their interaction the three normally keep themselves in fair nick, but we tend to intervene, cutting one off, neglecting another. If any aspect gets blocked within that normal, healthy homeostasis, then the system may begin to break down. Hence the need to have a fourth position, from which we can listen to what is being said by any one of these aspects. A great deal of pre-signalling is given before actual illness occurs; we need to check ourselves, to listen to symptoms as a symbolic language, as messages advising us to make adjustments and adaptations. Then we can help to bring back the homeostasis of that circuit, adjusting lifestyle and attitudes *before* illness strikes, concentrating on preventive rather than remedial medicine. The more we study the symptoms, the more we see how explicit is the language; the symptom is frequently an absolutely clear statement of what and where the problem is.

Early signs may come in pre-signalling, pre-warning dreams. The garden overrunning the house is a typical dream theme; the invading jungle; the house crumbling; spinning and having the thread drop out of the shuttle; the fabric tearing. These things may not mean a physical ailment, but might well do. The linking of the dream with the psychosomatic factors makes a most beautiful, awesome and wonderful picture.

I don't believe *everything* is psychosomatic. That way lies madness. In the middle of the twentieth century, to say 'it is psychosomatic' was to suggest 'therefore it's only imaginary, therefore it doesn't have to be heard. Let it then be *dosed*.' Now, there's almost a swing in the opposite direction; many of us fall into the error of thinking that absolutely everything is psychosomatic. People are made to feel that their broken arm – falling downstairs, being hit by a tree, struck by lightning – was a psychosomatic factor. In addition to the physical problem, the client ends screwed up with the guilt that each week they're paying somebody to load on to them! Very frequently they finish up worse than when they started.

Accidents do happen. If I don't keep my eyes open then I'm going to get run over. Right, I may have a psychosomatic reason for not keeping my eyes open in that moment. But, again, I may not. If someone beside me is hit and falls sideways on to me, and I lose my balance and break my leg, that is not psychosomatic, that is my interaction, my risk, as part of the collective. There are genetically-based and hereditary patterns, inter-uterine accidents, predispositions within the individual. Collective and family tendencies have to be borne in mind, raising as they do the question, 'Why did the Self choose those particular parents to be born to, that society, that time, that particular damage?' Here are mysteries greater than we can answer for.

Back to Jung. We can presume nothing; each person is a fresh experience. First we listen to the *person's* individual language and take their associations, not overlaying our own. Later it can be valuable to lay our experience in beside them, offering it in parallel to amplify and accompany their pain, or their joy. But, particularly with the interflow of psyche and soma, we do that only at the end. There is nothing more individual than the individual's own experience.

Here are a couple of examples. As I sat with one man, having invited a string of associations to some familiar, shared words, I was thinking about the word 'love', making connections in my own head. For me, love has to do with the heart, the abdomen, the Feminine Principle, the left-hand side. And what's 'love' for him? 'Desire!' he says. 'Where do you feel that?' Straight down in his genitals. 'Food?' Straight to his stomach. 'Urge?' 'What sort of urge?' 'An urge to express – where is that?' 'Bowels, abdomen, throat – and library, and ideas,' and his hand went to his head. If I'd concentrated on bringing the focus to the heart (where *I* would have put it) I could have blocked off every one of those areas. Only with the word 'joy' did he point to his heart, saying that, for him, it was less important than the rest.

So all my assumptions go to cock! They need that sort of widening by the image-making process. Checking back on the history, he spoke of a whole series of symptoms – genitalia, stomach, bowel, throat, heart, head

– building up in a pattern. The life-history of the person's ailments is almost the history of his inner development, right up to the moment of crisis which is a breakthrough.

Again, I personally associate the word 'loss' with eliminatory problems, lack of blood-clotting, loss of heart, loss of courage, the recognition that 'courage' and 'heart', *cœur*, come from the same base. I sense it has a lot to do with the navel, that deep-down instinctual area for loss and abandonment. But I asked my client what loss meant to *her*. 'Freedom,' she said, 'flying, release, letting go, sunshine, play, flying a kite!' Who would ever guess that those were associations with 'loss'? It's the same with all the words we share ('rejection, bereavement, grief, redundancy, pain, acceptance, home'); remember that the sub-tones, the *nuances*, the half-shades are theirs, not ours. All these words are containers, and the associations we make to them are out of our own personal experience. This is why we have to listen, presume nothing, let the symptoms speak their symbols. We have no idea of their music until we begin to listen.

It's no joyride to work with something psychosomatic. The body is a great symbol-carrier; for years it will hold experience so painful it was left out of memory, in order to make it possible for the person to go on. But the body has gone on carrying it and carrying it, and it shows, not only in particular organs but in posture and stance, in the muscle tone, in the expressions on our faces. As the body slowly lets go its tight hold, its responsibility, so the symptom may well open up; people often feel worse physically during the process of counselling than when they started. 'What on earth am I paying you *for*? To feel like *this*?' Early on I say, 'Let's work away from the symptom itself, because that will probably be among the last things to go.' It may not be, of course – people are unique and different – but generally they'll remember that and find it helpful.

So we listen to the body expressing itself through bodily symptoms, psychosomatic factors, posture, stance, expression. Symptom can also be seen as symbol in psychological dysfunction, the clinical states of hysteria, depression, schizophrenia. From a Transpersonal perspective, there is a symbolic language directly related to the person who has created these symbols, expressing them as they emerge through their body, or their words, or their attitude to life. Learning the language, we can map more accurately both ourselves and our clients.

CHAPTER TEN

Polarities and the
Transcendent Function
Barbara Somers

What on the lower level had led to wild conflicts and
panicky emotional outbursts, seen from the mountain top
seems to be a mere storm in the valley

It was twenty or more years ago that I first read Jung on the Transcendent Function. Since then I've seen it at work. Over the decades I've evoked it intuitively, on hunch, often in sheer desperation. It's always remarkable when it appears. What is it about?

Paradox

Everybody has within themselves the paradoxes of their own nature. Over and over we find ourselves caught in some kind of tension of opposites. There is a pull between spirit and flesh, order and chaos, masculine and feminine, head and heart, doing and being. If one end of this opposite pair feels negative and the other positive (which is how consciousness appears when we're dealing with such a polarity), it's extremely difficult to handle. One of my own images for it is that marvellous figure of Hercules struggling with the snakes, being pulled in two directions, trying with all his muscular tension to get the balance. There comes a point at which the opposites are almost equidistant; try as we will we're dragged off, failing to hold a point in the middle.

The difficulty is that a lot of us try to hold a pair of opposites at its own level, the horizontal level. Suppose that in a relationship we feel both acceptance and resentment. We both love *and* hate the other person. There will be times when the pull towards acceptance is very strong; days, weeks, even years in which it is possible to hold the ground and move towards the area of love. But then suddenly we get caught into the opposite pull. The movement is towards resentment, and the more we try to be accepting and loving, pushing our irritation into the unconscious, the more likely is the resentment to burst out. What started as a 'horizontal' polarity becomes 'vertical', with love and acceptance trying desperately hard to stay uppermost. Resentment goes down, picking up lots of energy from the unconscious, and comes out behind the scenes in all directions. While we're still doing our best to feel loving and accepting, we hear our own voices speaking from our shoved-down anger. A battle then begins.

On the other hand, it may be the resentment that we're conscious of. We may be acting it out all the time. Then, down go love and acceptance into the unconscious, where they in turn pick up energy. And that bothers us too: we can't hate, dislike, loathe, resent this person constructively and creatively and energetically if we also love and accept them! So we're in trouble again. Either way, given a pull and an equal counter-pull it's well nigh impossible to stay at the centre; there has to be some other way of handling it.

Projection

The most normal, human, earthy, natural way – possibly the most healthy way, for a period at least – is to project it on to the outside world. 'It's my partner who makes me feel like this!' As one pole struggles into consciousness, the other has gone down below, and it's much easier to project it out on to 'them', get rid of it, off-load it, than to accept it back into ourselves.

But, in the nature of life, sooner or later we have to withdraw our projections. As we are helped (or forced by our own experience) to accept responsibility, the energy naturally tends to go into the unconscious, from which it comes up in dreams, and possibly in psychosomatic illness. Better begin to take the projections back. But it can be very painful; very often we find ourselves in a worse state than before. 'I was quite all right till I began on all this!' And we were, because we were hanging our own rubbishy old clothes on other people's coat-hangers.

And now there really is a deadlock. If we are to be in any degree conscious, we'll be faced with the polarities within our own nature. And the more conscious they are, the more difficult to handle. The pulling opposites are equidistant, and the person in the middle does not know what to do. The ego, the everyday self, simply can't manage. The will that once held up one of the ends is withdrawn; it can no longer hold. We lose libido, our energy is drawn *down*, perhaps even taking the form of a depression or a psychosomatic illness. It is drawn back, as Jung says, to its source, going down into the unconscious, activating it, taking another form.[38]

Continuously throughout history the battle between spirit and flesh has been waged, and it's still being fought out in each of us. Every one of our positives has its counterface; for every light its shadow, for every shadow its brightness. It's in the nature of human experience that we all wrestle with these polarities. There are many examples of this struggle between an equidistant pair of opposites, two apparently equally-matched powers: Osiris, dismembered by his brother Set, was put in a lead coffin, enduring the period of scattering and the descent to the deepest before the gathering, and his raising as a god. Here we have Jesus in conflict with Satan in the desert, caught in the struggle between the powers of this world and the powers of the next, and his crucifixion between the intolerable tension of spirit and matter. Then came the descent into hell, his giving up and submission of the will, and out of that struggle the Christ emerged in the resurrection. Here is Luther still fighting it out with the Devils; St. Anthony struggling in the desert; Faust and Mephistopheles in the tension between heaven and earth. The Western church has simply split the two apart. Again, the young Buddha, struggling with Maya – illusion – following the Noble Middle Path, exploring life and death, to arise as the Enlightened One, the Buddha.

The transcendent function.

How is it done? Out of the unconscious there now emerges *another factor*, which holds within itself the energy originally contained within the two polarities.[39] This is the Transforming Symbol, the Transcendent Function, which includes the pair of opposites and takes them to a higher level. The resolution lies in our hope that it can be resolved. Out of Jesus's descent into Hell after three days there emerged a new factor, the Christ – and that resurrected Christ has been resonant for two thousand years. The transcendent function lies at the heart of Alchemy. Jung pointed out that it unites the pairs of psychic opposites in a synthesis which

---

38 When the opposites are exactly equal, and the ego absolutely involved in both, there is a suspension of the will. When every motive is balanced by an equally strong countermotive, the will can no longer operate. Life cannot tolerate a standstill, so there follows a damming up of vital energy.
    See C.G. Jung, 1921, Para.824.

39 Jung goes on to say that this would lead to an insufferable state, unless out of the tension of opposites could come a new, uniting function to transcend them. Since the will has been completely divided, no progress can have been made; so the vital energy streams backwards towards its source. So the opposites give rise to something new, which has arisen out of both the thesis and the antithesis. Compensating each of them, it becomes a middle ground for the uniting of the opposites.
    Ibid., Para.824-5.

transcends them both. This is very close to the definition of the Transpersonal as that which includes the personal but also transcends it. The
Transpersonal is very much concerned with this transformative symbol,
this Transcendent Function with its synthesis of opposites.

But there's a tendency in Transpersonal and spiritual work to try and
push people too quickly towards the synthesis of a polarity, before
they've explored the nature of the polarity itself. That cannot be done,
because of the pull of the energy down into the unconscious. The
polarities can't be dealt with by consciousness; that's why the libido
withdrew into the unconscious in the first place, there to gather energy
and to bring out a new transcendent symbol. The *mind* can't do it. We
can't *decide* to let the energy withdraw, we can't direct it down into the
unconscious and assume a symbol will arise, nice though that would be.
It's an entirely spontaneous happening. Often it comes through dreams,
whose images and motifs help ease out the intolerable tension and bring
in some third point between the pair of opposites. Speaking of the degree
of consciousness and individuation which we can begin to reach – at least
a little – Jung observes that a problem which at a lower level had led to
wild conflicts and panicky emotional outbursts, seems from the mountain
top to be a mere storm in the valley. The storm's real, but instead of being
in it we're above it.[40]

When this Transcendent Function, this transforming symbol, appears,
the balance between the ego and the unconscious is restored. And of
course as soon as it's restored a new imbalance will begin! Then we'll
have to go through the same thing all over again at a higher turn of the
spiral, until another balance is reached. However, many of us *haven't* had
the transformative symbol which would carry us up the mountain track.
We have to climb it ourselves by steps and stages, however much we feel
dragged down by the conflict of the polarity. But as we ascend above the
valley we can work with it more and more consciously, helping ourselves
prepare the ground. We may keep a notebook, a dream book, explore our
dreams on tape. We must allow *time* for the cooking process to occur.
Then, even if the transformative symbol hasn't yet appeared, we hope it
will come and take us up the mountain. Here is the story of one of my
own polarities.

One of the biggest conflicts in my own life came through my inability
to say No, my urge always to be there, to be around when anybody

---

[40] C.G. Jung, 1929, Para. 17.

needed me. At the other end was the inevitable voice of irresponsibility: 'Why the hell should *I* have to do it? What about *me*?' When somebody is always available, always trying to be able and active and aware and conscious and all the rest of it, there must be that polarity. Obsessed with this end of it, I would actively and fervently have denied my lazy, lie-about, easy-going side, but it was certainly there. And I knew roughly that it came out of another triangle.

It started in childhood. Quick and agile, I was very lively, interested, usually fairly sunny, but with the most awful temper. I'd go white with rage and hurl myself physically at whoever or whatever, knowing no bounds. It wasn't courage or anything like that; I simply leapt at the person and attacked them. My parents' marriage was not a happy one; it was a marriage of fire and water. I used to come out against my father, at three and a half kicking him in the shins, seeing even then that the best way to deal with a bully was not to fight him on his own ground but to stand up to him. However, my mother's voice was always behind me: 'Don't you do that to him or he'll hit *me*!' Always that voice!

I adapted. I learned to handle my own temper so well that in the end it lost its energy; it went into the unconscious and was not allowed out at all. I tried to be calm, equable, peacemaking, always checking the side effects of any action. Only in adulthood did I realise the degree to which a Transcendent Function had quite spontaneously emerged for me: I was always lined up against a big 'them' of some kind, in favour of somebody out there who was, I thought, less than able to handle it. First in journalism, then in the Society of Authors, I was fighting *for* the freelance *against* the big 'them' of the Unions. (I got on very well with 'them', too, and enjoyed it enormously.) I did the same thing in relationships, becoming more conscious of it as I went along. I saw how, if there wasn't another person out there, I'd invite somebody in so that I could look after them against the rest.

I had to swing the map around. If I put *me* down at the base, I would have to find out what father stood for. And he stood for inner authority and vocation, the ability to lay claim to space and boundaries and hold them, to say some creative No's. Without that, I wouldn't be allowed to say any positive Yes's. I saw that instead of looking after my mother, I had to see to my own feminine needs. And I had to try to do it consciously.

Here is another example, this time from a man terribly caught in a polarity. He came from an upright Scottish, very rigid, Puritan-ethic background. Over the fifteen years of their marriage, his wife had been 'the feeling one'. While it was accepted that he did all the thinking, looking after the structure and the mapping, she did all the flowing. But now his own feeling side was emerging. As it spontaneously arose, their roles and functions were badly thrown and the nature of the relationship changed. He started to speak in a slow, blurred, way, with a time-lag. 'Don't be silly,' she would respond in effect: 'That's my area. You don't know what you're talking about!' In other words, 'Keep off my grass!' A familiar story, as one of a pair begins to change and the roles and structure are blown. This was his dream:

'I am looking after the gate of a palace when a gipsy girl comes and asks if she can give me healing. At first I ask for whom she is collecting money and tell her to go away. I go into a field where figures like the Mummers are enacting a symbolic dance in the shape of a figure-of-eight.'

He drew this as the shape of infinity, sideways rather than the upright figure-of-eight.

'A fight breaks out between a strong man and a weak one who has apparently insulted him. We all watch transfixed. The strong one hits the weak with a club which turns out to be a roll of hollow paper. The fight becomes symbolic, like a dance. The strong man is changed by the weak and vice versa. I rejoin the dance, which turns into a sexual orgy. I don't stay, but go off in search of the gipsy girl. She's transformed into a beautiful woman whom I know quite well. We discuss how this can be, and she reminds me that I saw her at Belsen at the end of the war. She was the only one in her family to survive the gas chambers. I feel that we are to be united and that the union is shortly to be consummated.'

Here is the Transcendent Function coming in. This was one of those dreams that you simply wait on. You couldn't force this dream. We looked at the various motifs. The young anima-figure of the gipsy girl, representing the feeling side, close to nature, an instinctual, intuitive motif, was an interesting figure to emerge for him at that particular moment. At first he asked her, 'Who are you collecting money for?' (very much his tight-sporraned approach to money and energy and libido) and told her to go away. But then the dream brought in the figure-of-eight and the ritual quality of the dance, the traditional, distinct steps, and the dancers like Mummers. Next, the fight broke out, and the strong man hit the weak with a roll of hollow paper. There was an exchange of energy via this roll of paper: the strong man became changed by the weak, and vice versa. I asked him for his various associations to that, and he felt that it had a good deal to do with his sexuality; his penis was really a roll of hollow paper. In terms of what his wife said about him it unquestionably was! We recognised that the roll of paper and the exchange of energy pointed to a change of function.

Next, the girl was transformed into a beautiful woman whom he'd seen at Belsen at the end of the war, the only one in her family to survive the gas chamber. 'What *did* happen to you at the end of the war?' I asked. He hadn't been to Belsen, he'd been at university. But that was the time when, with a complete change of mode, he'd switched subjects – from the Social Sciences, which had been his original choice, to Law. He'd gone against his own feeling nature at that point (it was the feeling side of him, the side tending towards the Social Services, that was emerging now). Just at the end of the war he had married a 'feeling' wife in order, he said, to flesh out the polarity within his own nature. But now he was unable any longer to hold apart head and heart in himself, or to project it out on to his wife or his daughters. And this tension within him was facing him with the reality of his own predicament. He had all sorts of symptoms: the typical stiff neck and rigid shoulders that follow when head and heart are split.

He didn't know what his lovely dream meant, but he felt a lot better after it. The dream had carried the Transcendent Function. It came up out of the unconscious with a dance, a flow, a figure-of-eight which could unite at the symbolic level the pull of the polarities. The roll of paper exchanged the energies, and head and heart came closer together. He had previously been driven inwards, holding all the tension down in his body and trying to project it out on to his marriage. Now, a great release of energy came. The body, as Jung said, has to be in the experience too. Going down, we draw up the instinctual side. The Transcendent Function includes everything, the lot. It goes down and it goes up; the horizontal struggle is put at peace, brought together, making the perfect, equal-armed cross, and Earth is taken up into heaven.

The gipsy figure began more and more to play a part in his life. He was made to look at the difference between a 'weak man' and a 'strong man'. In the view of his Scottish background and his paternalistic clan, older-style 'weak man' meant a feeling, heart-based man. And his wife was of course expressing her view of what 'strong man' should be. That one dream stated the situation, led him, gave him his Transcendent Function, linked the two ends of the polarity and began the healing of the split.

Inner alchemy

It's only while working with somebody, trusting the process, allowing the time required for the incubation process to take place, for the cooking in the *alembic* – the alchemical flask – to occur, that we begin to see the Transcendent Function coming up. It's then that the conflict comes to seem like that storm in the valley seen from the mountain-top. People who have been in tension, taken down into their own darkness, made to face the reality of their own responsibility, have over and over again had the transforming Transcendent Function emerge out of the darkness to lead them to a different place. This is the secret of Alchemy.[41] It's a mysterious process, and it happens endlessly, drawing to our attention that there is some great Alchemist at work and that all life is alchemy.

Another man, in his late fifties, had been in the Royal Navy for the early part of his working life, joining at the age of fourteen. In due course he married, as we shall see, though they had no children. On retirement he took a small technical, clerical job in a company where he looked after all the engineering drawings for the group. The story can't be understood without reference to his mother and his wife. He was the youngest child by quite a long way. His father was physically present but psychologically absent. His dominant mother hated men. The son's eldest sister would dress him up and play dolls with him. He was the doll. He fought his way out to get into the Navy, where by the age of about twenty he'd become one of the youngest Chief Petty Officers, serving in the war and afterwards. After his very emotionally-deprived childhood he now linked up with a young WREN. Of all those available, he'd found a girl whose parents had separated when she was three; the mother had gone off and she had been fostered out to an unbelievable number of foster homes – a most appalling story. She was looking longingly for father, and felt she'd found him in her fiancé.

He had a very close friend who had been to him almost like an objective Transcendent Function. When this friend died, the tension was no longer held and he fell into a neurosis. The breakdown followed a dream: he and his wife were on a ship in a storm and he let his wife slip over the side while he saved himself. This dream disturbed and distressed

---

41   Jung said clearly that the transcendent function *is* the secret of alchemy. In its light the noble and the base parts of our personalities, both conscious and unconscious, are blended and fused, as are the most with the least differentiated of the four functions. Thus the personality is transformed.   C.G. Jung, 1928, Para. 360.

him greatly, but it was a movement towards the Self, towards his own identity, which he was no longer projecting on to her.

Meanwhile, his wife was seeing 'good father' in him, letting him run the roost, saying how terrible it would be if he ever left her and at the same time keeping him under very strong control. She had had a breakdown herself nine years previously and he'd 'been very good' in looking after her. Part of his dilemma was that he simply couldn't speak out his feelings in case he sent her back into that state. She was terrified of returning to hospital. He was caught helplessly in the double bind of it. 'I married my mother,' he said ruefully. 'The only way my wife's different is that she doesn't blow my nose for me.' Having fought his way out and away from his mother, he'd come right back to her. Of course he had sexual problems, impotence and all the rest of it.

Now he became aware of an enormous tension between his wife's control and his own masculine side. He drew a picture of a figure perched on a ledge; it was both the shadow and the innate masculinity which he'd been projecting out. Up to that point he'd solved the problem by taking everything up into his head, but his feelings were running around in the unconscious and he was driven as if by an engine from down below. Eventually we discovered within him a fascinating polarity between two childish figures: a boy of four desperately trying to kick mother, and an eighteen-month-old desperately trying to find mother. That was at the very root of this poor guy's situation.

He drew a picture of fire from a volcano, with the castle of the Self showing the possibility of the Transcendent Function. The drawbridge was up and the portcullis down, so there was no entry. The burning was all through his life, the alchemical fire externalising itself in pain, the heat under the flask, the cooking process of the stuff of his life that would eventually bring out the possibility of growth. This man had a particular fascination for dreams, remembering them from years back with very keen insight. In imaging, he saw a small figure down in the volcano he'd drawn, surrounded by blood, desperately trying to get out, saying, 'I really don't want to kill anybody, just to love them.' The smoke of the volcano was an extraordinary example of an unconscious motif emerging. It would eventually lead him home, but his story was not resolved quickly; there was a long way to go. 'What's trying to get out of the volcano ?' I asked. Spontaneously he drew a woman's head from behind, and the full moon. Only afterwards did he see it was the back-view of the Transcendent Function. And the doors of the castle were open and the lights were on.

I am almost overwhelmed by the quite spontaneous way these things come up. These are graphic examples, but just look at the dreams, the motifs that crop up, the things that happen in our lives – the people we bump into, the film we saw last night, the book that falls into our hands. It may take a very long time, but after a period of tension and withdrawal, after enough time in the unconscious, that redeeming factor emerges to take us through. Here is another example.

An American Jewish girl I know was brought up in the most appalling circumstances in New York. Her mother was left pregnant after a one-night stand and she never knew who her father was. When she was three her mother married a man who brought in two stepsons, one ten and the other six. She was raped by her new father and by each of the brothers just about alternately. There was hardly a time when this was not happening. Not surprisingly, in these dreadful conditions, by the time she was in her forties she had a very marked anxiety neurosis. But all the way through she remembered one thing. She'd been hiding one day in a doorway in the windswept streets of New York, curled up in a corner not knowing what to do (she didn't want to go home and there was nowhere else to go) when she'd seen a splash of yellow in the darkness of the street-some half-dead flowers lying there. These flowers were the one motif she could hold on to.

Sexuality loomed enormously large in her life. Every image, every dream, came up as distorted sexuality, and it had begun to obsess her, though it became apparent that it was tenderness rather than sexuality that she was looking for. As do many people with a very wounded background, she became a social worker. By the job she chose she was unconsciously seeking a Transcendent Function, looking for a way of pulling together this split in herself. She was fully aware that she was trying to do for others what hadn't been done for herself. Such a movement in the unconscious often leads us to adjust our own healing. She became a sexual counsellor, both fascinated and repelled by her work.

We looked for something in her job that would hold her and by degrees draw her up. People can't go straight up the mountain. One of the dangers, as we've seen, is to rush them, not letting them penetrate their darkness, not allowing time for the healing factor to emerge, pulling it out too rapidly into consciousness. Where people have too suddenly come up to the light, there is nearly always a throwback. Better rather find a motif of light, and take the light *down* to explore the darkness.

We also sought some anchor-point in the outer world where she could begin to express herself. She kept a notebook for a while, then she began to 'dabble in paint', as she called it; she'd never touched a paintbrush in her life. Art was spontaneously emerging. Her first picture was of the dead flowers, with a red ball representing her sexuality as it had now become. The picture showed the new relationship between it and the flowers – a remarkable thing to have emerged from somebody so incredibly wounded. It wasn't just on canvas now, it was in her life, her own redeeming, salving motif. It had been with her in that doorway when she was about seven, and it had stayed with her all through the years. Again and again people come out of the depths of their hell and it is as if somebody has said, 'Lo, I have been with you all the days of your life.'

Five years later she drew a final enchanting picture. It's when she broke out of the egg – one of my most-beloved emergings: a chick with one leg in the air, standing in a puddle, not very footed yet – and very, very beautiful.

Gestalt with objects

When someone is struggling, when they can't hold the tension any longer, they're going to glissade down. Therefore we can't wait for the transformative symbol to appear. I work as if it were on its way. The art is to help the person become more conscious so that they can at least hold the balance as they seek the integrity of the Self. And over and over, in their dreams and images, there comes a sudden 'click' and *something* appears. I've found a good method of working towards this. I use a Gestalt technique, letting *objects* rather than chairs or cushions stand for the issues of choice. I add another object to be alongside the person, which stands in for the integrity of the Self, the Soul, the spirit. Here is an example.

There was a man who drew 'chaos' and 'peace' at the two ends of a pole. He said that at one time he'd been unable to tolerate any upset or anger anywhere. He'd adjusted to the impossible pull by going for *peace at any price*. But after a while he became aware that the peace was set against the chaos of his original background. 'When *they* get into trouble with each other, my wife and my son,' he said, 'I dive straight in the middle – and then they both come in and bash *me*.' A member of a partnership of three at work, he would leap right into the fray when the other two went for each other, and again they'd both bash *him*. He saw how often he had leapt into the fracas and always been hit (reminiscent of the sketch of the husband and wife caught in a drunken brawl. One small policeman is hanging on to the two of them, they're both bashing *him*, his helmet's dented, and he's shouting, 'Help! help! Somebody do something!')

We used this 'Gestalt with objects' to explore it. Since he had family problems, the objects I put on the table stood in for family members. I began with my rock crystal: 'That's you. Now, here's your wife. This is your son. What's happening here?' By this Gestalt method we got the feeling of the energy-flow between the three of them. Next I said, 'Now, here's you as one end of the polarity. What's at the other end? Why do you react to your son and your wife in quite that way? What out here makes you react so to that scene going on between them?' 'Fear of being the outsider!' he said.

This visual Gestalt, these three objects, had enabled him to see it. A memory: he'd been evacuated away from his family, while his younger sister had been kept at home. We talked about the chaos of his parents, and himself as the rejected little outsider. We used those objects now to stand for mother and beloved baby sister, and for him being put out. When he was brought back after the war he'd felt he belonged nowhere. His family seemed complete without him, a set-up family from which he'd been pushed out. Longing for a way into their containment, he didn't know where to relate. It hadn't just been love of peace: 'I was afraid of being the outsider!' The rejected child pushed out of the family, he'd tried to become the insider by being peacemaker and harmoniser. And it had worked very well; the family indeed called on him when they hit problems, so he did feel to some extent included.

It was the visual movement of objects on a table that enabled him to see. I asked, 'If you could handle things differently, how would you do it – if you had the choice?' 'I'd like to be able to stand in a different place, see it in a different way.' 'If you could stand *there* instead of here, and not be drawn back to the earlier stages, how would you like to handle it, now in your maturity?' 'Well, I can see my wife's point of view – she has a lot on her side, but I can also see my son's – yes, there are some positive things between them.' Eventually he said, 'But it's *their* business!'

As he moved the objects around the table, we could see the energy-dynamic going back and forth. At last he understood what he was doing when he leaped into the middle and tried to handle things from there. He realised it was because he was that fearful child (frightened of chaos and disorder, frightened of the breaking-up of the harmony of the family) trying to get in. Leaping in without a transformative symbol took him continually backwards and forwards and down. Together we tried to rebalance. He saw how far he split off; he was so afraid of reactivating that childhood chaos that no price was too large for peace. He had to recognise that in speaking his truth he risked being an outsider.

His dreams suggested that a transformative symbol was about to appear; but until it did he started to act *as if* it had, *as if* there were the possibility of a new harmony. He took the positive values of the peace-maker, and also the positive values of allowing chaos to happen. 'What is the energy within chaos which you can use creatively and constructively?' No longer feeling he personally had to 'do something about it', he found that he could tolerate a lot more chaos both in the world and in his personal relationships. He'd never allowed himself to look at the nature of his own chaos. The peace and the chaos each lay within himself.

From that moment things improved in his home. He realised he had an alternative. Before, he'd either reacted from a childish base, or struggled to be the adult in the middle, always getting bashed. Now, he began to act *as if* he could stand. It affected his style of work. He remembered the old familiar pattern. But, 'No, I'm not going to dive in now; I'm just going to hold on and do what I choose, not what I feel impelled to do.' On reading Jung for the first time, he declared, 'The individual is the most important thing. It's through the individual that the collective will be redeemed. Peace has got to start in me !' In the bringing together of peace and chaos, he discovered his own usefulness and his own transformative symbol.

At the beginning, while the polarities are still there in the unconscious, there is no split. The two sides of the coin are married together, and we aren't aware which side is operating. It's when the thing first comes out of the unconscious that they split and we have the conflict. To begin with we aren't sure what the poles of the conflict are. We know we've got trouble, there's a multitude of feelings, but we can't quite identify them. The person and I will work with that, hoping to move on towards the Transcendent Function.

Using Gestalt

I may use the more conventional Gestalt here, with chairs or cushions rather than objects. Giving a place to each of the critical *feelings* as it emerges, moving from one position to the other, getting into the two that seem to be conflict, may lead to a sudden clarification. Or we may give a personification to two *figures,* finding perhaps that this one is conventional, traditional ('My partner's not behaving very well – it's time he was punished!') while that one loves the partner. Till now there's been no clarity; using Gestalt will bring the split into consciousness in a most remarkable way, identifying the poles that are fighting. Then of course we have to move on towards the transformative symbol.

Some people, needing to be in control, would refuse absolutely to move themselves around in this way on cushions or chairs. But, seeing the table as an energy field, they'd be willing to work with objects, which they can move about in the middle of a conversation. We need to use both methods: first the polarities need to be identified, and then a tableful of small things can in an extraordinary way give people the sense of having a choice, having alternatives, being able to move things around on the board of their own life.

Two figures came up for me once when I was doing some imaging, one male, one female. I intended to discuss with them the problems they were posing, but instead these two figures took me firmly by the hand, led me out into a meadow and discussed *me*! As their problem! I became happy with that and accepted it. But in the middle of their discussion, a little bull wandered by. He meandered around, Disney-style, sniffing the daisies and holding a buttercup under his chin. I looked at him and thought, 'There's nothing in me that has anything whatever to do with this bull!' It took me seven years to see it. The laziness – 'I'm not *allowed* to be like that!' – the idleness, the love of just *being*, dozing around all over the place. He was the perfect counterpoint to my polarities and my tension, a lazy bull just doing nothing. He was my transforming symbol.

Hubris and inflation

All these symbols are containers of energy. We may have a sudden emotional conversion and believe it to be a transformative symbol. We may go wild, go into *hubris*, fly up, lose contact with the ground. Catholics become Communists and Communists become Catholics overnight, but the groundwork hasn't been done. We haven't been through the suffering and tension of opposites, the struggle to raise that which is unconscious up into consciousness, and there can be a very dangerous sense of inflation. If we're lucky, it dies away; otherwise it can take hold of us and make us into fanatics, cosmic boy scouts.

The transformative symbol

However, St. Francis, very much enjoying life, was obeying a sudden inner vision when he built his little church. What he'd seen as just a small building turned into a whole movement, because it brought with it the energy of transformation. The truly transformative symbol changes our attitudes, our lives, because it brings with it the energy required in consciousness to transform the whole situation. If anybody had described my little bull to me or given me a reason for him seven years earlier, it might have meant quite a bit to me at the conceptual level, but it would have meant absolutely damn-all at the life-basis level. We have to be very, very careful of interpreting for people. Let them do it for themselves. Otherwise, as well as the problems they come in with, we send them out with the burden of our interpretations. We need to wait upon life. The transformative symbol comes to each of us when the moment is ready. The Transcendent Function is its own explanation.

It's said that the prime energy of our lives gets lost in the system. To be caught into the mass is to be caught into the shadow side of the group. We come into incarnation and embody ourselves in the mass, but many of us know that it isn't quite right; the unity in the group means that the shadow side is not experienced. It was necessary to be born into our families, be enwombed in the womb of unconsciousness. Many people are enwombed again, but this time in the womb of consciousness, to be reborn. But before that we muddle love with desire. What we call 'love' is very often the need for possession of the other to give ourselves a sense of identity. It is a desire that comes from the solar plexus. But out of the upper cusps of the heart comes love of the whole, love of the One, the love which enables us to go back to the original group – but consciously, having had the experience. The individual journey is to find the line home to the original place we came from. We come from the One, we return to the One – the faces of God, the faces of the One – and the energy of the One is life.

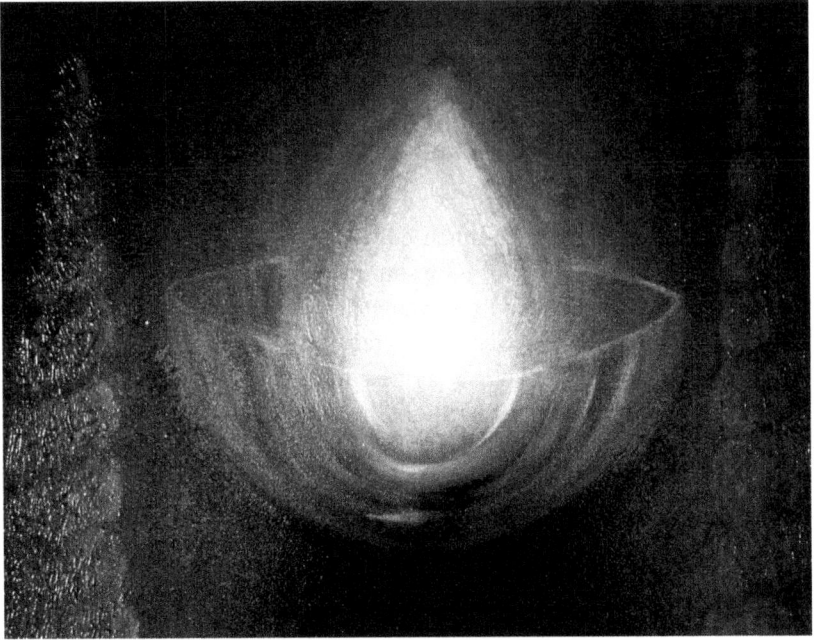

Plate 12

Millenium Bowl

CHAPTER ELEVEN

Projection and Collusion
Barbara Somers and Ian Gordon-Brown

Certain it is that if we remain unconscious
of the initial projection,
we will marry the same problem again and again

Projection

We saw in the last chapter how while, as Jung says, there are no opposites in the unconscious, yet any particular energy holds together like a single coin. Both sides of the penny are united. When the energy first comes into play it splits into its two sides, its two halves; it becomes heads and tails, masculine and feminine, all the polarities you can think of. Through the interplay of these polarities and our attempt to get to grips with them to resolve the conflict, eventually there emerges the Transcendent Function. Then we integrate them and consciously understand their relationship.

Projection is very closely related to this. We see the world through our own distorting mirror-images, our own pink spectacles. If we're feeling good, well put-together, if the sun is shining and we've had a decent holiday, we will tend to pick up the good bits in the outside world. The world is a mirror of the condition of the inner self. If on the other hand we're depressed, we will pick up the greyness, see the black spots, feel that everything's wrong with the world. Obviously the aim is to see things as they are, clearly and without distortion, and to handle them according to reality.

Jung pointed to the psychological rule which says that inner situations left out of consciousness happen outside as fate. So when we remain unconscious of our inner contradictions, the world must be torn into opposite halves as it perforce acts out the conflict. We project our locked energies, unresolved conflicts, unsatisfied drives to wholeness on the environment. What we see there is our own condition mirrored, and individuation is the process of internalising these projections.

Suppose we don't quite know how we stand with authority. We haven't yet sufficiently discovered our own internal authority, so we can't easily stand up to those in charge outside. We project this on to all manner of people. Some of them will be quite suitable: the boss, say. Others will be most unsuitable, not really authority-figures at all. We're projecting our own unresolved difficulty, making people out there into a mirror of the unresolved conflict within us.

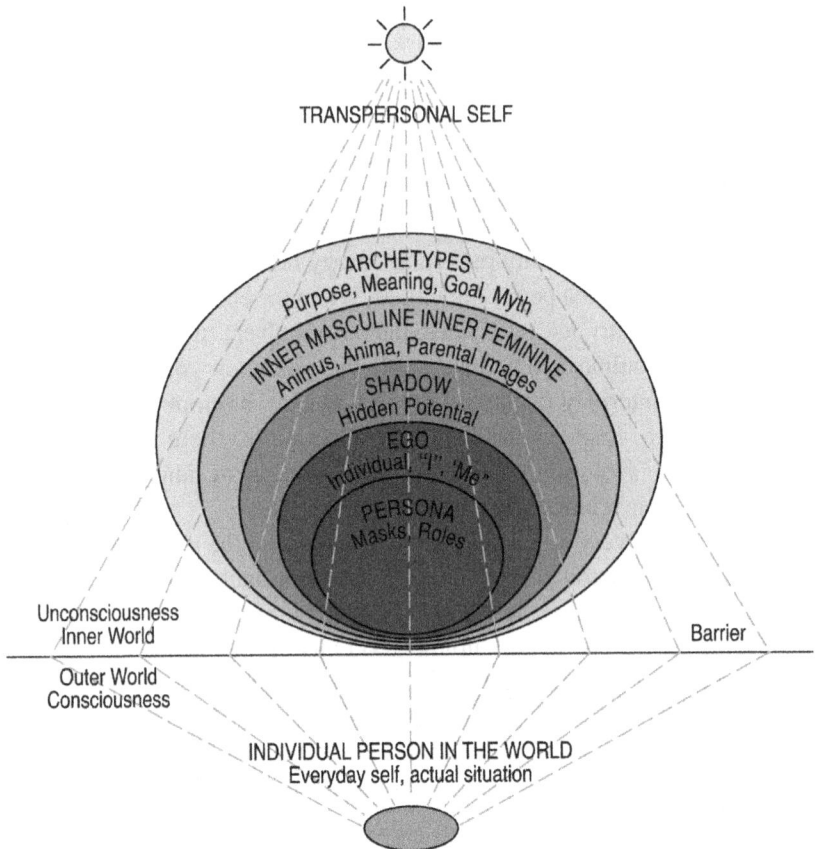

Figure 15 The Onion Map

Levels of projection

It's as if there were a barrier between the inner and outer worlds. On the outer side lies the the ordinary, everyday *person in the world*. On the inner side are layers, like those of an onion. The first is the *Persona* which we present to the world; in fact we are wearing a whole series of masks, playing a whole series of roles. Then there's the personal centre, the 'real me', the individual 'I', the *Ego*. Our exploration begins here as we seek to discover the nature of the personal 'I'.

But then we begin to move further into an area of unconsciousness where lies the *shadow*. Here we're unaware of the situation, don't know what's going on; there may be conflicts as yet unresolved, potentialities as yet unrecognised. Through and beyond the shadow we come to the *contra-sexual side*, the parental images and the inner animus and anima. Beyond that lies the level of *purpose, meaning and archetypes*, right through to the *Transpersonal Self*. The path of individuation, of initiation, is about the relating of the Transpersonal centre out there to the centre down here in the world. All the diverse images which are reflected out and brought back into our individual situation need ultimately to be integrated, so that the outer and the inner worlds are harmoniously related.

We shall look at the onion layers of the map at Figure 15 opposite, starting from:

The person in the world

Imagine a young child, or someone very primitive in their consciousness: there's often a total identification of the inside with the outside. The outside world is animate, full of spirits and energies, fairies and devils who do things to you. When ego-consciousness is just beginning to form it's quite a while before the child can say 'I'; the distinction between the inner and the outer is not yet fully realised nor properly developed. In primitive people the concept of the *participation mystique* between the inside and the outside can lead to their making some fascinating identifications of themselves with animals or objects or places. The personal centre is so involved with both the inside and the outside that a person quite easily identifies with animals, totem poles, stones, physical promontories, mountains, hills. If it's a tree, then when the tree is cut down, the person dies. When the child's identification with his hurt teddy -bear is great enough he cries, genuinely feeling the pain of the bear. These are elements of Projection.

The Ego

As the personal self develops, girls in childhood and adolescence project on to older girls, teachers, stars; young boys on to parents, on to teachers, musicians, sporting figures. They want to believe in these people, in what they do, in how helpful they are. If there isn't an adequate father around, the young person may find someone on whom to project their need, their lack, and this can be a very healthy and constructive projection.

The Shadow

Having established ego-consciousness, we next explore all that boiling stuff that lies just beyond it. Shadow projections can be both positive and negative; not only emotions such as hate, dislike, shame, suspicion or envy, but also love, belief in the hero, worship of someone else. Almost anything that is part of the inner world of the psyche can be projected. We usually think projection is a problem of the *dark* shadow, but the *bright* shadow can be projected too. Till we recognise gurus and wise people for what they are (only partially wise, mostly), we attach a hook to them and hang our joy, beauty and wisdom upon it. If we're not fully conscious of our inner urge for an ideal to which to devote ourselves, we will project that as well, and they'll become a hook on which to hang the bright shadow of our idealisation. Then we worship them!

Many movements and organisations spring up where the bright shadow and the ideal are projected in this way. There is a general agreement to perpetuate the myth of the Leader, the Teacher, the Chosen People, 'the best group in the world' or whatever. If people looked, they would be conscious that it was not so; but at the unconscious level they have so much invested in maintaining the *status quo* of the group and its importance in the world that they cannot face the reality and, as we shall see, collusion prevents them from doing so. Gurus from both East and West, while seeming to meet people's needs, are often very far from being what they're cracked up to be. In the end they're found not to fit the public image; they're mostly very ordinary, with feet of clay. Many of them, not knowing this, make the mistake of allowing or accepting the hero-worship that is hung on them. So while much group energy results from a collective projection of ideals, in the end the projectors find the hook won't hold any longer. As members of the group see the true nature of the leader, they have to face the shadow within.

The Masculine and Feminine within

Moving behind that, we come to an area where projection particularly thrives: the *anima* and the *animus*. Falling in love is a classic example of projection. The person of the other sex constellates your ideal image of the feminine if you're a man, of the masculine if you're a woman, and there's an explosive coming together. If you're lucky you find (probably after a difficult process) that you can live with the reality eventually discovered behind the projection, and you stay together. If unlucky, you continue in conflict, or you part.

We often get together with our inner opposite, someone who lives out the part of our nature we don't yet know about. Most of us are hooked here, at least in Western culture. A man may not really be conscious of the feminine side of his nature. Having difficulty in living it out, he hooks it on to a woman who is appropriate in various ways, but who also constellates that unknown feminine side of himself. Thus he can live out whole aspects of his nature, his *anima*, which would otherwise have to be contained. The woman too, when the shining projection wears thin, has to come to terms with reality, learning to live out and become conscious of her inner *animus*. Relating to the opposite in her partner, she discovers that the image she projected is not really his, but her own.

It's now that, in order to allow our own inner side to grow, we may after all need to distance ourselves and separate from the other. This is the point when either or both may find a different partner to carry the same projection. Or, if we have begun to be aware of the inner, contra-sexual side, we may find somebody who more appropriately fits our nature, someone with whom we can have a more real relationship.

Our parents are often involved in our projections. Frequently we see them in our partners. If a man has an unresolved problem with his mother he may well project mother on to his partner. She may not be much like his mother, but suddenly he finds himself behaving in relation to this woman as if he were her child, and she his (maybe critical) parent. She doesn't necessarily deserve it. It's very difficult to have a relationship with a husband who thinks you are his mother, a wife who treats you like her father. Each projects on the other their image of the parent, behaving towards them as if they *were* that, allowing the projection to take them back into childhood so that instead of two adult people living together, you have a boy and his mother, a girl and her dad. The other partner may go along with this, unable to handle it, colluding. 'She can't manage without me.' 'He thinks I'm his mum, so I have to be.' Unhooking is easier said than done. Perhaps aware that the other is being a child, neither knows why it's happening. When a woman says, 'All men are boys!' she's really admitting she doesn't know what to do about it. Each is saying, 'My partner needs help!'

'The Enchanted Cottage', a novel of the 1930s, told of a blind woman and a hideously deformed man who fell in love. The story was about the interplay between the pity of others who saw them as they appeared from outside, and their love. Enchanted each with the other, they lived with their inner images; in their cottage they were two of the most beautiful people in the world. But then, in the story, her sight was restored and he had his face re-formed and they saw each other and couldn't bear the reality of it. (Since after all it was a novel, what they had in the Enchanted Cottage had to be able to stand the test of time, and they were made to come back together again!)

But we fall in love, and though we've always said, 'I could never live with anyone untidy!' we find that the beloved *will* leave their clothes all over the floor. Along came this person, and in we fell. Fall *out* of love, though, and the first thing we complain about is... socks everywhere! Again, there's a lot of projection on to the partner; where we once saw beauty, now – ugliness.

Jung said, interestingly, that because the nature of the masculine is *outwardly polygamous*, looking for the many, it is *internally monogamous*: a man tends to seek one woman, one face among the multitude. You see it in great artists and writers who depict always the face of the one beloved. Whereas a woman, being of the feminine, is naturally more *outwardly monogamous*, and so she is *inwardly polygamous*: she will have a number of masculine faces within, which she seeks. A man seeks one type, she seeks many. Her ideal man is a montage of several. She needs somebody who'll drag her out by the hair, gallop off with her, beat her, but also a knight in shining armour, but also a daddy-figure, but also a responsible bread-winner – all put together to make the ideal man.

There are certain women who typically constellate the *anima* for men, offering the most beautiful hooks for male projection. If a man thinks over his image of the ideal – the perfect woman, the star, the singer he loves most – he will probably find a common thread or theme (a couple if he's lucky) running through. A woman who is such an *anima* figure calls forth the projection. One colleague told me how she met a woman who strongly reminded her of an old acquaintance of the same name. 'Are you by any chance her sister?' asked my colleague. 'No,' said the woman, 'that was my husband's first wife.' Certain it is that if we remain unconscious of the initial projection we will marry the same problem again and again.

We can try to note the qualities of people we like and dislike *very much indeed*. 'Those are the kind of people I really love!' we say, or 'I absolutely hate people like that!' There's an exaggeration, a great affect. Look at the qualities, and we'll have a near-representation of the inner conflict within ourselves. In general, projection is marked by an *inappropriate* degree of emotion, whether anger, hate, fear, anxiety; or an unjustified ideological identification, an inappropriate amount of hero worship, for somebody who is not a hero.

It can be instructive to shut your eyes and invite images of two people of your own sex. The first you actively like and approve of. You're drawn to this person, find them most attractive and magnetic, perhaps even fascinating. The second you strongly disapprove of, finding them difficult and awkward, perhaps untrustworthy; they generally turn you off and you'd go a long way to avoid meeting them. Then get two more images, this time of people of the opposite sex; again, one image for the kind of person who turns you on, whom you find appealing and greatly enjoy spending time with, and the other whom you frankly dislike and avoid whenever possible. They're not at all your type, you find them distasteful, you don't really trust them, they give you an uncomfortable taste or feeling. Finally, invite two images of yourself, the first when you're at your best, the second, at your worst.

It's worthwhile to check through those six images and see whether there are any connections between how you're reacting to them all. What element of projection may there be, and is it involved with your past and present relationships?

It's interesting to see how what we dislike is often the very thing we invite. We may greatly resent being seen as, say, a doormat, but then, that's the way we're acting. When we don't like other people's idea of us, we need to check whether we're giving out an image of ourselves which causes them to see us in the wrong way. And when an inappropriate degree of feeling surprises us, that's projection; perhaps we bumped into somebody at the bus stop and amazed ourselves by exploding with rage, letting out a whole lot of stuff that had been boiling up inside. Perhaps we realise we're always having problems at work, hearing ourselves constantly complaining that we can never get a satisfactory boss, turning every manager, even the meekest and mildest, into an authority figure and hitting out at them. That's projection.

The Archetypal level

This is an area for projection in action. We see wise persons, healers and teachers, saints and heroes in all kinds of popular figures; and there are wise people to be found. Someone we think is wise will say things which give us a kind of 'Aha!' inside ourselves. It's an evocation of something already known; we say, 'I realised it wasn't new to me – I knew it already.' Wisdom is a process of remembering, 're-membering' again, re-gathering to ourselves the parts which were projected out. But the truly valid wise person or spiritual teacher *evokes an environment* in which that chord begins to strike within us. We can hear it vibrating, like the sound that follows a plucked string. The wise person's value is that the inner note is made to thrum. The wise person is not for us a wise person if the thrumming doesn't happen, but it won't unless the thrumming is already in us.

The landscape of projection is a very shifting one. We meet our Wise People at the interface; they may come in the form of psychosomatic illnesses, or devils, or angels or whatever. But they're all making the statement which causes that thrumming to happen, lets the spring arise, makes sunflowers grow out of sunflower seeds.

The Self

And so we come to the Self. The normal view is that the personal 'I', the Ego, possesses some aspect of our nature called soul or spirit or atman or whatever. But from a Transpersonal perspective it's a very interesting possibility that it's the other way round: that the ordinary everyday 'I' is a projection of the Self, that the Self possesses us. Then the business of withdrawing projections takes on an added dimension. The images we project are related to the partial, distorted views of the personal centre. When we recognise and make them conscious, trying to understand what the reality is, when we cease to react to someone according to the projection, then the small self, the personal 'I', begins to be taken back to the Centre. People refer, sometimes obscurely, to 'processes of identification and dis-identification', 'distinguishing the I from the Not-I'. But to talk about the withdrawal of projection, the shattering of false images about reality, makes more sense. It's very fundamental. It has to do with strengthening the connection of the outer with the inner, the self with the Self.

Collective projection

We have looked at projection as it affects the individual. A great deal of what happens in the world has to do with inner conflicts which surface collectively as projections of energy on groups or peoples or particular situations. There are many collective stereotypes. As we saw when looking at the family, there are typical *scapegoats* upon whom people will round in anger. Whole peoples have been picked up and used as such scapegoats right through history; there's been a collective projection of the shadow over to them. For example, the explosive wars and violence we see come out of a projective mechanism. People become agents for war, unaware of the forces which burst out and move them in the collective moment. We saw it in Second World War propaganda; while the Russians were our allies they were seen as 'marvellous, beautiful, brave, noble, kind, generous'. Later, when they were on the other side of the Iron Curtain, they became 'that hugging, treacherous bear'. Manipulators twist images on a mass scale so that they can play their own cards. The whole of advertising, presumably in the hope of collusion, is based on projection.

Projection in organisations

We've seen how polarities operate in groups and movements, both at the conscious and the unconscious level, and are projected out. One newly-trained analyst had been in industry. Talking about the unconscious power struggles in the analytic field, he said, 'These groups are outwardly all about love and understanding, and it's very interesting to note that in the unconscious there is such a tremendous jockeying for power. The members are quite unaware of it'. He compared it with what went on in the industrial field, where everyone knew about the games being played, laughing at so-and-so who's 'on a power-trip'. 'Power is *conscious* there,' he said, 'and something else operates at an *un*conscious level. Could it perhaps be love of humanity?'

Groups have to have an enemy on whom to project the shadow. When they split, as groups often do, one of the parties is generally seen as the bright ideal and the other, consisting of those who break away or cause the split, becomes the evil figure. Again, the degree of emotion signifies how much projection there is; in groups it's very easily stirred up and provoked. People have great expectations of the leaders. They wish impossible ideals of perfection on those who are in significant key positions, and huge projections are placed on them. The love that some leaders and ikons receive is suffocating and smothering; and as for the criticism that goes to others, or to the same ones after they have been found wanting, well, which is worse, the love or the condemnation? Both are projections. We need to stand outside the whole mechanism. Plenty of small boys are needed to say that the Emperor has no clothes.

Collusion

Collusion is closely related to the mechanism of projection. Two people can become locked into what is often a not-very-fond embrace. It's about entanglement at the unconscious level, and it's very difficult for each to disentangle what is theirs and what is the other person's. It's almost as if there were a shared unconscious. For instance, there can be collusion between a parent and a child. We've seen how sometimes the un-recognised problems of the parent, aspects of their shadow, may be carried by the child; or the parent may hold the child close as one means of avoiding what they will have to face when it grows up and leaves them. Collusion comes when some over-responsible child co-operates with the parent and stays close because, at an unconscious or semi-conscious level, they feel responsible for helping the parent and carrying their burden for them. The child is colluding.

In families with an identified patient, one of the children will be carrying the shadow for the parents. That child will be an essential part of the psychological mechanism of the group. As we saw with the family, take the identified patient away and the whole structure falls down. Fighting breaks out between people who've otherwise been very happy, and full of love and caring for the patient on whom they'd put their shadow. The child had become their safety valve. Here we have a small group colluding – unconsciously, of course.

With couples, collusion happens when the scales fall, reality emerges, and the struggle to adjust and come to terms with each other begins. Consciously, they may both try to *suppress* the problem, thinking that by holding it below they can stay together. However, the initial attempt to keep the thing together may have led to a tight hold that is suffocating for the inner *anima* and *animus*, and needs loosening in order to let these two aspects emerge. When we live together as couples we become very close. In sharing the same bed there will often be a sharing of aura, of psyche. To become an individual, to strike out on our own, is extremely threatening. We may feel that, if we separated, part of us would be torn out; so much so that, although we may push and pull with each other, at another level we're both holding on as tightly as possible. Our symbiotic relationship is better than the struggle to become an individual and to relate more consciously.

However, at an unconscious level separation is being forced by the psyche. It's no good staying together unless the difficulty is resolved. So we collude; the unconscious constantly raises the trouble and it surfaces in fights and battles. This collusion may cause us to split apart, but no healthy relationship is possible in the long run unless the thing is brought into consciousness and dealt with.

On the other hand, at the conscious level the couple may *want* to split, but be unconsciously colluding to stay together. In this case, the psyche knows very well that if they *do* split the problem is not going to be resolved, but will have to be faced again later. So why not do it with the existing partner?

Collusion happens in work groups. If, say, we keep missing buses or trains, or have continuous dreams of doing so, we can ask if there's a part of us colluding to *make* us miss them. Is it a train we really want to catch, or is there some part of us which appears to be working against us? One employee stayed on, nobly and gallantly, in an ideological work-place where he was not happy – till he was sacked. Though consciously he tried hard to stay loyal and employed because of the emotional and ideological tie, his behaviour ensured his contract was ended. He was colluding with the sackers, helping them to get rid of him. If he had listened to what was going on, he would have chosen to get out years before. The amount of emotion attached to ideologies of various kinds makes them one of the ripest fields for the mechanisms of both collusion and projection to operate.

Again it can be instructive to sense which ideology we strongly go for, and which we strongly hate or dislike. Then take some national group or people for whom we feel an affinity and another we dislike very much indeed. Discover what all this tells us about ourselves.

Avoiding collusion

We collude when we are unaware that we have a hook. But if we refuse to keep the hook out, then beyond a certain point no one can hang anything on it – the coat falls off the peg. The projection comes at us, and we can say, 'Well, so what?' and pass by. Christ's teaching is to turn the other cheek and let the aggression happen. And the Zen master *allows* the aggression to come towards him; instead of coming out to counter it, he flows in the opposite direction so that it carries on by its own force. Someone who worked in a gaol told this story: 'There was a very aggressive prisoner sparring up to two policemen who wanted some information from him – big strong fellows quite looking forward to a fight. I looked at the prisoner and said in my ordinary voice, "Look, this is what we need to know." He turned to me and said, "Oh yes, well, this is it..." and he told me. Then – comically – he turned back to go on sparring at the officers.'

Once you've taken the hook, you're in the collusion. One story has stayed with a friend for always: she'd seen a very young, gentle-looking Indian man being come at by a whole Encounter Group. They'd picked him out as scapegoat. He remained very quiet, didn't join in, and eventually the whole wretched group attacked him about his lack of participation. He was a thorn in their flesh because he wasn't playing the game – and by the end there was a great game going on! One by one they honed in on him. He just sat there, being real, saying absolutely nothing. It made them feel very embarrassed and unreal, and they came right up to him, going for him. Still with that same gentle look, he took it all. When they'd finished he said, 'So?' Then the group collapsed. They couldn't go on, they split up, and that was the end of the whole great melodrama. He didn't collude. He simply didn't hold out a hook. His truth had made their untruth look ridiculous.

CHAPTER TWELVE

Archetypal Patterns and Story-Making

Barbara Somers

The masculine is the Hero on the Quest;
the feminine is the very Journey itself

So far we've been dealing with the individual: as seed, as child in the adult, with mother, father, brothers and sisters, with the family dynamics. We've looked at the individual's need for space and boundaries, at polarities, projection and collusion, at the reaction of each person to their own intimate environment – and, as individuals, we can't be seen in isolation from that environment. However, whether or not we are conscious of it, each of us has also an ethnic and historic tail (or tale) coming behind the quality and substance of our outlook. When two people meet on a journey and one listens to the other, the listener hears an individual voice speaking about where the teller has come from, where they're going – a very personal history. But behind that single human voice are many others, the voices of the ground from which they emerged. Sheldon Kopp says that such a contemporary pilgrim is separated from the mythical heritage that supported his ancestors. God is dead, and man is isolated in his secularity. Man belonged when God lived, and story-telling and myth-making left no need for psychology. To regain our identity, we must work at the telling of our own stories.[42]

It's only in the really big, archetypal, resonant moments – life and death, birth and high danger, rebirths, crisis, ageing – that we have the sense of being part of something inevitably bigger than our souls. A note is struck in us. Then we walk through corridors somewhere between time: a time-warp, a space-warp. Inner and outer come together. Here is also the language of the mystics. Suddenly, apparently for little reason, something comes to them and they see the outside world as if through a glass. They can touch it, even hear themselves talking and manifesting in a reasonably usual way, and yet they have a tremendous sense of the 'otherness' that is there.

---

[42] See Sheldon Kopp 1974, Page 15.

In a major crisis (the death of someone, deep illness, shock) we talk of being in touch for perhaps the first time with something infinitely deeper. We walk through the world aware that people are talking, living, doing the world-things we were once so much part of, yet feeling as if we were also in another space, consciously walking the interface between inner and outer. These are big resonances; when we have to tread these borderlands between life and death, it seems as if an Archetype walked through our lives. Firstly, I will respond to such circumstances as a person; however, I will also react as part of a Collective. If I'm Greek I will respond like a Greek; I may not feel like a Greek in ordinary conscious living, but in one of those moments I am likely to react in the way of my nation. As a Tibetan, who may have taken in a great deal of Western culture, when life, death, birth hit me I respond also as a Tibetan. The mask cracks; I emerge from my context and link again with my roots.

Someone I knew remembered a fragment from a dream and took it forward into guided imaging. She felt it showed up very sharply how she responded as a Jewish woman. Although consciously she considered that being Jewish mattered very little, scarcely touching her life, she saw that only a Jewish woman could have had this image. It was of an old man whom she felt was a wise person. In taking the dream forward she said:

'The image makes me think of my grandfather; though he wasn't particularly wise. I see the scene; it's after my brother died. Grandfather is praying – chanting – praying. Seeing her father like this made my mother cry, as if to say, "Poor man, it has hit him hard," as if she felt not her own loss but his; she wouldn't cry for herself but she'd cry for him. Grandfather was a very mild, quiet person; he just sat there, quietly chanting and praying.

'Grandmother was being hysterical, doing her ritual wailing. My mother was against all that – so controlled. My grandfather made a bridge between the melodramatic behaviour of my grandmother and our real grieving. He was crying while chanting, very quietly contained within himself. He didn't understand the Hebrew prayers, but it didn't matter because they were the vessel for his feelings. He died himself a few months later.

'Such different reactions: mother repressing, grandmother hysterical, grandfather praying. They divided man and woman. I could hear my father sobbing in the other room. My father was a bridge, too. He let himself go at the beginning in a heavy bout of weeping, supported by the men. But, when the first news had come that my brother had died, he had put the phone straight down and telephoned the rabbi. I had broken down and cried then; it was so horrible that he should telephone someone immediately after hearing about my brother's death. Father later said he gave himself time to cry, and then he stopped and didn't cry again. My mother was consciously suppressing herself, letting herself shed no tears.

'As for me, I didn't understand why my brother had died so suddenly. I was just an observer, detached; nothing made any sense. For years I've not been able to make sense.'

That was the story as she told it, but also as it was told by someone Jewish out of her remembering of time past, still very much 'time present'. She and I had worked with an inner figure representing her wisdom (which I presume was also Jewish, since such a talisman carries part of our psyche). It said:

'That was your first experience with death. It came very close to you; you had the chance to see what effect it had on the people you love. They all dealt with his death in their different ways. You were still trying to deal not just with *his* death, but with Death. And Life. You are still trying to work something out about it. What matters is that you should live your own life and penetrate it as deeply as you can. It matters to you if you go through meaningless ritual, like your grandfather with his Hebrew prayers. These are the wrong vessel for you, though they were right for him. Your grandmother's hysterics were her vessel, but not yours. You are still looking for yours. Sometimes you think you will find it in your relationship with a man; perhaps you will, but it doesn't matter. What matters is that you want to find it and that you keep looking.'

That she couldn't deny. She agreed that touching her roots had carried her through to a completely different understanding of life. That sense of the ground of her being, though she didn't understand it and it wasn't to her apparent taste, showed she was part of something richly coloured, very *other* and yet *family*. A really sophisticated Western woman, who had denied the roots of her nature and that it meant anything at all to her to be Jewish, was hit by the extreme Jewishness of it. She came to herself. Had she been Tibetan, it would have been in the Tibetan idiom, and so on. And now she celebrates the fact that she is Jewish.

The ancestors

Throughout his life Jung was consistently aware of our connection with the ancestors of the past, with the present and with what is to be. Working in the here-and-now with individuals, whatever their personal crisis or problem or glory might be, he knew they carry with them all that has been, and for a moment become a focal point for all that will be. Jung said of his Tower at Bollingen that it was as if he lived there in many centuries at once. It would stand well beyond his lifetime and yet because of its style and setting it pointed to the past and to things of long ago. It did not much suggest the present. People of the sixteenth century would know their way about without difficulty, finding only the kerosene lamp and the matches new to them. There were neither electric lights nor telephones to disturb the dead. The atmosphere of the house would sustain the souls of his ancestors, for he was addressing for them their lives' unanswered questions, carving out rough answers as best he could, even drawing them on the walls. A silent family, greater, stretching down the centuries, seemed to be peopling the house. Living there in his 'second personality', he saw life in the round, forever coming into being and passing on.[43]

Going home

So when working in these areas of power, with these moments which are part of the Collective, the individual will often tell of a sense of connection with the ancestors, for whom they may not otherwise have been concerned at all. Going through some important rite of passage, some initiation, some opening in consciousness, they frequently dream of returning to the ground of their being. Over and over they will make a return to their roots, going back to the old home although they may have been away for years and 'home' is some other place. One colleague told this story:

'I revisited the United States for the first time in years, having rejected it totally, even spurning anyone with an American accent. It was a very moving experience. I visited my old home, I visited the graveyard where my parents are buried, I visited the church that had been an extremely important and symbolic part of my life. And, standing in the church, suddenly for no reason at all I burst into tears. I went to the place where I had spent all my childhood summers, and there I met my sister again.

---

[43] C.G. Jung, 1963, Page 264 – 5.

Our summer place had been a very central and important part of my life. Almost every aspect of the roots of my childhood were touched. I was overwhelmed. I came away thinking, "This is good."

'Now a little bit more of me is in America. When the hot weather comes I listen for the crickets – and of course there aren't any in England. I mourn that. But still I can hear the song of the crickets in the song of the trees, the wind. I've caught that current of the depth of my own feeling, and found to my surprise that my roots are still there. A child has any number of ways of leaving home, and I came out into adulthood in a very dramatic and painful way. I left all that was secure and ritual and safe. But with this acceptance and discovery I've found a new identity, a new harmony. It will take time, but there's certainly something working: rediscovering, re-identifying, revisiting the roots in order to bring them in in a new way.'

We may or may not revisit the old ground in waking life. People do go back to the old school, the old country, back to the ground of their nature. But we frequently go back home in dreams. It comes up in Earth Mother motifs; we find ourselves returning to a spring of water, sensing a need to gather up what was left behind and bring it forward. It's a regathering, a gathering-in of lost parts of our nature, bringing them into the corpus of our own present. The word 're-membering' is very appropriate here: as well as the great inner rites of passage, minor initiations take place when we gather something back, and they round us out.

Archetypal levels

Jung knew how tremendously important is the context. He knew the ethnic tail that each person carries behind them. It's as if the individual is peeking up out of the ground of the Collective, carrying their roots behind them. He believed we had many layers sub-standing our psyche at any given moment. We begin with the Individual, the bit we see of the iceberg in everyday consciousness. Behind the Individual is the immediate Family, then the Tribe, then the Nation. He begins to connect them with each other where, behind the Nation, lies the Ethnic Group, then our Primitive Human Ancestors and behind that the Animal Ancestors. Going back further still, an unfathomable Central Energy underlies it all, the rhizome from which all have sprung. Jung never forgot that behind each individual, and behind the apparent consciousness of any nation, lies all of that. We can understand neither the individual nor the nation except that we explore these deeper possibilities.[44]

How can I amplify Jung? Well, following the elephant comes the small bucket and spade! Playing around with it, asking what happens if you take our dear old friends the Personal Masculine and the Personal Feminine, I made this map (Figure 16) to be read upwards.

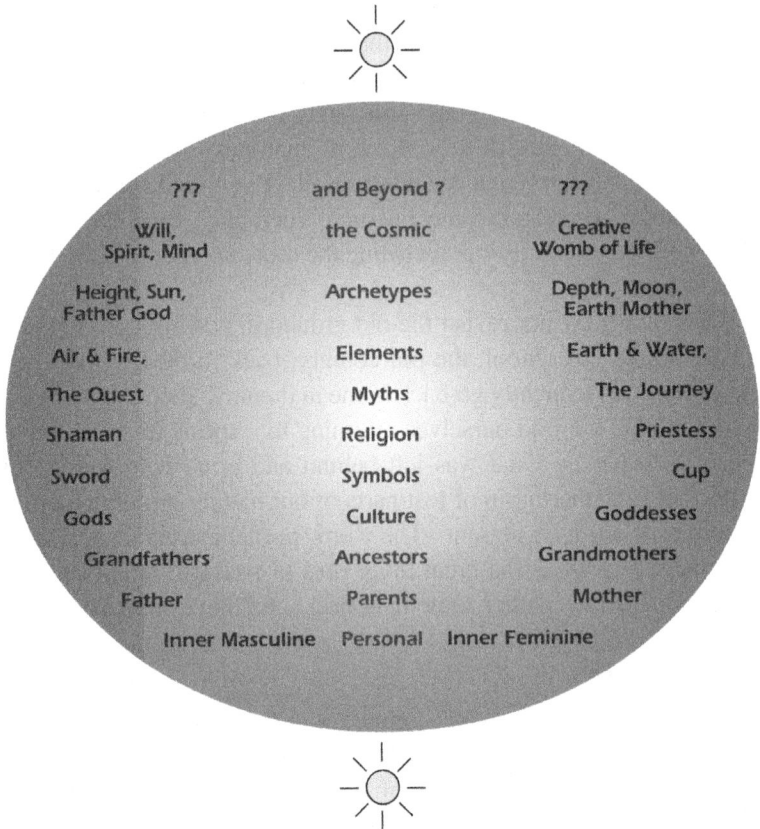

???	and Beyond ?	???
Will, Spirit, Mind	the Cosmic	Creative Womb of Life
Height, Sun, Father God	Archetypes	Depth, Moon, Earth Mother
Air & Fire,	Elements	Earth & Water,
The Quest	Myths	The Journey
Shaman	Religion	Priestess
Sword	Symbols	Cup
Gods	Culture	Goddesses
Grandfathers	Ancestors	Grandmothers
Father	Parents	Mother
Inner Masculine	Personal	Inner Feminine

Figure 16 Archetypal Levels

We start at the bottom, with the individual. Mapping up one side, we begin to explore the Personal Masculine, sweeping round and right the way back to the Father God and beyond. The Personal Feminine goes round in another sweep, from the Mother and Grandmothers right back to the archetype of the Earth Mother. My suggestion is that if we trace any

---

[44] See Jacobi, 1942, Page 34.

archetypal image in a person, eventually the Two will come together. It will lead to the One. Alternatively, we could start from the One, looking at an archetype and working the other way round. Then we'd see how the energy of that archetype comes down and emerges here as the individual whom we know.

Archetypes of the Masculine

In more detail: the map shows first the *personal* Inner Masculine within an individual, whether a man or a woman. Telling of masculine things, we begin with our own personal experience of it. Explore that, and we come to the *parent* level: what we have inherited from our personal father or his equivalent, the first meeting with Man in this lifetime.

The *ancestral* Fathers lie behind that, the ground of the Grandfathers and the uncles and the brothers. This is the widening masculine – teachers, policemen, judges; they too are out there for us as individuals, carrying the *mores*, the law and order of the culture we were born into. They become ours by our being born into a particular culture as a child of our own times. An uncle in India, for example, has a very different function from an uncle in Britain; in the Middle East, if the father dies, the uncles often have a taking-over function.

Behind them is the *cultural* father. Here are the great masculine energies: Jehovah, Shiva, Christ the Saviour, The Prophet, Sri Krishna, whatever in the culture are the forms of the gods. Somebody who's had Shiva as the masculine image of their God will feel differently from somebody who's had the Buddha in their background. Take a person whose God is the Jehovah of the Old Testament and one whose God is the Father of the Jesus of the New Testament; they are going to have two completely different and sometimes opposed views.

Next we discover the *mythical* masculine, or the image of the masculine for that individual. People telling their story are all affected by the legends of their people, their hero-myths, their folk stories and fairy-tales. Pointed objects – directional, purposive, phallic things – stand in many cultures for the masculine. Certain animals are shared all over the world – bulls and stags and lions. Over and over, a black stallion will stand for energy, libido, yet there will be a different *feeling* about the black stallion according to how he appears in the legends of the particular culture. We may think that we personally have nothing to do with all this; and yet deep in us, in our very souls, lie these backgrounds. We each of us carry this history within us, despite ourselves, telling our favourite fairy stories, tuning down through the sound of the words into the resonances of our far past.

Deep within us and behind all this lies the *religious* aspect of the masculine. Here are the mediators of the god: the Priest, the Shaman, Guru, Witch Doctor, Devil, Tempter, Trickster. While throughout most cultures these have the same function or quality of feeling, they differ for different individuals, conditioning and colouring our understanding of religion – never mind how it may have been immediately put over by our personal fathers. Tell our stories, and something of our background, of how we have been scripted, perhaps weighed down by the masculine side of religion, will come through.

The masculine *elements* of Air and Fire come next. They too are mediated through the exploring individual, who may come out with a stream of images. This is the level of the hero. The quality of the quest always has to do with the masculine principle. (Why are there so few feminine heroes? Well, while the masculine is the hero, the feminine is the journey itself, as we shall see.)

Behind this lies the *archetypal* level. Light, Day, Sun; these images of the masculine run through many cultures. They are conscious, active, right-handed. Here are the Creation myths, the Father Gods, of all peoples. And then, the Creative Phallus, the One who creates. We have finally returned to the One. And when we're looking at the masculine, all of this sub-stands the individual!

Archetypes of the Feminine

Working on the other side of the map, we start with our own *personal* Feminine. Behind that is the *parent*, our own mother or whoever was her replacement. Next we have our *ancestors*, the grandmothers, aunts and sisters, teachers and nurses; but also the ancestral figures of grandmother, aunt, sister and what they represent in the family, which would be very different for a Peruvian from, say, a Scot, and very different from the Scot would be a Chinese person.

Beyond this are the *culture's* images: the Madonna, Kali, the Earth Mother, Sophia, whatever the Goddess may be. What do these figures represent, culturally as well as individually and personally? These lie behind the *ancestral* mothers; here is the place of the roots, the very soil out of which the culture of that person has grown. Given a Japanese or a

Norse background, we will speak of the 'Ground of the Mothers'; the Tibetans have the 'Realm of the Mothers'; every culture has its equivalent- the Indians, the Malays, the Irish....

Next comes the *mythical* mother, the Mythical Feminine. The animals and plants, flowers and figures of the myths, helpful or negative, will be of a person's own terrain, but also of the internal landscape of their folk legends. Here are to be found container shapes: the cup, the vase, the flask, the basket, box, shell, chalice, breast, purse; which ones depend on the culture to which the myth, folklore, folk-history of the place have given rise. Here are the cat, the cow, tigress, rabbit, deer. They're bound to affect our current nature and psyche, even though we may not consciously have heard the stories. (Or perhaps we did hear the stories in childhood, and forgot. We drank the Water of Lethe and knew its amnesia.) Yet princess and queen, devouring sea-monster, witch and virago, fairy and nymph, spider and octopus, mermaid and siren – all are in our culture, and all the myths behind us emerge in what belongs to us, which we inherit by being children of our culture.

The *religious* ground of the feminine comes next, represented by the Priestess. How is the feminine within the religion? [45] Everything to do with the Feminine Mysteries still sub-stands the individual. It raises the unanswerable question, 'Does the Self choose to be born into a particular culture at a particular time, with a particular background?' Obviously this is something we each have to come to personally; I feel that it does – that there is an element of choice.

Elemental motifs of Earth and Water follow. From a very dry terrain, we'll have a different feeling about water from somebody who is surrounded by it, and yet it's still water. Here are the greater containing shapes: the whale and the womb, the cave and the mine and the labyrinth, the place of springs.

We saw that the male is the hero on the quest. The masculine is heroic in the sense that he's the one on the journey, questing towards light, day, sun, consciousness, that which is active and moving towards the future. But the feminine is the very journey itself. What is the nature of the journey of our people? Were they a wandering, nomadic, travelling

---

[45] Pope John XXIII in the twentieth century raised the Virgin Mary to divine status, declaring her to be assumed into Heaven. Jung said that the feminine element is added to the masculine Trinity by this dogma of the Assumption of Mary. It brings a terrestrial element into the spiritual, and thus 'sinful' man is brought to the Godhead. In doing this, however, the Church was still making an almost shadowless quaternity, with the devil remaining outside. This, he said, yet constitutes a major problem, even though the Divine wholeness has now had the masculine and feminine opposites smuggled in. C.G. Jung 1977, Para. 1552, 1607.

people always looking for a place to be; or a people with a stable ground, who perhaps set out over the seas to conquer other territories? Were they an island people or a landlocked people? It will be there in our story. What is the nature of our own journey?

The feminine is the road; she is the trees on the way, the rocks, the water we cross, the path beneath our feet. She is the forests we pass through, the valleys and hills, mountains and streams. The feminine is the dragon. She is also the traveller we meet on the road. And very often she is the goal of the quest. Journey's end is frequently a feminine object: the Golden Fleece, the Grail, the pearl of great price, the pot of gold.

So here is the conjunction of all our myths, legends and folklore. While the hero is on the quest, the feminine is the journey. Behind her lie the constellations and galaxies of space. The feminine is everything that draws us towards the dark night, the moon and stars, the left-handed, the unconscious, all that's receptive and can act as womb to the past. Here are the *archetypal* ocean, the depths, the caverns, the labyrinth, the underworld. And behind the Earth Mother with her lunar face, dark or light, will be the Creation, the creative Womb of Life itself.

As far back as we can go (though there may well be more beyond) lies the *cosmic* level, pre-verbal, as old as human beings. Some of the tribes who seem to us most primitive are still around, with their own refined and sophisticated culture. Their Creation Myths tell the story: the creative phallus penetrates the creative womb of life, and Earth rises up and disports her lovely self with the Divine Father through heaven. The sun comes down to the earth at evening and goes into the earth, penetrating it, rising up again in the East. And then, as a celebration, in their marvellous disports of joy the Gods roll right the way through heaven, presumably falling out of bed on the other side! And so the Earth is made. And the day which comes out of the night through light and joy is carried across the heavens till, tired out, they sleep, and go down through their dreams until, in the morning, they come up in love once more. Black Elk said that the work of his people was that they should forever celebrate the sun. Should his nation stop doing that, the very world would stop.[46]

So they come together, the Creative Phallus and the Creative Womb. The marriage of Masculine and Feminine takes place within the alembic, the container formed by the individual. Oneness is brought about, the person is remade. All creation myths take us back to the beginning, and

---

[46] 'Black Elk Speaks', Neihardt, 1932.

in the beginning was the One which divided into Two, male and female. Through the myths we are searching for their coming together again, once more to make a One. Whether we work from the archetypal One towards the individual, or from the One represented in the individual to the archetypal, either way we come back to a Oneness. The true woman, the true man of no rank knows how to combine the two spirals, the two principles. And that is enlightenment.

Story-making

Archetypal patterns are also about storytelling. They belong together. Say to someone, 'Tell me a story', and you'll hear them speak with a different voice. Their favourite story is for them magical, strange; it has the quality of myth. What they've made of that story has stayed with them throughout their lives. In telling it, they tell us what's missing in their nature, what is the healing balm to put to their wound. We can hear the counterpoint to that myth, the missing myth. For one, it's the Icarus story, or the tale of the flight of Phaethon, Apollo's son (both of whom fell from the sky),[47] that ring bells. Such stories tell of their need to come down to earth. For another, it's Pegasus the winged horse whose mother was Medusa and whose father Poseidon, Shaker of Earth, God of the Sea. Pegasus finished up yoked like a carthorse to the chariot of Zeus (however, to start in the realm of the God of the Sea and end by pulling the chariot of the King of the Gods must mean some growth in consciousness!). For me it's 'The Wind in the Willows'; the ground, the earth, the little creatures, the Mole popping out from his hole, the Badger.

Right from the beginning, story-tellers have mediated through myth, legend, folklore, fairy-tale, the great things which come out through individuals. Travelling from place to place they gave them form, shape, word, bringing these stories into the everyday awareness of people who couldn't read. The stories have travelled. They are hybrid; there's been a wonderful cross-fertilisation.

Each of us has our story. The telling of the story is therapeutic in its release of energy. Almost the key point of Freud's work is the 'anamnesis': to remember – to re-member – to put together again the

---

47 Icarus, son of Daedalus the craftman, disregarded his father's warning, took the waxed-together feather wings that had been made for him,and flew too close to the sun. The wax melted and Icarus fell into the sea and drowned. Phaethon, son of Apollo or Helios, extracted from *his* father a promise to allow him to drive the chariot of the sun for one day. Too young and too rash to handle the horses, he lost control and almost set fire to the earth, before Zeus finally struck him with a thunderbolt and brought him tumbling down. Ed.

body of our inner and outer journeys. And it's said that the task of the poet and the story-teller is to listen as well as to tell, to 'dwell in the ecstasy of attention to words'. This quality of re-membering, of listening, of paying attention to the spoken word, is at the very heart of therapy. Whatever story someone is telling (her-story, his-story), however small a story, it has for some reason stayed with them, caught their imagination. To listen to the way in which the story is told, to attend upon the teller, is tremendously important, for behind it will be a chorus of voices from way back. The *therapeutes* are such attenders.

Encounter with the archetypal

The psyche has us, we don't have the psyche. Some people are involved with archetypal material which, over and above the personal, smacks of the Collective. It may come up in a dream, a vision, or through the imagination, or it may emerge spontaneously as an irruption from the unconscious. It can be pretty frightening, so it's important to ground ourselves. We need help to learn to walk the borderland between inner and outer, unconscious and conscious, light and dark. All initiates walk that borderland. Nowadays a lot of people are undergoing their own initiation by the unconscious; the rites of passage are happening internally.

It's a dangerous area. It's very numinous and beautiful, but the danger is that we can get too easily caught into inflation rather than enlargement. Archetypal images carry a lot of power. When somebody starts talking about their sense of the energy of an archetype, there's an unmistakeable quality, a resonance about it. As, in a temple or under a vaulted ceiling, when you reach that clear point in the centre the sound comes back to you, so the room becomes powerful with what is being said, and begins to resonate, and you feel you're in the presence of something larger than just the two people there.

That can be both divine and malign; it is possible to be overtaken by an archetype! There's all the difference in the world between experiencing something of the *energies* of an archetype, and actually getting in touch with it – between saying, 'I feel that I now begin to understand what Christ must have gone through in Gethsemane,' and saying, 'I am Christ in Gethsemane!' To say, 'I have a very shrewd idea of the nature, the quality, of Mary Magdalene' is different from saying 'I *am* Mary Magdalene!' 'I am' means that the person has identified with the archetype, one of the signs that they may be in danger of an inundation from the unconscious which they can't hold.

A number of people are in touch with *something*. It may be a necessary opening, a rending of the veil between consciousness and the unconscious-as in the break up to break down to break through. A rigidity has developed like a veil around somebody's ego-consciousness, for some very positive reason to do with their own inner development. Now that veil is being allowed to grow thinner, even be ruptured, in order that they can go on to some larger development. In their ordinary daytime consciousness they may have a very strange feeling of being in two worlds at the same time, or they may sense a great presence, or see a vision.

If this happens to us, it helps to have a witness, someone who will do the extremely delicate work of sensing and feeling it with us, acting *as if* it were true, accepting how valid the experience is for us. Such a person needs to be able without fear to hold the tension of light-dark, good-evil. Far more important than anything they say is their quality of being able to face what may come. We need to map what that energy is doing in our lives, how far it has begun to take possession of our consciousness, perhaps overwhelm it. A numinous vision of something supra-conscious puts us for a while 'beside ourselves', outside ourselves, not ourselves. But there is a return. If we can be helped in the grounding and earthing process by someone who at least *looks* undisturbed by anything, our lives may become enlarged by the vision – the vision is going somewhere through us. We are channels for an energy which is 'about its Father's business' – or its mother's business for that matter!

If people seem to be having experiences larger than themselves, it needs to be treated with respect – and awe. Some of those labelled 'schizophrenic', perhaps even locked away in hospitals, may be among our most creative people, but their ego hasn't been strong enough to hold it. They might anchor it by writing or drawing. It's important for them to anchor their dreams as far as possible; to get the dream from inside themselves and put it out. Painting, sculpting, dancing, drama become exceedingly important when the energies which sub-stand the individual are beginning to come up to the surface of consciousness.

A marvellous image came to one young woman in a dream. She had been labelled 'schizophrenic', but I felt she had been breaking up to break *through*, not to break down. Suspecting she was on a journey, I asked her to anchor the image. It took the form of a Green Man. I told her a little about the Green Man, but also withheld a great deal because it was her Green Man and I wanted *her* to find out about it. She anchored it first by writing, then brought out a very powerful drawing, full of motifs of Earth and Water and of the Journey. She'd done a circle with a cross in it: 'That's the religion I've lost, but I'm bringing my own religion into being'. At first she'd spoken of her 'schizoid split' and of her struggle to hold that split together. Now she learned to use the word 'polarity' instead; this was the polarity within herself.

She came across a book on Demeter, and we talked about the Earth Mother. The breasts in her drawing she said stood for 'nourishment'. The dish she had drawn was herself being held, and also the nourishment she'd like to give over and beyond herself. 'I don't want to be always going back to my wretched mother!' She'd talked about the vagina, and the original womb, and the movement forward to a more creative womb. I took one of her words: 'What about the vagina?' She said, 'Sex', so I put the word 'sex' in the middle of a sheet of paper. 'Could you, very quickly, fill in all sorts of words that you relate to it.' I didn't allow her time to think it out – free association, but grounded. Writing is one of the ways of anchoring.

Round about that word she wrote very quickly: 'guilt, love, lust, meat, power, manipulation, frogs, umbrella, porn, pile of letters'. 'Frogs' we looked at. 'Seeing frogs copulating in the pond.' 'Guilt, love, lust, meat' – that was how she felt she'd been used sexually at one time. 'Power, manipulation' were fairly straightforward. With 'umbrella' I just raised an eyebrow at her, and she said, 'If you close an umbrella it's sort of phallic and if you open it up, it's like a breast.' 'Pile of letters?' I was thinking, deep in my darkest thoughts, 'French letters?' but, though it took a little while, no, she'd seen somebody in an office with 'one of those fingerstall things' going through a pile of letters, and she'd thought that was how babies were born! I might next have put any one of those words – 'guilt', 'meat', 'breast', 'Green Man' – getting her to anchor it instead of coming back to the imaging.

Looking at the Demeter figure she said she felt she should go out to work – a very good impulse for her. She asked me what sort of work I thought she ought to take; I said that she must really decide for herself, but perhaps it would have something to do with the dish and the nourishing? And I told her to make sure that she herself was nourished. She telephoned; she'd taken an office job, what did I think about it? I

said, 'You tell me what you think about it when you've done a bit of it.'
After ten days she'd done another drawing, which later she called
'Persephone'. (Persephone is the daughter of Demeter; she was taken into
the Underworld.) The drawing had something of a schizoid feeling about
it, to say the least. I saw from the fantastic talent beginning to emerge that
she might be splitting again. Was the new job pushing her back up into
her head? We worked a lot on grounding. She took up dancing; she got
some clay and produced her very first effort, which had in it all the motifs
of her Green Man.

It was a tremendous release of energy. The important thing was to
hold it down, to keep the thresholds there. She drew a crocodile. She
drew a wheel with compass-bearings, saying it had grown out of the
circle with the cross in it; she'd talked of her need for a compass-bearing.
She drew an owl-cum-falcon, with something of a baleful quality. I think
she was struggling between the chthonic – the Underworld – and the
Overworld.

She said, 'Any gift that I can give people from what I have learned
from within myself...' She didn't say, 'from what I've been helped to
do', she said, 'from within myself.' I found it completely gripping! She
would say, 'I've had a dream in which I am...' 'Might it be that you are
that, but not yet? That is the potential within you,' I would ask. 'First,
you need to come to terms with your mother.' 'But I've killed the
dragon!' she announced. 'I'm finished with mother now; I'm really on
my way!' However, that is not how we dispose of dragons; we need to
talk to them, understand them –'What do dragons mean to you?' I told her
a bit about dragons; she considered it, but all the time she was anchoring
her own meaning.

Working with archetypal images

I've heard of therapists doing awful things with images : 'Get an image
and kill it!' If 'it' comes as say an elephant, they tell the person to 'Shoot
that elephant!' It's a dreadful thing to do! 'Club it down!' they say. It
can be exactly like killing an aspect of oneself. If the elephant's charging,
more creative by far to side-step it, and then say, 'Hello, elephant!' *Talk*
with that energy which has personified itself as a charging elephant,
discover what it's about, why it's charging, where it's going. Then
become the charging elephant, get the feeling of what it's like to be a
charging elephant.

If someone says, 'I've got this thing coming at me, it terrifies me', then I say, 'Well, just what would happen if it *did* come at you?' My lack of fear and my own willingness to set up an environment in which such a thing can happen without too much fright will very often let a person confront their terrors. It's exactly like a child waking up still caught in the nightmare, and in comes Mum. If Mum accepts the nightmare but puts her arms around the child, then the images are usually brought down to size, whereas if she doesn't accept the nightmare, they're enlarged.

Later, this lovely girl stopped drawing and bought a kiln. She told me, 'I'd like to work with handicapped children: mentally handicapped.' I said, 'With all that work you've been doing – all the grounding and earthing – there are so many *physically* handicapped in the world!' And she said, 'Oh, I like that. I feel that's right. That would put me much more in line with my body.' She gave up the office for pottery. Eventually she took to working with physically-handicapped children. And she'd originally been labelled 'schizophrenic'!

However, others become inflated, full of hubris. They don't channel the energy but hold it, block it. Their ego, too small to expand under it, instead begins to crack; there's an inundation and an overwhelming and they are taken over by it. After a while, inevitably crying, 'The world does not understand me!' they come to think they are somebody divine. This is followed by a sense of dissociation and isolation.

Then there are those very gentle, frightened people who by nature have a rather fragile veil between conscious and unconscious, inner and outer. Such a person may come to believe that they are the anti-Christ or the Devil and will quite definitely pollute whoever they touch. Clinically they're said to 'have a psychosis'; but they may be opening up to something in a new way. Those supporting them need to handle it gently and lovingly, *as if* it were true, yet always earthing and grounding the person; asking 'What effect is it having in your life?', anchoring them back to *this* reality, which for them has become the 'other reality'. They need to anchor, to earth, to get a sense of grounding. Like a falcon flying, they need to be gathered back to the firm base of someone's wrist again.

Potential helpers often back off at this point. One psychoanalyst said, 'That is a load of bloody nonsense! Now let's get on with some living.' Well, I would say that it isn't a load of bloody nonsense. Whether a person can hold the power of the energy of this profound level of archetypal meaning or not, the fact remains that this level exists, or appears to exist. It's been existentially spoken about by generation after succeeding generation. The initiations we once had, the rituals, the religions, helped to contain these things; perhaps in earlier days we could have come into the body of Mother Church and said, 'I am Christ!' and perhaps the priest would have said, 'My son, we are all Christ,' and begun to enhance it out. Or we could have said, 'At last I am enlightened!' and the Zen master would have been able to say *something*.

But these days people have to try to handle it themselves with nowhere to go, no bigger containers to hold them. It's highly speculative, but perhaps a lot of our 'psychotics', 'neurotics', 'schizophrenics' are Geiger counters of a great change of consciousness running through the whole of humanity. And sometimes they can't hold it. Or perhaps they are containing it *for* us, until we can contain it collectively. But if these images come through, long, gentle handling is needed, possibly slow but certainly full of common sense, to help the person's own innate common sense (there's also an archetype of Common Sense!) It's very important for us to be working on ourselves, travelling our own journey, reading and knowing as much as we can, being open to the myths, legends and folklores of our cultures. Then we really can listen to the images, both other people's and our own.

We may be concerned because a lot of energy is coming from our images; it may be very powerful. Then there is always a sense of awe, of the *tremendum*, of something bigger than the ego. In normal healthy circumstances we are so contained within our ego, so sure of its boundaries, that to have those boundaries shaken can be absolutely terrifying – maybe we can't stop shaking all over. If we are so shaken, perhaps the vision we need will be held at bay and won't come to us? Then we need an object which can act for us as a talisman of power, something we can wear, perhaps, that will remind us; so that if at night we feel this something coming to us, be it benign or malign, we'll have a talisman which we can hold, giving us a sense of grounding and anchoring *here*.

One writer (fortunately able to use the written word to anchor his images) had been in hospital having ECT shock-treatments for several months before we met. I asked him whether he had some *thing* that he could hold on to. He brought a rock-crystal, and we put it between us. He sensed it was gathering strength from the work that he was doing on himself. For a period that rock-crystal kept the dark and the nightmares at bay. Eventually he didn't need it any longer; he'd keep it in his hip pocket. At last he forgot altogether to bring it. He took that as a very important landmark, and so did I. After a while it was just a memory. He has an internalised rock-crystal now, but it was extremely important then to have a real object he could hold on to.

It's not just fear – it's *awe*, it's reverence; different reactions to the same energies. It can be very helpful to put three cushions for Body, Mind and Feeling, but with a *fourth place*. Put a fourth cushion for this awesome force. Sit on the first and get the feeling of how 'the Body' feels about whatever it is that's coming towards you. Then move. What does 'the Mind' think about it? How do 'the Emotions' sense it? Sometimes they all feel different things; the Emotions may sense that a force is dark, while the Mind sees it as light. It's very revealing. Then sit on the fourth cushion and become this force, whatever it may be. It can be exceedingly powerful to switch in this way, flipping over, taking the fourth cushion and *being* the force that's coming out at you.

Some people have developed the practice of putting circles of light, perhaps with crosses in the middle, around themselves. Caution is required here. I think the mere fact that you feel you have to put up such a protection can make you more frightened. It's like starting to run on a dark road; once you've begun, you go on running like hell and everything out of hell comes after you. The greatest protection is the radiation from *inside* you, outwards to something. And it's tremendously positive to know there is something out there towards which you can radiate. Take one simple image of countryside – a meadow, a tree, a mountain, a valley, a stream – into the inner world of the psyche, and it can become archetypal in its potency.

A really powerful archetype can come up as ambiguous, ambivalent. What do we do when an archetypal energy seems both benign and malign? They do have this polarity. First, personify it if you can; get a shape and a form for it in your mind. Then you'll be able by amplification to find out that everything has its two faces. Nothing is complete except that it has its light and dark sides. Calling something beneficent or maleficent is really an ego-decision. You don't know it – you haven't yet mapped it – it is an *energy* that is being dealt with. Setting up a dialogue with it helps, or, even better, painting the two sides, exploring the two faces.

Is there good, is there evil within the universe? I have to hold a question-mark here. I haven't come up with a suitable answer for myself.

I work *as if* there were. In dealing with these big forces I quite often talk in energy terms. A lot of people who might be frightened of images understand energies quite well. I find that there are certain energies within the warp and woof of creation itself, some of which are moving towards life and others towards apparent death – some towards the light and others towards the dark. But in the round of things they come together, and the interplay of these energies is as necessary as in a tapestry, or in the warp and woof of woven cloth. Once again, we need if possible to have these realities accepted by someone else; it helps tremendously to have it recognised that we can handle only so much. If we're helped to gather it in, we can begin to handle the bit we *can* handle; then what seemed horrifying is brought down to manageable size and ceases to be so horrifying.

A truly big figure can easily appear as dark, and is certainly not to be tampered with. But it's rare indeed that we are dealing with an archetype, a god, the power of the One. If we had that full energy we'd go insane, and presumably the whole locality would be blasted out! More likely, it's whoever happens to be knocking around within our psyche. If we get a terrifying figure, it's probably not Kali the Destroyer Goddess, but our archetypal grandmother. The Christian is more likely to be confronted by his threatening uncle than by Jehovah. We play with the word 'archetype', and none of us knows what it means; I commend you to Jung who borrowed the term in the beginning.[48]   But if I were with somebody who felt they were in direct confrontation with a god, I'd put them under my arm and bolt out of the nearest window!

When an image has that deeper energy behind it, we are in the presence of something bigger and more powerful than the sum of the one or two people in the room. As we go down into the *sub*-standing stuff, something new comes in. It has a God-likeness – or a Devil-likeness – about it. If the other person calls it 'God' or 'Devil', I treat it as if it *were* God or Devil, since for them it is! And I'd hope we wouldn't have to go too far back to find out exactly what it was. Their primary need may be to link with Earth, so having the ground under their feet and the light around them is very valuable. A sword comes in handy; though they needn't necessarily do anything with it, they can stand against this force and feel they have a power.

---

[48]   See Jacobi 1942, which gives a very good breakdown of the nature of these archetypes. And Jung's lectures on 'Four Archetypes: Mother, Rebirth, Spirit and Trickster' (C.G. Jung 1938-54). Also 'Ego and Archetype' by Edward Edinger, 1972

It's important for them to say, 'Part of me may be childish; I am not childish. Part of me may be devilish; I am not the devil. Part of me may be godlike, though I am not God.' They can take an aspect, be it fearful or that which would fill them with pride and hubris, and give it a shape, a form, to contain the energy and help it to filter through into their lives in a creative, positive way. Then, no longer afraid of being overwhelmed or taken up by it, they can come to see it as only an aspect of life.

The inner sanctuary

There are times when an inner sanctuary is the only place to which people can go. Those in prison-camp have found in that archetypally nightmare horror, caught within a collective as children of their history, that many of them were able to survive only in such a sanctuary; perhaps a memory or hope which had become for them a place of recourse and a haven.

One colleague told me of a woman who had spent over twenty-five years in mental hospitals with very severe psychotic breakdowns. Labelled 'a manic depressive', the story went that it used to take five nurses to hold her down. But she had another side to her, wonderful to behold in someone who'd been to hell and back. There had been help there, and struggle, and always a searching to stand alone and on her own feet. She would often say, 'It's because I've been ill.' So after some months, because she'd also been showing many signs of inner strength, my colleague asked, 'Do you feel you want to talk about this time of illness at all? You never really have.

'She just sat there for what felt like fifteen minutes; it was probably a minute and a half or three minutes, but it seemed a long time. And she said, "It's so horrific!" And I said, "Well, there's no need – we can, little by little – or it's perhaps not important." And then she started to talk. She spoke about padded cells, and about being in one twenty-five years ago. "It was so horrific I can't begin to tell you," she said. "There it was, all the walls lined with padding, and on the floor a mattress – and a tin chamber pot that was dented and dented and dented – and I had a long woolly nightgown and that's all – and there I was, for day after day after day. And it was so horrific –"

'"You see," she said, "I didn't like to eat in the same room in which I peed. So I put the mattress on end so that I would have two rooms, and one day the mattress fell down, and I was so terrified."

'And I heard her say this and I said, "But you put the mattress on end!

Did you hear what you were saying, did you hear that cry within you for dignity?" And then she said, "And I went back again and again and again. And always they tried to put me back into that same padded cell. Once they realised padded cells weren't necessary, the padding was taken down and the door was open. But because they had no other bed-space they still wanted me to stay in that padded cell. I said I would only go in there if they put fresh flowers in it and a cross on the wall."

'And there she was, having another psychotic breakdown, back for perhaps the dozenth time. But that cry of help, that cry of the light out of the darkness, it was so beautiful that I'm still moved by it. But the light was coming out of what was for her an archetypal darkness. However negative the image, the memory, the experience, she walked out knowing that there in those blackest times was that light. And now she laughs a great deal. She wrote a tiny poem:

> "There was a need
> > but there has been a crisis
> > as everyone knows.
> I took stock,
> > I made some cuts;
> > I found I could run my business
> > single-handed."

'She's been on a journey,' said my colleague. 'Who was guiding whom?' It's of great value to have a skilful guide on such a journey, but the fact remains that the healing power was within herself from the start, fighting its way up to be revealed *through* it all.

Rites of passage

These have an *internal* form; they go on within the psyche. A 'neurosis' or a 'psychotic breakdown', seen as illness because no one knows how to handle them, can at the internal level be very, very similar to the mysteries and initiations undertaken consciously and by an act of choice by many people throughout the centuries. Once, the shaman or priest or hierophant was the holder of the therapeutic end of the process. Now, story-telling and listening are at the very heart of therapy and the word 'therapeutic' has a wider bearing.

The therapeutes

Originally it referred to initiations having to do with the Gods and with the Mother. The initiate was lowered into the ground and hung mid-air in a deep, deep hole for three days and three nights, there to face his own light and dark. After initiation he was drawn out of the incubation hole by *therapeutes*, or attendants. The *therapeutes* would sit the initiate on the lap of Mnemosyne, Memory, mother of the Muses.[49] There he was helped to remember – to re-member, to be gathered again in a new way. (This is 'anamnesis'.) They brought him back to life 'by asking of him all that he had seen and learned. Then when they have heard it they put him in charge of his friends... for he is still in the grip of fear and unaware of himself and those around him. But later on his wits will return to him unimpaired and in particular he will recover the power of laughter.' [50]

A Shaman in his training went *down*, fighting out the fears and tensions in his roots, finding and relating again to the ground of his being. Then for the first time he was allowed to be a child of the universe. Many people now claim to be children of the universe, but not until we've touched the ground of our true being does a redemption occur in the re-membering and the re-gathering, the re-centring of our nature. A redemptive stream passes back through the roots of our being. We find that our parents become people – we are people! Reading the history, working on these things, we begin to posit responses to the unanswered questions of our ancestors. So the most apparently un-mysterious of us touch mysteries and seed the line of the future.

Words of power

In telling their story, people begin to use certain words which are for them immensely powerful. We saw how different people react differently to the same words. Take the word 'power'. A psychologist might define it as 'directed libido'. Early Man would say, 'earth and sky are charged with the anger of the gods'. Someone in the Middle Ages might respond, 'She is a witch! You can see her power.' Different people, different idioms, all reacting to the same word. There's benign power: manna, charisma. There's negative power, ruthless, dominant, authoritarian, implacable. There's the authority of power, the power of authority. For Einstein, $E = MC^2$ meant 'the world is charged with God'. Those are his words, not mine; except that you asked Einstein himself about it, you couldn't know that that was how he saw that formula. The languages and

---

49 Mnesmosyne was a Titaness, one of the wives of Zeus. Larousse, 1979, Page 119, Ed.

50 See Pausanias, quoted by Nor Hall, 1980, Page 24 – 27.

the idioms change, but the archetypes remain the same.

Words of power carry something deeply individual to the person. You don't know who you're talking to until you discover what they mean by the words they use. We can see our own reactions to certain of these power words, these big words, these words which unite us. Write the word in the middle of a sheet of paper, and around it chart your connections, your free associations to it. Watch yourself pausing – it's fascinating! For instance, try the word 'man', putting every associated word you can think of. Do it rapidly; speed yourself up. Try 'woman'; see what comes out.

One person put the word 'God' in the centre and made rapid associations : 'blood, sky, wound, guilt, father, wool, tombstones, fear'. Another, still with the word 'God' in the centre, put 'rare, wise, earth, love, understanding, belonging, piglets, dove'. I couldn't resist the piglets; they were his first experience of what he understood as 'love', his key word for God, small piglets hanging on to mother's teats in the sty, giving him a sense that there was after all such a thing as mother-love, which his experience hadn't taught him. So piglets appear when one is talking of God, and God and love are connected. The theme is the richness of the language, the quality of listening. When people tell their story they're telling something infinitely greater than themselves.

So the *therapeutes* recorded what they heard. It's a very, very old skill. Paying attention to words was the primary task of those attendants, and with the re-membering came the regathering into a new kind of consciousness. At first the initiate was still out of his wits and frightened. But what takes my heart is the redemption of *laughter*. Though it may come along a bit later, it's amazing how it does come. Many today have been held in just such a hole in the darkness, and may only now be coming out of such an initiation. We must go gently and tenderly on this. Laughing, not hysterically but with joy, is the key to it all.

Plate 13

Sungate –Moongate

CHAPTER THIRTEEN

The Dreamer
Barbara Somers

*Last night I dreamed I was a butterfly. Am I a man who dreamt
I was a butterfly, or a butterfly dreaming that I'm a man?* [51]

What is a dream?

Dreams don't comment on life, life comments on dreams. For some,
Tibetans and Egyptians among them, this life is the dream and the after-
life the reality. The very Gods – archetypes, myths, legends, folklore,
stories – feed down to us in dreams. Nowadays, we feel that at night, or
whenever we let go and set on one side the supreme mastership of the ego
and our intellect, these other levels and aspects come to us. But from
earliest times it was felt to be the other way round. This 'ego consciousness' was seen as the dream, as death, and what we call 'death' or
'dreaming' was seen as life. When the Egyptians pictured the Underworld
(what we call Death) they tipped the whole thing over. Their friezes show
a figure walking upside down. They called it Life. Here are the dark
dreams, the nightmares; here are instincts, racial roots, the three kingdoms
of nature, the animals. Are we asleep or awake? Which is outer and which
inner – which life, which death?

It's only relatively recently that the language of dreams has dropped
away. With the Age of Enlightenment and then the Industrial Revolution,
with the movement away from Earth and nature, from so-called 'supersti-
tion', the 'if it's rational it's real' attitude became over-dominant. However,
our folklore and fairy stories and the gods in myth and legend have en-
capsulated the language of dreams and kept it alive. Now, when chaos
arises and rational formulas and panaceas are seen not to be working, many
people turn to it again. Everywhere the Hero's Journey is reinstated; myth
and legend and fairy tale, not to mention the soothsayer and astrologer
reading the entrails of the unconscious, are turned to as rationality fails.

Dreams are bridges

Not only from the unconscious to the conscious, from the inner world to

---

[51] See Chuang Tsu, who followed after Lao Tsu. Chuang Tsu, 1974.

the outer, but dreams bridge between past, present and future. The dream is always relevant to the present. It allows an overview, as from a mountain we can look down on to a road and see its beginning and its end and everything that happens midway. It comes in the dreamer's own idiom with something to say about our current, external living, rectifying an imbalance or presenting a viewpoint from the unconscious.

James's brother was, in his dream, a drunkard on a bench in the park. 'It's not really my brother,' he explained. 'Sure, he does drink, but not heavily.' He told me how much he admired this younger brother. Yet he'd grown up in his shadow; the brother's actions had been self-serving, to James's detriment. Now, the dream motifs were diminishing the brother, showing James needed to re-estimate, to value himself more. Afterwards, having first seen him as brother, James was led to look at this tramp tippling spirits on the bench as himself. Eventually he associated the dream with his own thirst – his thirst for Spirit.

Working with our dreams

The more we work with our dreams, the more they seem to come to us. We become conscious of a process going on the whole time. There appears to be not only co-operation but a sense of love in it; something that bends over backwards to help the process. Keeping a dream notebook helps us to open up our intuition and remember what's important. However, if something significant occurs and we rush to get to sleep so that we can dream about it, of course nothing happens. There's an almost thermostatic cut-out; at certain points dreams just stay away, go underground, lie dormant. They don't knock on the door at all, so that we have to anchor down in the outer world. They start up again the moment there's a need for rebalancing, in-breathing and out-breathing in their incredible rhythmic process. We can't bully the unconscious. We don't 'have an unconscious'. The unconscious has us.

Working with dreams, we need to bear in mind the age and stage of life of the dreamer. There is a consistent pattern, and it's important to know the nature of the thrust of someone's dreams. We can't treat a child like an adult, or somebody in their fifties or sixties as if they were thirty, thinking, 'Well, the imaging doesn't change.' It does, though a child may have an adult's dream, and an adult or adolescent may on occasion dream the dream of a child – or a dream of the child*like*; such dreams are always partly for the Collective, and are given to those with an innocent spirit.

So I ask, 'And how old are you in the dream?' I've hardly known a dreamer unable to tell me. They don't believe they know, then they say, 'seven and a half!' – 'thirteen and a quarter.' It's most exact! Talking about the present moment, the dream also triggers them back to that age. It may be looking forward too. If somebody of forty is, say, three and a half in the dream, I ask, 'What was happening when you were around that age?' or 'What was happening three and a half years ago?' I also ask, 'What's going to happen in three and a half years' time?' Here's the value of the dream notebook. Looking back to it three and a half years later, we frequently find something absolutely relevant. 'Didn't I have a dream nine months ago that mentioned nine months forward?' Yes, and it often ties in somehow, since past, present and future are all the same thing.

Childhood

The dreams of childhood tend to be remarkably straight, uncomplicated and accepting. Frances Wickes [52] tells how children before five haven't had much laid on them, nor much experience to draw on. They're not bent too far out of their *naïveté* by the educative process. The dreams of the child, as also the reported dreams of primitive peoples, use a straight language in which trees talk and the Earth shakes, water has something to say and the clouds in the sky are part of a *unus mundus*. Only by degrees does the child build in its little ego-centre, its everyday awareness, and lose touch with that closeness with the inner world. As they grow, this has to happen; the spontaneous wisdom of the child has to be overlaid with acquired knowledge.

Yet before this, children often have dreams of insight which directly link inner and outer, giving an absolutely straight rebalancing of whatever is out of true. I had a dream at about six, repeated three times. Half vision, half dream, it came to me in the daytime. It was of a great figure sleeping, huge, in a short toga. As I watched, the eyelids flickered and the beautiful figure threw up a hand, just coming out of sleep. I didn't know what it meant – I still don't know what it means – but even then I knew it was not just for me. It was wider than me. At the time, my mother and father were in high tension with each other and my inner and outer thoughts were in conflict too. The dream brought a quality of hope, although I didn't understand it.

In Indian culture there are marvellous paintings and sculptures of the

---

[52] Wickes, 1927.

great God Vishnu asleep on a cosmic barge shaped like a lotus, sleeping while he dreams the cosmic dream through countless aeons. When he begins to awaken out of his sleep, he dreams another dream; though the planets and Solar System remain, that is the end of that age and the beginning of the new. All this had had little impact on me until I saw the sculpture at the India exhibition in London in the 'eighties. Then I started to read. My brain and intellect had kept my child's picture of the dreaming Lord away. It began to come back when I saw this most tactile piece. For the first time I really connected with Vishnu. I still don't know the connection with my childhood dream – an Eastern dream that came to a girl in a Western land – but I expect to be working on it for the rest of my life.

How frequently people weep at the vision of clarity they once had, but lost! They weep with joy, discovering through the mediation of dreams that it hasn't left them. Dreams bring this reconnection, this re-membering, re-gathering of things once known in clarity but not yet earthed or anchored. Their life has been a journey to rediscover a potential, actualise a vision which was once clear. Very frequently people's work, their vocation, is a response to the call they heard very early on. The life they live is true to the early vision, and looking back they suddenly see it: 'The whole thing *did* follow that original vision of mine!'

A child will normally and healthily begin to have nightmares at about five, six or seven, when the dark and the light begin to confront each other. This has to be. The inside world to which they've been closely related is beginning to clash head-on with the increasing pressures of the outside. At school there's an impact with the natural growth going on within. Nightmares are very healthy, very normal. I would worry about children who *didn't* have nightmares at around that age (perhaps overprotected, still held at an earlier level; perhaps given too much responsibility too soon. The 'nightmares' of such children, instead of taking the dream form, may well show in the body in such things as nervous tics.) But a child who's been sleeping perfectly well suddenly wants a night-light, or won't go past that door in the passage. The imagination, rather than being internal, begins to wake up and externalise itself; there are pirates in the cupboard and dragons under the bed.

Some adults become terribly interested in dreams and then they make their children terribly interested too, getting them to note everything and draw everything and tell everything. It isn't healthy for the child. Listen, yes, but it's best not to work too much with a child on its dreams or put particular importance on them. To listen to a nightmare, draw it out, to sit by the child and hold it when it's disturbed by a dream – that's fine. We may invite a child to talk to a dream character: 'Maybe he wants to talk to you, or laugh with you?' We stay close while we're doing that, and our presence is very important, but then we anchor the child to outer life, let the dream go and let it work itself out in play. Much better the steady flow of interaction between unconscious and conscious. The child needs to be supported in frightening dreams, understood in non-frightening ones and, most of all, be anchored through play to the outside world.

Adolescence

Adolescents have to confront dragons to establish their own place in the world. They must establish ego-consciousness, pulling away from the subjective towards the control of the outer. Dreams, desires, wishes have very often to be let go of in the harsh reality of life. As yet more tension is set up, the threshold between inner and outer is again being strengthened and a strong door built in. Attitudes, training, education decide whether this is a threshold or a split. In some people inner and outer are split apart and don't come back together to the end of their days.

However, for most adolescents (if those who care for them can be aware of it) it need not become a split. It's not inner *or* outer; rather it can be inner *and* outer. Inner and outer knowing are tested against each other. Given an education system where head and heart were treated equally (as I guess education in the future needs to be), then the threshold need not become blocked. But for too many people it does, unless something spontaneously occurs which causes them to erupt out of it.

Adolescents dream a great deal, and so they should. Their dreams tend to be extremely rich in material, often having to do with growth and development, the need to break away from the nursery and the dominance of the childhood gods, to escape the parents and pursue their own heroic quest. There's a tremendous interaction between the collective images of myth, legend, folklore and fairytale, and the outer world in its more imaginative form.

One young woman used to dream she was moving house, but there was always a pressing need to go back and look at the old one. 'I was dissatisfied. There were odd belongings which I hadn't picked up, things left; the old house was empty, desolate. I knew I was moving out, but not where I was going to move to.' Three and a half years later she was still dreaming about renting flats and actually finding a place of her own. One dream was delightful: 'I went along with the agent to a marvellous house, sumptuous, Edwardian, a mad place full of plush and wrought iron and hanging plants, not at all the sort of Georgian primness that I thought I liked. This place was an absolute riot. I loved it.

'The owner, who was in bed when we arrived, got out in his pyjamas. He said I could have various bits and pieces which I loved – Baroque! A lovely Baroque bed. "It's only £10,000," he said. Then, the blow: "There's only one thing. There isn't a bathroom." I thought, "That's it!" I'd been so enthusiastic and now there's no bathroom! I set about trying to compensate, using a gutter-pipe. I have no feelings about that bathroom. What would a bathroom be?'

The bathroom is presumably a place of cleansing and purification, of contained water, to do with washing and clearance. 'What kind of bathroom would you like to have had?' I asked. 'We could have had a hip-bath. Getting rid of the water was the problem.' We looked for the emotional content – the mother – because of the bath shape, the contained water, the place of the emotions. 'You tried to accommodate by putting a gutter-pipe down. Perhaps you're seeking a place for your emotions within you? Are they still a bit hooked back?' We saw that now she was building up an outer environment which had infinitely more to do with her. Baroque it was, her kind of Baroque. It was funny, it really amused her, but still she hadn't quite got the bathroom!

Middle years

In the middle years, it's a totally different matter. Caught by now into the outer world, we are too externalised, inner and outer realities have split too far apart, and much encouragement is needed to work on our *inner* life. Dreams are the royal road here, the great bridge. Many people dream very important dreams around this time, though few will admit to remembering them. These middle years are high up in consciousness, furthest away from the deep unconscious. People are far too busy dealing with outer situations to worry about the inner life. This is when we need to become more and more conscious of the interaction between inner and outer, of our inner dialogues, inner figures, our dream-life. The whole thrust now is to reconnect the bridge.

Often in their middle years people feel they've reached the end of something. That which was is no longer sufficient. If they are to have somewhere to go, if they are to go forward into it, they will dream. They may find themselves in a no-man's-land of abandonment and desolation, amid desert places, barren ground, arid country. This is the burning-ground, the middle place, the desert. They dream of watchmen on doors, of railway porters, station masters, frontier officials, of meetings at cross-roads, of passings, borders, thresholds. This is the drying-out – or the inundation – of all that's known. A stripping process goes on (and in our kind of work we can only welcome it). If they're to cross a new threshold of understanding, they're stripped down, *hoodwinked* in every sense. To be hoodwinked means to be betrayed. They are betrayed both by having a blind, a hood, put on, and by that which had been and no longer is.

All this may come out in an unusual way. In 'The Tempest', Caliban, the Shadow figure of Prospero the magician, had to emerge on the island to show the nature of the totally other. And all the fairy voices of the island began to speak. An island very often appears in dreams and an awful lot of people don't go beyond it. It's much much safer to stay with the known, with the blocked threshold.

Dream motifs offer choices. The dreamer has pricked her finger on a needle and is going to fall into a deep sleep for a thousand years; or he's been banished into a hill, Rip Van Winkle-like, to vanish from sight. Parsifal goes for the first time into the Grail Castle; we don't see him again for a while and when he reappears he is inwardly changed. In myths and legends of every kind the hero makes the first approach to the threshold, and it challenges him. Is he going to go through it – or not? The majority of people don't and won't and can't, and maybe shouldn't. If anybody wishes (if we ourselves wish) to choose to stay asleep, that too has to be honoured. Don't waken the dreamer before she is ready to be awakened! She may be choosing a conscious death, setting her values by the outer world, choosing to die to the inside world. But usually, before she does that and goes into the sleep, a whole lot of dreams or psycho-somatic aspects, synchronous happenings, comments from people, will come to her to say, 'Stay awake, stay awake!'

But someone who lurches into our ken is concerned by the threshold; she is between two pulls, an inner and an outer, and her dreams will very often mediate the nature of the pull. She is just coming out of sleep, stirring in her sleep. This will often be heralded by nightmares, psychosomatic factors, people's comments, synchronicity – the same things! Part of the art of working with dreams is knowing that some people are breaking up to break down, while others are breaking up to break through. By the nature of the dreams, and the dreamer, we can tell whether she is opting to sleep or opting to wake up, and it's important to have the sensitivity and respect for the psyche which honours her choice. We develop an interior sensitivity, listening to what the dreams are saying. Do we need to stay with that person, accompanying her through her dream material, letting the dream carry both of us forward, or do we just quietly let her sleep? Sooner or later she's going to wake up. After a while, we learn to know the sleeper, the half-awakening, and the totally awake person.

Charles told me, 'I never dream!' He was troubled about his marriage; it was pretty poor, in his view. 'That's my responsibility,' he said. 'I'm a mediocre man! That's what my wife calls me.' She had aspirations. She came from what she considered a better background and felt herself to be more intelligent than he. Always pushing him, she made him feel even more mediocre. She would tell him he was impotent – and eventually he damned nearly was!

He had a number of dreams in which he was making love to a beautiful woman. However, just as he got to the key point of the copulation she would vanish from under him, and he would be left more or less in mid-air. Then came the day (hilarious fortunately for both of us) when he'd been making love again to this dream-woman, very beautiful and seductive. 'It was great!' In this particular dream the vision below him vanished as usual – but, to his horror, so did the bed and so did the floor. And there he was, caught in mid-action, hovering over his wife's dining-table, *in flagrante*. She was throwing a dinner party. She looked up at him over the glass in her hand: 'Oh Charles, you are a fool!'

I fell about with laughter; I just roared. Charles looked startled, then he started to laugh too. For the first time he recognised how his wife's view of him had pushed him and his sexuality right out to another level altogether. So startled was he that he began to remember his dreams more freely, and we took them forward in active imagination. He dreamt that he was running along behind a dark, cloaked figure on horseback, who had one face looking forward and another face looking back. He, Charles, was racing along behind this figure, together with a whole run of rats – a most horrible, frightening dream, especially since he was 'nearly phobic' about rats and horrified about running with them.

He asked me if the figure was Death; was he going to die? Re-envisaging it, he realised that the face looking forward was male and the face looking back, female. He said 'It's like running in a rat-race!' Acting out the dream, he became sorry for the rats. When he was four he'd had one as a pet, and it had been taken away and put down because it was 'dirty and horrid and made messes and my mother had had to clean up after it. My wife's like that too.' The pressure he felt she was putting on him kept him in the rat-race. Did he still feel the figure was Death? I asked. 'No, but it does have something to do with dying, with an important part of what might be the life in me beginning to die'.

In the next dream he was on a floor 'being thrashed and threshed with flails', feeling he was being shattered. Then a wind swept across the floor, and all the parts of him blew away. He was very struck by this dream: 'I just don't know what it means!' I asked, 'What could it mean?' He felt the pain of the flails and associated this with his wife's lashing tongue, but it wasn't just his wife now. This was the image of wife who was also mother and also God – every authority figure you could imagine. And the flail was the 'continuous beating out of his guts'. As he said, 'It's knocking the stuffing out of me.'

We re-lived it together. The very strong feeling of the wind blowing across for the winnowing concerned him a great deal. He didn't understand how parts of him could be lifted and blown into every quarter: North, South, East and West. 'But isn't there something in the Bible about corn on the threshing floor?' he said finally. 'Yes. It's unbelievable – that I could not only have the experience but remember the wind so strongly! And it's biblical!' [53] He'd been so extraverted, so suspicious of anything to do with the unconscious. He'd dragged himself into this so much against his will!

'Could you gather together the parts of yourself that have been scattered by the wind?' He visualised a potter's wheel, something centred, to which things could be gathered. He worked the wheel, shaping what he would like to become – the life that had been thrown away and distributed. And, imaging, he made a shape in the air in front of me. Though it was most unusual for him to image strongly, let alone to bring his hands in, I saw his hand creating the outline of some lovely shapely thing. Then he began to laugh. He laughed and he laughed and he laughed. He shook all over. Finally he came to himself. 'There I was with this beautiful thing coming up – I got it right up to a key point – a gorgeous female shape. And suddenly it dropped away and became just an ordinary pot – a beer mug! I'm tickled pink!' So once again the female figure had fallen away from under him; he was an ordinary beer mug. 'What's wrong with a beer mug?' I asked. 'There's nothing wrong with a

---

[53] See Daniel 2, 35. 'Then was the iron, the clay, the brass, the silver, and the gold, broken to pieces together, and became like the chaff of the summer threshing floors; and the wind carried them away, that no place was found for them: and the stone that smote the image became a great mountain, and filled the whole earth.' Ed.

beer mug. Here's what it is to be a beer mug!' Telling me, he was appreciating himself as he was. 'I *feel* a lot, I really care about earthy things, I like to drink beer, I don't want to do all the things my wife tells me.'

Now Charles became very much quieter and deeper. He began to be who he was. The wind had blown across his dream and a new spirit blew in him. He changed his job, he changed his life-style, he knew he would probably have to change his wife. 'From that moment forward I could never be the same person again.'

Such dreams mark inner initiations. Charles went through this when the wind blew across the winnowing floor; he could later say, 'The person I was then is different from the person I am now.' Joseph Henderson cites a number of dreams which were later proved to be distinct stages of an inner initiation.[54] For some, it's quite clear and marked and recognisable; the quality of the dream draws or leads the person. Others see it only later. We can but guess at the implications of such a dream for the individual. It has an inescapably compelling quality, it won't leave them, it has a resonance. Like a compass bearing, it gives a direction and their lives are changed. There's nothing we can do in the presence of dream as initiation, except honour it and not presume to analyse it. We realise that the dream has us; it will continue to dream through us. We get our dream-book, note it and date it, and are grateful.

One woman had a series of three dreams over several months. In each there was an old woman. In the first:

'There was a rabble outside my house and I was afraid they'd get in. I was trying to lock the door and keep them out. A woman who was very close to me came into the house; a mother – she'd got children. Then this old woman knocked on the door, and I had to open it to let her in. She said, "Have you got any dirty washing for me?" I closed the door, and her finger got stuck in the crack of it. That was one dream.'

'I met her again in the second, several months later. I was in the street this time and there were three women, including me. I was the mistress of a man out there somewhere and the woman I met in the street was a wife. The wife was about to shoot me, the mistress, when suddenly this old woman intervened. She took something out of her coat which I thought was a gun and it turned into an Easter egg.'

After a further few months came the third dream. 'I had been in the house and had gone out. The same old woman came right in to the utility room, where she performed a weird rite, taking off all her clothes and

---

54   Henderson, 1967.

painting her body. She was wanted by the police, too. I worked on that for a long time!'

Discussing the series, we agreed it might have been partly about the dreamer's attitude to authority (the old woman wanted by the police; the rabble outside; the theme of inside/outside; her asking for dirty washing, suggesting business to be done). But the old woman was presumably a laundress. The laundress is very much a figure of wisdom, the wise woman who comes around. She can also be a midwife who goes from place to place, or the person who lays out the dead. She's very familiar in fairy stories. The two aspects of the dreamer, the mistress and the wife, were probably in conflict with each other, and the old woman came in showing the possibility of a third, transcendent, function. The performance of a rite in the place of utility suggested valuation and initiation. The dreamer certainly felt she was important.

Maturity

As people grow towards maturity, so dreams may come to them far more strongly than ever before. Their quality seems to change, having less to do with the outside world and more with the interior life. Dreams like those of adolescence (when myth and story were confronting the outside world) often return in dreams of people around fifty-six to sixty-three, bringing out the idiom of folklore. We have to try to bring inner and outer together more consciously if we're to go on maturing. Otherwise we can begin to die psychologically. Stuck in an outer reality to the detriment of the inner, we don't build the bridge – or can't go over the bridge which has been built. One man dreamt of a big sailing ship, all wood and rope and canvas and brass, beautifully fitted out:

'I was the mate or first officer getting ready for a sea-journey, checking the crew, making sure everything was all right. And everything was perfect. Then the captain's wife gave birth to a sickly child. And I gave birth too! Holding on to the rail and squatting down, and helped by the crew, I gave birth to a beautiful, healthy baby. It was a landmark dream, or rather a sea-mark dream!'

His sea-mark dream was preparing for a sea-journey. He said it was to do with acknowledging the feminine aspect, and intuition. It was his own child, not one 'out there'. The captain's wife produced a sickly child, he produced a healthy one. He felt the captain stood for the old order. 'It was hopeless. The child wouldn't live. It may have been to do with the emerging Captain.'

We usually mature through this process, whether it comes in mythical and dream language, or just in the sheer bloodiness of life. Looking bruised and having white hair are, as Jung said, signs of maturity. Somebody walked into Abraham Lincoln's office for an interview. When he left, Lincoln remarked, 'I don't like the look of that man's face.' His secretary responded, 'Well, he can't help it!' And Lincoln said, 'Anyone over the age of forty can help the look on his face!' A wise man who spoke and got shot for it! We go in young and beautiful, we come out grey and battered. Enough people have gone through it to suggest that a lot more could come through. And they are coming through. They are wounded healers; bitten by the poisonous serpent of experience, they also carry the antidote.

Old age

And after maturity, the dreams of old age itself have a quality very similar to the dreams of childhood: out-of-time, out-of-space, having much to do with the collective. Here, dreams and experience often seem to be strangely dissociated from ourselves. This is a losing of ourselves in order to discover and come to ourselves. It's a late stage, a not-knowing of ourselves, and it may hold a great lovingness for the whole world. A beautiful example is offered by Jung. Clear as he was right into the last stages of his life, yet he said that, feeling uncertain about himself, yet there had grown up in him an ever greater feeling of kinship with all things.[55]

So people who are very conscious and in fairly advanced old age, having known themselves rather unusually well and explored the nature and meaning of their lives in an exceptional way, will often become less clear, less certain, less aware of who they are. Experiencing the extraordinary natural kinship that the child has with all things (with nature, with earth), the outer and the inner realities begin to merge together. It's a very lovely experience to talk with somebody like that at a deep level, and to explore their dream-life. By degrees they cease to dream a personal dream and become part of the collective, aware of the oneness in all things. I love the feeling of this emergence and gathering in again. The old man, to whom there's no hope of tomorrow, goes out to plant a tree.

---

[55] The very last paragraph of 'Memories, Dreams, Reflections'. C.G. Jung, 1963.

CHAPTER FOURTEEN

The Dream

Barbara Somers and Ian Gordon-Brown

*In dreams, as in stories as in life, we have
all that we need for the Journey*

Where do dreams come from?

Dream motifs emerge from certain rough areas which Freud called the 'subconscious' and Jung the 'personal unconscious'. If we take the Egg Map (Figure 1, p.10) we can begin to map them. Some dreams seem to be a mish-mash out of the Middle Unconscious, snippets of the day, soon forgotten. Then there are the rather more anxious, perhaps nightmare-toned, dreams out of the Lower Unconscious; they do hang around for a bit. And thirdly may come the resonant dreams which stay with us, sometimes for decades, perhaps for a whole lifetime. These may well be deeply Supra Conscious dreams.

I shall start with dreams from the Middle and Lower Unconscious. For example, we may be looking at our *rejected attitudes*, bits of ourselves that we need to have in consciousness. James, who dreamt of his drunken brother emerging as a tramp (see page 226), discovered it was also himself. We all have such neglected attitudes held well down. We would rather push them out of consciousness and not face them. Given half a chance they could burst into consciousness. If we dream of thieves, drop-outs, tramps, drunks, or of neglected animals, plants, children, objects, we can begin to recognise rejected, neglected aspects of our own selves.

One person recurrently dreamt she found 'the room I didn't know I had'. Dreams about finding another room in a house, perhaps locked, lead us to look for *undiscovered potentials* within the self. The dreamer may be minimising her own capacity because of past patterns: 'I'm the kind of person who never would, never could, never should, do that kind of thing', or, 'I know I'm not a practical sort of person'. We lock ourselves in by what may once have been valid but is so no longer. Finding extra rooms, we find extra dimensions, extra values. Given some quiet time, we can begin to build the dream room into our inner space, visiting it, exploring it, finding out exactly what it is saying to us.

I had a house in my childhood dreams, and I've come to it over and over again throughout the years. Consciously, I forget about it; yet in the dream I always say, 'Oh, *this* house again!' Each time, there's something different about it, something I hadn't noticed before. By degrees it has become a motif of the very first order for me, and I go to it whenever I need security. Originally, two men were there, parent figures. They took a very strange form for a child who didn't know anything of the East, for, seeing flagstones, I later realised I was on a Zen training floor. I saw the shape of it; I saw my feet wearing strange boots that as a child I knew nothing about. And these were the Sword Master and the Teaching Master! I couldn't possibly have read of such things at six, not in my environment. Perhaps we plug into the collective? Perhaps sometimes there is a place waiting for us that we need to explore.

Cut-off motifs will come up when parts of us are split apart – often our heart from our head. One woman did a marvellous drawing. 'It's me being extremely angry,' she said: a round, plump, furious duck, squawking out its needs for the very first time. 'Do you notice anything about its feet?' I asked. Most ducks are duck-footed – their feet turn in, but this duck's feet not only turned in, it had its right foot standing on its left! Work on this duck taught her a lot about the 'ought and should' parts of herself. She learnt that what she was expressing she was justified in expressing. The dream was moving her towards exploring the truly rejected, cut-off attitudes of her own nature.

Unlived life may lead to dreams of things dead, maimed, dying. Here we find not only neglected but crippled children, animals and plants. These figures are cut back, dwarfed, maimed, distorted, hunched; potential life-energy which wasn't lived out earlier, distorting the shape of the person, leaving parts of them untouched or causing them to over-emphasise and malform themselves. Here are dreams of impotence, of darkness and trapped places. The energy that is rightly required in consciousness hasn't been lived through, hasn't come up into the light, but has stood still, held back in the unconscious area. Loss of the use of eyes or mouth or feet or hands or tongue follows in the dream. Here is *thwarted growth*. Here too are lost values, lost valuables; dreams of losing handbags, purses, wallets, luggage, letters, which are the unlived bits of ourselves. Looking at what is locked up in these motifs, we can help bring the energy up into consciousness for a more rounded life.

Unresolved conflicts come out in dreams of attack and defence, perhaps of being forcibly immobilised or held down. Here are energetic thugs, attacking animals or people, rapists and burglars, break-ins and assaults. There's a lot of energy in dreams of unresolved conflicts; we're in the house battening down all the windows and doors while the tiger prowls outside. The dreamer is both the person struggling to bolt the doors and the tiger breaking through into the house of consciousness. The tiger is trying to bring in an energy. In such a conflict dream two aspects of ourselves are brought together in battle.

With this kind of dream I love to work with the various conflicting characters. When we *become* each of the two sides and allow them to come into conflict, we recognise that we are looking at two aspects of ourselves. The clash of opposites is within us. We can't put it 'out there', because the dream has shown that it's in here, inside us. Take the tiger; to reconstellate the mood of the dream I invite the dreamer to be the person inside the house, running around trying to keep this thing out. I ask, 'How does it feel to be this person? What do you imagine is coming at you, what are you trying to keep out?' The body-language will begin to make a drama of it. Then I flip it: 'Become the tiger. What is the tiger doing? How do you, *as tiger*, feel?' Very often the tiger turns out not to be at all fearsome – it may feel itself to be a very small cat. Or perhaps it's Tigger, trying to bounce its way into the house of consciousness to be accepted. There may be the contrast of its wild, untamed, probably very instinctual energy, and the domesticated energy; it may in fact be seeking for a way in, longing to be domesticated and recognised.

Real-life situations can themselves be like dreams. One Saturday night a friend caught a burglar half-in and half-out of a window of his house. Afterwards he did some imaging, working on the rage he felt at the intruder. Quite clearly, his image of the burglar did raise much anger in him. But, later, it was sadness rather than anger that came out. He saw that he himself was half-in and half-out in practically every situation in his life: he was not only the householder, but the burglar too. It was a beautiful, synchronous thing.

Synchronicity

Such things happen because we are dealing with one reality. We may say, 'I had a dream and, lo and behold, what do you think happened in my life?' Or we say, 'Something happened in life, and then I had this dream.' Things are one. They appear to be synchronous, but a synchronous happening is our recognition of the oneness, that all things do belong together. What is outside is also inside, what is inside is also outside – and at the same time. It's our consciousness that holds them apart. The nightmare quality of the conflict, the clash of opposites, nearly always follows because conscious and unconscious are at war. They need to come to-gether within the individual and to be seen as parts of the one reality.

Synchronicity can be seen everywhere. Jung was discussing with a woman her dream about a golden scarab at the exact moment when a scarab-like beetle flew in through the window. Laurens Van der Post, in his film on Jung, was just about to speak of the synchronous storm that occurred when Jung died – how lightning had come down and struck Jung's favourite tree – when, at the very moment when Van der Post was telling of this rare storm coming off Lake Zürich, a damn great thunder-crash happened. Viewers could see Van der Post quake! Gathering himself, he talked of how his hair stood on end at that moment.

Talk about synchronicity, and lo and behold, something synchronistic happens! A lecturer had just mentioned synchronous time when there was a tremendous crash at the back of the room. A very large, Big Ben-like clock had fallen off the wall at the precise moment he mentioned the words. And did the people jump! Again, a young scientist who specialised in analysing synchronous happenings was infamous for making gadgets go wrong. Things happened around him, objects fell apart; it was always known when he was coming back to the lab because the equipment would malfunction. On one occasion his colleagues organised a party in his honour, and they'd arranged for a chandelier to fall just as he entered the room. He came into the room. And the pulley stuck.

Dreams of death

When people have dreams that include motifs of death (dying trees, corpses, coffins, skeletons, skulls, tombstones) they quite often say, 'My God, am I going to die?' But rarely, hardly ever, does it have to do with the death of the person. It's the death of old attitudes, or the passing out of structures that need to go, with death as a transition, a going from one place to another. In dreaming, death itself is rarely presaged by things we would normally associate with dying, because the psyche doesn't see it like that. It's the other way round. A birth-channel may come in, a tunnel the dreamer goes through. It may have walls that show it's about birth. Birth can also mean death; death and rebirth are very close together.

'Nightmares'

People usually call a dream which gives them a frightened feeling a 'nightmare', and yet it may be just as potent a dream as one which gives them a sense of awe and bliss and rapture. It's we in our reaction who call it 'night-mare', the horse, the mare, of the night. Or not. These dark-faced aspects, when befriended, so frequently reveal their light face (just as the light very often reveals its dark side. The dark and the light are one and the same reality). The nightmarish quality is a Shadow side of ourselves, that which is being withheld from the light or is about to emerge into the light, seeking conscious recognition and acceptance. Within ourselves we often have two voices: the one being punished, and the punisher. Hence the victim-saviour, sadistic, masochistic stuff of nightmare. Yet at its heart lies the opportunity for redemption. The Transcendent Function emerges, needing, wishing, longing to be – perhaps already being – redeemed.

Transformative dreams

And so we come to dreams of transformation. Whatever the symptoms, however dark the nightmares from the repressed material of the Lower Unconscious, here lies the seeding of a new potential for the dreamer. Though dreams from this area may start out with a nightmarish quality (cut back, repressed, dwarfed, paralysing), yet it's from them that something new may emerge for the future, a transforming motif suddenly bobbing in, making it a transforming dream.

How do we recognize the motif of transformation? In retrospect it's very clear: certain key figures, images, lift the whole content of the dream. The series may be talking personally about the individual's need for rebalancing, for a movement away from lopsidedness. But the truly transformative motif will inevitably have to do with the Collective. It brings us into the region of myth, legend, folklore and story, lifting us towards a different area of dreaming, Transpersonal in that, while still very relevant to the individual, it is far beyond the realm of the strictly personal.

Look again at the man who dreamt of being flailed, the wind blowing across and the seed scattering (page 232-233). Winnowed by the great wind, he changed the whole shape of his life and followed a totally different line of his journey. Fundamentally earthy, he'd had the experience of something infinitely bigger. In the light of that moment, he stood at the centre, becoming who he was.

It takes an open heart and a fiery imagination to work with the emergent symbols of transformation. These may come from the top part of the Egg (Figure 1, p.10), the higher unconscious. Here are dreams of frog, ape, seabird, fire, eggs, seeds breaking, light from the darkness. Here the threefold begins to give way to the fourfold. Shapes change, a circle or a triangle moves out to become a square, perhaps a town square. Trees are flowering and fruitful; the child is newborn. Here are the rose, the lotus, the sun-wheel, the lapis, the diamond, the jewel. They don't always take obvious forms. One man was half-staggering, half-swimming along a sewer in his dream when he came to a diamond-shaped trap acting as a filter. Who would have thought it was a diamond? (I missed it altogether.) Only eighteen months later did we see it: a diamond was fixed in the dream turban of a male figure, who was talking about his intuition. We went back to the sewer, realising that the next stage had been predicted a year and a half earlier.

Green Man dreams

A transformative dream is one that you remember, marking a passage in your life. Many years ago I dreamt of being led down into the deep basement of the place where I was working at the time, by a woman who also worked there. There was a rectangular table, and just a bit of dim light which fell on to the most wonderful little figurine in jade, a monk with joined hands, a little Green Man. In the dream, I wanted, I desired, I lusted after this figure. I said to my companion, 'That is the most beautiful thing I have ever seen!' She said, 'You've broken it. See, you broke it!' I picked it up and looked at it: 'I can't see where it's broken.' 'It was standing on horseback,' she said. 'You broke off the rider on horseback.' I still couldn't find a break. 'It looks absolutely perfect to me,' I said. 'I would give everything I have in the world for this, it is so beautiful. If I broke it, then perhaps I can buy it?' She replied, 'It will cost you everything that you have.' 'What is the price?' 'Two hundred and thirty-one pounds.' In the dream I knew that that was just a bit too much. I woke up.

That first dream wouldn't leave me alone. About four months later, waiting in the queue at the post office to see how much I had in my account (at that time all I had in the world), I saw the colleague of my dream lining up in the other queue. I'd never once seen her in that post office, although we'd worked together for years. And, yes, although I'd been putting money in and taking it out, the account held – two hundred and thirty-one pounds.

This dream took years to explore. I read a lot about it. The rider on horseback, I found, was to do with the personality, the horse being the animal nature and the rider the one trying to get control of it. That was fairly explicit and clear enough. And the little figurine certainly caused me to explore the nature of the Green Man, indeed, to become quite an expert! But the two and the three and the one? Then, years later, another dream: feeling now that I might be able to buy the figure, I was heading for the steps outside my old work place, intending to see if the Green Man was still on the table in the basement. I whipped round the corner, and there he was – my Green Man, now fully human size, standing at the bottom of the steps. He said to me, 'Why do you look for me inside, when I'm out on the street?'

I'm still working on it. It won't leave me. It comes up over and over again. How like myths these transforming dreams are! In dreams, as in stories as in life, we have all that we need for the journey. We face the shadow, the side of ourselves that we don't wish to admit, and we pass it. This is where we find the Keeper of the Threshold. Then there is that flash of the quest, the vision.

The ally

Next the Friend, usually of the same sex, appears; just a friend, sometimes there and sometimes not, bobbing up in different forms with that befriending quality. Of course, in time the friend proves to be – ourselves; but in the beginning it feels as if there's someone different out there. Such doubling figures (like David and Jonathan) come into various stories: a pair of twins, two daughters, two sons. One is often dark and the other light. As the threshold becomes more permeable, conscious and unconscious factors turn up side by side, sometimes with flash images or an occasional sense of dissociation.

If somebody has a lot of this doubling, or if big, resonant dreams come too often, then I watch in case the interface is becoming too permeable too fast. The art is then to work with the person to help them stabilise and anchor. But usually the slow progression of dreams, together with the doubling, suggests that the two worlds are coming together.[56] One woman dreamt: 'I was down below, underground. It was full of light, total light,

---

56 There's a German word, *Doppelgänger*, which means that you see your own double. German folklore says this occurs when you are so ill or feverish or sick that you're almost dying. This is not quite the same thing as this doubling, where the two images are not ourselves. Maybe the Keeper of the Threshold is the *Doppelgänger* too, for life or death?

no shadow; and yet it wasn't a true light. No doors or windows, no way out of that tunnel. There were two stick-figures, totally the same, exact doubles. They were obviously guarding some sort of guardians.' Stick-figures, having no shadow, perhaps indicate a need to incorporate the shadow, to fill out figures yet unseen. And wherever you get the Guardian you know there is a Threshold.

The beloved other

A figure of the opposite sex may have come to us and been glimpsed in our dreams. Strangely enough, in the Underworld the beloved can often come with a dark face. It is that which has to *become* the beloved, not that which is lovable in itself. Part of the work in the Underworld is to embrace that which we had not thought to be embracing. It's easy enough to embrace the *beautiful* beloved, but this is to discover the nature of love in very much detail.

Little Saint

I'm particularly fond of this story, of a little man who was thought by so many people to be a saint that even the Devil heard about him; his saint-like qualities were being booted abroad a bit too loudly. So the Devil, the illustrious Fallen Lord, got himself arrayed and went and visited the Little Saint. He said, 'I'm hearing a bit too much about you! You watch it!' The little man said, 'Sorry, can't hear you, I'm a bit deaf.' The Devil thought, 'Can't hear me? I'll give him something to hear!' So he whistled up his demonic angels – the Great Lord in full panoply, with all his host ranged behind him. 'Come now, behave yourself? I'm not going to have you messing up my business like this!' And Little Saint said again, 'What? – can't hear – bit deaf.' So the Devil bent down to shout the louder. And Little Saint kissed him on the mouth. And the Devil went sadly back to hell.

This beautiful story comes up in different forms among many peoples. The word 'sadly' is the key. The devil went sadly back to hell, perhaps (and this is me, projecting on to the devil, which is dangerous stuff!), but I suspect, maybe with just a little touch of the love that had seemed to be lost.

Big dreams

Even the most ordinary, commonplace dream may seem to have a number of levels. However, some dreams have the quality of more than a dream, as though they not only had form and substance in the outer world, but also an import from the inner. Such a 'big dream' feels more like a vision than a dream. It has great significance, as though sent purposefully with a deep message. It seems to refer to our whole life, our progress, our goals, but with a quality over and above just what has to do with the individual. It comments not only on the present, but on the past and also on the future, linking them, raising the quality of the dream to something beyond time and space.[57] These are dreams which seem to take the dreamer into a different dimension with a different resonance. The dream hangs around and won't go away. It's dramatic; it's as if we go through a different door. Such a 'big dream' may change with its resonance our direction or orientation or focus.

Do our dreams tell the future?

Is the 'big dream' with its special resonance saying something about the future which, in terms of horizontal living, hasn't yet happened? We can't be sure till afterwards. Never know better and never know first, as Jung said, and it applies particularly in this area. We cannot know if some people are not penetrating the future in their dreams. May they even have dreamed far, far beyond them, with much more relevance to their race, their era, their species than to their own personal lives? While only hindsight shows whether a dream was predictive, there certainly can be a predictive quality. In 1913 Jung dreamt of a fair-haired youth, drowned, in a jet of blood;[58] at the time it didn't seem there was going to be a world war, but there was. However, though the dream may be predictive, I work with it as if it were making a statement about current living – because it also is.

Certain dreams are unknowable; we come to the point where there is nothing to be said. We can only wait to find out what the dream is saying. As we've seen, from the beginning big dreams have been dreamt for the collective. We read how from time immemorial it's been in the nature and the training of priests and witch-doctors and shamans that they should explore dreams, penetrating the unconscious. We read that they suffer a lot of ill health, frequently what in the West would be called a neurosis or a psychosis. Jung himself, a modern-day shaman, is a recent example. He tells how, after his break with Freud, he began to explore the nature of his own unconscious, taking himself down by degrees into it, holding

---

[57] It's been said that the division of the time into past, present and future is but a human concept for our convenience. In the dream-world they're the same thing; they can't be divided out. In the language of dreams, everything is in the eternal Now.

[58] C.G.Jung, 1963, Page 203-4.

dialogue with his own dream contents.[59]   Beginning to feel that he was losing touch with outer life, it was only his recall of the fact that he was Dr. Carl Jung, with a wife and family, regular meal-times and a known address, that allowed him somehow to make a bridge between the outer and the inner realities. That's exactly what we read of the training of the shaman who is to become a 'seer', a carrier of the collective dream of the people, and to penetrate the nature of the tribe. There is a very, very fine threshold between outer and inner, and the barrier between conscious and unconscious can be extremely thin.

'Psychics', those who work from the gut or the solar plexus level, are rather different. In them, past, present and future seem to be close together and to have no normal divisions. While they live near to the unconscious, they are also very open to people around them and to the collective environment. And such people are notoriously inundated by their sensitivity. They often don't have control of it. The difference between the training of witch-doctor, priest and shaman on the one hand, and the 'sensitive' on the other, is that the former try to be in control of the exploration into the unconscious. Their sensitivity comes more from the third eye than from the gut level.

Someone with a great many dreams with archetypal symbolism – inundations, floods, volcanoes, wars, avalanches – may perhaps be on the fringe of a neurosis or a psychosis. These are very often pre-signalled by continuous dreams with archetypal matter in them. Anyone dreaming one archetypal dream after another needs to be cautious of what they are handling; they need to anchor it and steady it, working with each dream as it comes up.

However, there are naturally sensitive people who may be dreaming beyond themselves; natural modern shamans, they have archetypal dreams. Nobody knows for sure which is what; anybody who pretends they do is making assumptions not based in fact. We know very little about dreams, and most of that we are re-learning from the Egyptians and Greeks and Indians and Tibetans, who have a far more sophisticated and fundamental knowledge of dreams than we have yet developed. But someone being trained to dream dreams will have a particular quality which allows them to be a carrier of the collective.

How can such a person be strengthened to receive that amount of input from the unconscious? If they have enough support to allow them

---

[59]   Ibid., Page 214.

to open to their own unconscious, they will gain the strength to carry the dream. The dream comes to the one who can carry it. As certain forms of genius are found in those able to carry the extra charge of energy, so also with these archetypal dreams. Reasonably well hung together, they may have problems, but they aren't on the fringe of a psychosis. Support such a person, and they will begin to dream their own dreams. Then comes that threshold point at which time and the timeless, past and future intersect each other. Here we find creative artists, musicians, writers; if they have anything worthwhile in them, they will walk the threshold finding a creativity which they might otherwise never have had the courage to explore.

And every therapeutic person worth his salt walks the threshold too. Those whose life-training turns them into such people very often have to experience life and death, sometimes quite literally. They become therapeutic in the process of themselves holding inner and outer together. They walk the threshold, and there's something about the walking that raises energy. It's so easy to fall either side of the razor. Someone who might fall may, encouraged by a walker of the threshold, turn it into a breakthrough.

Rites of transition

When we're taken down into the place of the Devil, it's often in the quest of a different, deeper kind of loving. And, as part of the loving process brought us by life, we are stripped down. These are the Rites of Transition. We have to learn the nature of sacrifice. There's 'sacrifice' meaning to give up, to render up; we're stripped of illusion, stripped of strength, stripped of what we lived by, stripped down and oiled as the Greek runners were, to run free. And only in the transition stages do we become aware that there are two different meanings to the word: sacrifice as *giving up* has turned into sacrifice to be *made sacred*. It is a holy rite, even though it appears to be unholy; we're rendered down and then re-rendered, to be turned into something sacred.

After the giving-up process, we realise that in the sacrifice of being rendered up – or rendered down – we have to grow in order to make it sacred. Jung gives a lovely little snippet from a woman's dream, showing the need to grow.[60] She dreamt she came to a black wall and walked over to a tree growing near it. The tree gathered her up in its branches and lifted her over the wall. Jung went on to comment that she literally had to grow over the obstacle, and did it by taking the attitude and position of

---

60 See C.G. Jung, 1930-34, Vol.1, Page 109-110.

the tree. In order to get anywhere, she *had* to grow, standing still and waiting till she had become tall enough to reach over the top. There was no other way. 'You see', goes on Jung (I love this! You can almost hear Jung saying it – 'You see – simply this') You see, the unconscious always tends to create an impossible situation. As long as we haven't met such a problem – as long as we can promise ourselves some solution – we have surely not met the right situation, but a merely preparatory one. We need an impossible problem, where we have to renounce our own wit. All we can do is trust to the impersonal power of growth and development as we wait. The dream offers us a wall and tells us we can't get over it except by growing like a tree. Thus the major problems of life cannot be solved at their own level, they can only be grown beyond.

That seems to be what these transforming dreams are about. The threshold between inner and outer becomes permeable, and we are rendered down in the flask of our own nature. I know that when we're in these rites of transition – learning to grow through love, by love, to love – very many dreams come of abandonment and desolation, desert places and no man's land and middle ground. We saw this in the dreams of people in their middle years. We are neither in touch with where we came from, nor yet with where we're going, and there's an increasing battle, a confrontation. It feels like a struggle with the Devil, but it's ourselves we fight.

Such dreams often have a questioning quality: 'Is this person going to make it, or not?' This seems to be decided by the dreamer's attitude to the impossible problem. It's not the solution of the problem, it's the attitude to the burning-ground that guarantees that we are going to come through. Even quite a way in to these rites of transition the option is open. There seems to be a choice; the threshold may become permeable and allow us back, never to venture that way again. I've seen a number of people pull back from that point, close down, narrow. They're safe, they're in the outer world. But they start to die psychologically. Others stay on the burning-ground. Maybe they go a little mad for a bit, until they can be helped to realise that, just conceivably, they may be going sane. There are yet others who, in the right way, just stand and wait; they're already off the burning-field, though perhaps they don't realise it. The dreams reflect all this. Harry's dream is typical of the burning-ground. The dreamer went back for a pair of shoes:

'I'm with an old girlfriend and a male friend as well (both the Friend and the Other, *animus* and *anima*, as he said). We're going along a well-worn path through an open space, carrying our tents and equipment with us, looking for a place to camp. The more-travelled path ends, and we take off our shoes and go on into wilder country. I'm very excited about this; I want to keep going, but it's getting late. The other two agree it's too dark and that we should go back. I also think, "Yes that's right. Anyway we have to get our shoes."

'So we go back. I remember that these are shoes I wore as an adolescent. But on the way back I turn into a child of six or seven. The other people go and I make a friend of a number of boys, including a little black boy. I get excited by my friendship with this black boy. He's a bit wild and exotic. I'm extremely happy about my new friend; he's so different from me that I leave him and run to tell my mother. And I see my mother looking as if she didn't like it! As I'm running towards her I impale myself on a piece of iron that's sticking out of some rock. It goes right through to the heart. And I die.

'But then the dream continues and I find myself in an old walled city, an ancient town. I'm with a minstrel-philosopher who says, "Welcome!" There's a festival going on in the town. "Now we're all going to the festival," he says. He starts to tell me things: "Remember the number four – remember apples." I was happy. And I woke up.'

That was a brilliantly transformative dream! It had the lot, and penetration of the heart too. It suggested that the dreamer was on a journey. The dream stayed with him, taking a number of forms. 'It's the connection with the mother,' he said, 'and it's the breaking of something. Also, the philosopher; I feel there's some invitation to merge into him.' He went on, 'I took the number four as Jung's four functions.' Four is also, of course, one of the cardinal numbers of wholeness; when the four begins to replace the three, we have a number of potential, a mandala of completeness. He needed to go back to gather up elements, and he had to be penetrated by the breaking of something. Then there was the 'exotic' boy; an exotic figure is very often an unconscious one. He said that the impaling seemed to be done by the mother; she turned into a figure who penetrated him with his own penis, a challenge to his manhood. If he left it in her hand, he would sooner or later be impaled upon her. He needed to take it back into his own hand and slay the mother-image. A lovely dream.

Nowadays, without those early priests and shamans, mediators and initiators, the dream has even more of a function: it is mediating for us. Over the years I've met many different people, of many different ages and cultures, who wouldn't for one instant think they were on any kind of journey. Quests mean nothing to these dreamers. They can't deal with them, they throw them out. But the dreams won't be thrown. People admit with embarrassment, 'Oh yes, well, I suppose I did have a dream...' We may think, 'Well, I certainly haven't gone through any thresholds!' But maybe we have; we realise when we start to talk about it. The Self initiates us one by one. And that process goes on all the time.

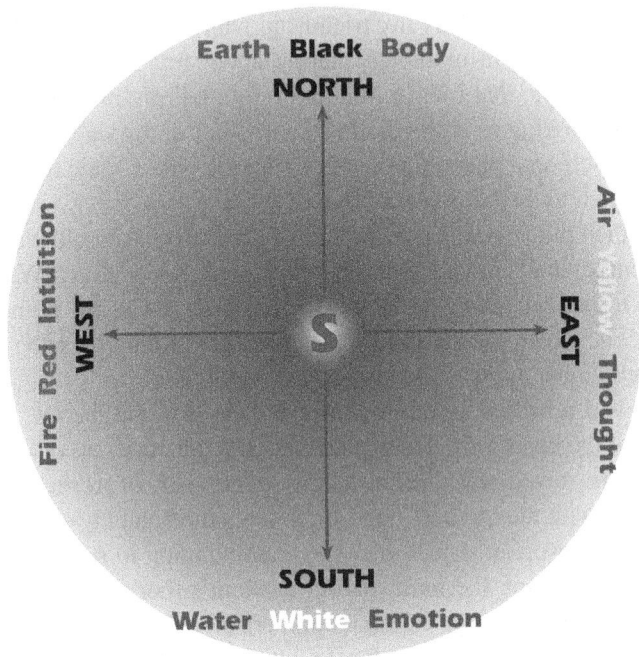

Figure 17 The Journey of Singing Stone

Singing Stone

There's a lovely story out of America about the initiation process. Once there was a young brave among the Sioux Indians, and his name was Singing Stone. This young warrior went to the Council of Elders and said, 'I've heard that somewhere there is a Singing Stone, and I'm determined to find it.' They said, 'Well then, you must travel to the North.'

He took his horse and travelled for months northward; he had lots of adventures and finally came to far and frozen lands, rocky and barren, full of black caves, earthy rough places, ice and snow. Here he had more adventures, some of them painful. Finally, fed up with the North, he sought out the only wise man of that place to see if he could help him find the Singing Stone. But he told him only that this was not the place. 'You must search to the East,' he said.

Despite the fact that he was remembering with nostalgia his home and his own people, he continued his journey in a wide sweep towards the rising sun. After many adventures and some years had passed, he reached the Mountains of the Morning, full of wide spaces and windswept hills. Here at last in this beautiful land must be the Singing Stone! Then his horse died. Deeply disappointed, he buried it among the people of the East where it had ended its days, thinking with longing of completing his journey and returning home to his own people. Sadly he sought the wise men of the Eastern tribes. 'You must go South,' they told him. 'That is where you will find the Singing Stone!'

By now the young brave was not so young. He was growing tired. Summoning his strength, he set out southwards alone and on foot to fulfil his quest. He had to ford many huge rivers in spate, cross or skirt great lakes. And when finally, after narrowly avoiding drowning, he reached the South, the Singing Stone was not there. 'Oh no, it's in the West!' he was told.

The journey to the West was hardest of all. Long and weary was this lonely push into the heat of the desert sun. He travelled mainly by night, sometimes accompanied by fellow travellers, mostly all alone. Heat and thirst befuddled his brain, he longed for the cool lands of home, he longed for his own people, he longed just to stop. But the Singing Stone compelled him, and he struggled on. Many a time he thought that he would die before he reached the lands of the Western tribes. And they too told him that the Singing Stone was not to be found here. He had reached the four quarters of the earth seeking the Singing Stone, and it didn't exist! Exhausted and in despair he turned back at last towards to his own home.

But what was this? His own tribe were waiting for him – his own people expected him! The children came out from the settlement to greet him. They knew him, although he was old. Calling to him from far off with welcome in their voices, they took him by the hands, they led him into his own place and let him be refreshed and rested. Then they made a great feast for him. And at the feast, the Elders in full panoply brought him to the centre and there they called him by his name. 'Singing Stone. We welcome you home from your search,' they said. 'Faithfully you have followed the call to find your true name, your sacred treasure. Know now, that you are your own Quest; you *are* Singing Stone.'

This is a story found in all tribes and peoples. One does not discover the goal, one becomes the goal. I've met a few Singing Stones. Very rarely do they know that's what they are. They may think they are a stone – but it's the others who hear the singing. There aren't many of them around; I'm lucky to have met one or two. This is what the individuation process is about: the mastery of matter, and the releasing of the spirit that lies within the matter. And they come to a liberation into choice, which is inevitably a liberation into responsibility. As we've seen, Jung said that the greatest freedom is to do willingly that which we must.

So finally we come off the burning ground. And the dreams and the actuality of our nature begin to re-member, gathering us back. Once, there were externalised rites of passage which helped people go through these stages of experience – growth in consciousness and penetration in depth. Such rites of incorporation would have been mediated to the individual by (according to the culture) the shaman, priest, witch doctor, hierophant. These made it possible for people to make a deeper penetration in consciousness to the god, and also to come through and be re-incorporated into their outer lives.

The Rainmaker

Like stories, our dreams often give us just a little touch: the simple person we ignored somewhere, the unnoticed word that may mean something so much bigger, the little overlooked bit that was there somewhere in us all the time. The story of the Rainmaker tells what happens when one comes out through this process. It has something to do with *being* Singing Stone, being the quest and the goal that one thought one was in search of. Jung said of this story, 'Tell it as often as you can.' So here it is.

The place (which place doesn't matter; it's anybody's psyche) was in disarray because there had been such drought for so long, and still no rain had fallen. And so the people of that place went everywhere, calling in the wise people and using their prayers and their chants and their fetishes and their talismans to try to bring rain. But nothing happened.

At last someone said, 'Well of course, there is that old rainmaker we've heard about. Don't know what he'll charge, but we could try him?' 'Yes, better bring him in.' So they laid out a feast to welcome him, and in bowled this small character, not at all what they expected. 'Probably isn't worth his price, either!' they grumbled, disappointed. 'Well, what is it you need?' The Rainmaker sniffed the scenery and said 'Nothing, nothing much, thank you. Just a small hut. Come back in three days.' So they put him in a small hut and waited three days' and so came the rain. And it rained and it rained and it rained, and great was the rejoicing at it.

Then they went to the Rainmaker and said, 'What did you do? What was this great magic?' The Rainmaker said, 'I didn't do anything. I didn't like what I found when I got here. So I went into the hut and came quietly to myself; I got myself in line, and of course it rained.' [61]

I've sat in the presence of dreamers and heard them tell this same story. 'You don't do anything. There's nothing to be done. You just get yourself in order and the whole climate changes. You come to the place where you find and remember yourself, and then things move.' People change, miracles occur, deserts begin to flower. And yet the rainmakers didn't know they were doing it (and maybe if they had they couldn't have done it).

Very often people nearly have to die to have this experience. I'm lucky – I nearly died twice, and managed to get back again. I clinically 'died' being taken to hospital in an ambulance, and I had the most extraordinary experience within it – a lifting-out-of-the-body feeling. I could hear a beating sound which I learned later was the heart system that they put on me, and I was in agony through my back, lying on this lung thing. And I clearly heard a man's voice say, 'Christ, she's gone!' Suddenly it all went away, and there was a sense of coming right out of my body – a lovely feeling! Partial consciousness remained which displaced me out of the body; I still heard people's voices and things going on. However, there was a consciousness of being in an inexorable 'pull'. And then the 'inexorable pull' got me and – as far as I'm concerned – I went. All possible fear of death has left me and has never come back, except, presumably, when I meet the Keeper of the Threshold itself!

It was part dream, part vision. And the changed consciousness was extraordinary. It must be, I guess, how eagles feel when they're flying straight to the sun, that wonderful sense of golden light and air and cleanness. It was so beautiful, and I so wanted to go! Talk about music of the spheres! It was to do with sound, and this wonderful pull through. And then suddenly it was as if a hand came out of the sun and pushed; a

---

[61] See also Irene Claremont de Castillejo, 1973, Page 131.

great, dark hand pushing me back. And I came along the tension of the stream, of pulling this way and pushing that. I can clearly remember coming back into this world; it was as if the hand pushed me back on to this plane again. And then I passed out of consciousness completely and woke up in the hospital.

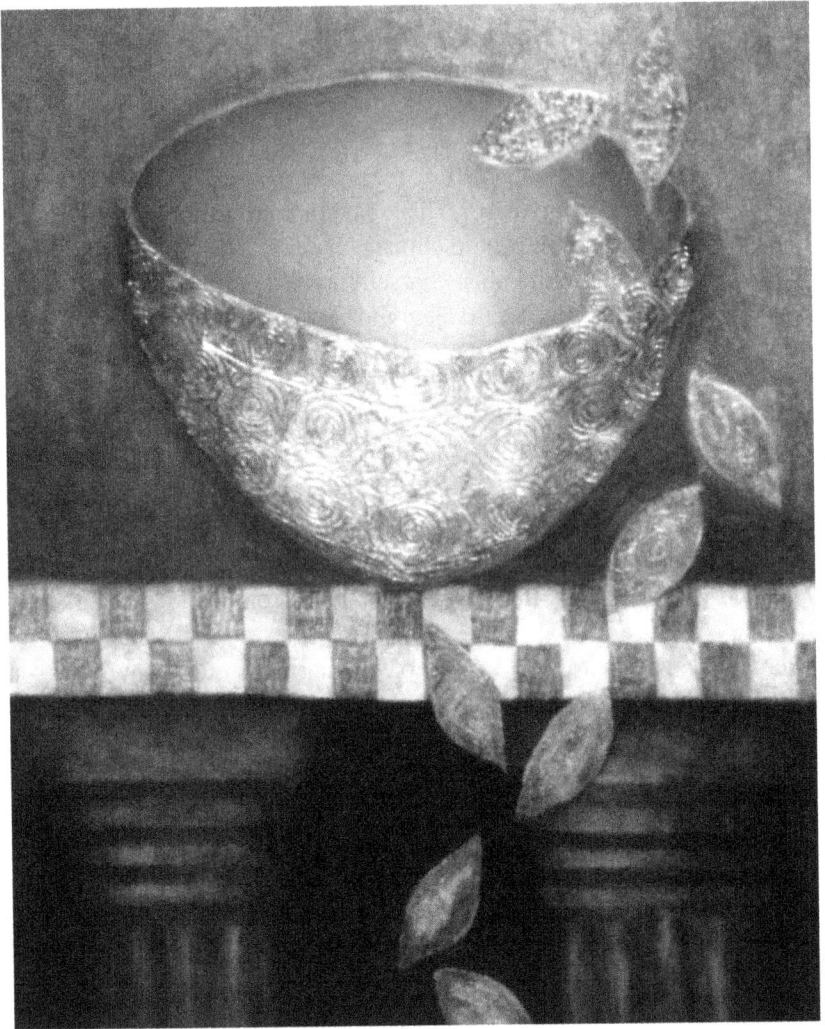

Plate 14

Between Two Worlds

CHAPTER FIFTEEN

Issues of Choice
Barbara Somers

It's as though we'd been living for many, many years in a
foreign country, having to learn the language of that people;
then suddenly we hear the voice of our homeland

Who chooses?

As we develop, we make choices just by nature of being a human being. Is it always the personality, or is it sometimes the Self that makes the choice? Jung coined the term *individuation* for our development from birth to our awakening as the Self. It's our coming into our own integrity of being, the integral part of ourselves, whatever we call it: God, the One. Jung called it the Self. Choice and individuation are the same. Issues of choice involve the processes of individuation, of becoming who we are: the greatest challenge in life. A lot of people choose not to be who they are, because that's by far the easiest path to follow. To choose to be who we truly are, and to live by it, is perhaps the greatest choice that any of us ever has to make.

There's a Hebrew saying that men and women were created for the sake of choice – quite a strong point. It certainly seems that the process of waking up to evolved consciousness is a journey of choice. In Buddhist terms it's to become awake, an awakening; the word Buddha means 'an awakened one'. So individuation, choice, awakening; those three parallel words each posit the others. Responsibility, authority, self-authority are all subsidiary to the three basic words: *choice, individuation, awakening.*

The Hero, the Heroine on the Journey has to leave the king's castle, the family cottage, the beginnings of things, and go out on the adventure of life, leaving the mass. And that in itself is an enormous choice. Most of it is done in the early days at a relatively unconscious level. If we are to become individual, we have to come out from the mass, and many choices are involved. We may choose to stand out against the collective mores or expectations of the mass, and it's only then, in the ancient esoteric wisdom traditions, that we can 'enter the group'. Lots of people think they are in a group when they're not; they are still in a mass.

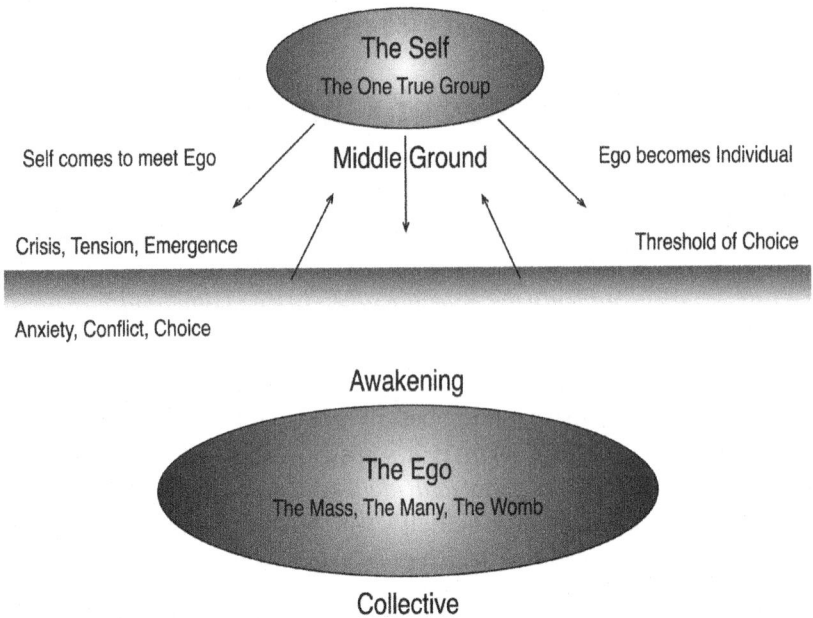

Figure 18 Evolving out of the Mass

The map at Figure 18, to be read from the bottom up, shows how we emerge from the mass, the collective unconsciousness into which we were born, in order to become individual. I evolved this map out of my own experience of life, and I would say that this is the impetus of choice.

As a race, we haven't yet evolved to be truly group-conscious, part of the real group. That is another movement onwards. It may be what the age of Aquarius is bringing in for us: to be working side by side in a real group of equal individuals who, coming from the mass collective, all share the same vision. I think we must aim as a race to evolve towards the group. In the old traditions, first we move from the mass to become an individual, and it's *then*, when we've made individual choices and taken the responsibilities of the individual, that we discover our true group, our soul group, our destined group of brothers and sisters with whom we will function to serve the one God, the Self. So we emerge from, individuate from, the original family, we create our own family, and then ultimately we hope to move into wisdom. Jung commented that, while the ego would say, 'There's something good at the top of that mountain, so I'll head straight for it', the archetypal way is not like that. Like a serpent, it spirals and wriggles its way towards the top. We feel defeated, brought to a standstill, we get terribly impatient, even desperate. Nothing happens, we get nowhere, we feel constantly hindered. But this is how it should be! It's our only way of reaching the top. All we can do is *grow* up to it. *Doing* doesn't work; it's an illusion, and proves nothing about our growth and development. As Buddhist teaching holds, we can't *attain* redemption, we can only grow up to it.

Even the Buddha himself had to go through more than five hundred incarnations to attain Nirvana. I think Jung might see that as a metaphor: five hundred incarnations in one! Especially today, with the speed at which everything is moving. But I love this theme of Jung's: that the only way we can reach towards the top of the mountain is to grow towards it.

Jung spoke many times of 'the serpentine way', of life being not a straight line from A to Z but a spiral development, a continuation. For each of us, the major choices are probably in every turn of the spiral: we come full circle and then we're faced with the choice. If we are to grow, this is probably the point at which we do it. Whatever we decide here, we choose whether to go on going round and round in it, or whether to move on to the next curve of the spiral. Our consciousness, growing more and more, gives us the impetus to go on till again we come full circle.

And we're likely to go on repeating the old patterns until we're faced with yet another choice. 'Oh no, I don't have to choose *again*, do I?' Or – (we don't always put it in these words) 'Oh surely I haven't got to face *that* lot again, have I?' Yes, we have. Are we going to deal with the repetitive old pattern in the old familiar way? Or shall we make a choice or decision that challenges the known and familiar, makes us grow, wakes us up? Something has to change. If we can't make the change outside, we can *look* at the opportunity of choice in a different way. How grown-up are we? Shall we once again find somebody else to sort this for us? Shall we go back over old patterns in the hope that, if we keep at them hard enough, things will shift? These intractable patterns of life will not shift at their own level.

Figure 18, left, indicates a road map from the *mass*, through the *individual*, to the *group*, to the *One*. And it's on the understanding that we start from the One anyway. The One is everywhere, the Self, God, meaning, purpose, whatever name we dignify – or undignify – it with. We are on a journey, a temporary journey, and it isn't just 'us' on this journey. For 'us' is both the personality, the 'I' of everyday, and also, 'us' is soul, that divine essence, that X-quality, that everlasting part of us that comes from God. I've mentioned frequently this twofold journey. But in the beginning the key for most of us is the emergence of the personality. This, I assume, is what incarnation is about: we take on flesh, choosing to experience on this planet at this point for the eternal part in us, the soul.

Here is the power of the eternal soul, the spark, the spirit. We are being called; that's why we are here. Many people come to the Transpersonal trying to get *out* – transiting, taking the next flight away. Intuitive people particularly can't accept the fact that they are incarnated at all. But that's what we're here for. Do we choose to stay, or do we go? If people take the choice of going they begin a slow suicide, looking for other people to role model their lives for them, even to live for them, rather than themselves living the kind of life they are being asked to live.

What chooses our life?

What is it in us that has the blueprint, the DNA coding of the soul, the genetic patterning of what we're about? The ancient wisdoms teach that it is our soul that holds that pattern and knows what it is. We forget, but the soul remembers. On this journey of choice we move again to wake up, to begin to remember why we're here. And what is our duty (that old-fashioned word), our *dharma*? What are we here for? What do we need to refer back to? Are we piping away on a little bugle, or are we drawing forth the deep notes of the bassoon? I once dreamt I was playing a large 'cello, working away like mad, having great difficulty with it, sawing at it, listening intently to the sound coming out of it. And suddenly, in the dream, I lifted my head from what I was groaning away at, and heard – the orchestra! I was in the middle of a full orchestra, everybody *else* was playing and it wasn't just me chugging away there. And my 'cello wasn't all that dissonant, as I'd felt. That was a very fundamental dream, teaching me many things I needed to remember: 'It's not just me; life's about the meaning of that full orchestration'.

The wise have said, as did the ancients themselves, that we are here for a reason, which is the meaning and purpose of our life. By living our life we endow it with meaning. It isn't just something out there that we reach towards, but something rendered from within our very substance. The creator of the process, like a great spider, renders the thread, the web, out of the soul, creating this most marvellous mandala-shape, and at dawn the spider's web is hung with dew. And so we render our lives, another of the forms of nature, out of the substance of the soul. The meaning of our lives begins to take on body and form. I believe – so I'm told, I'm working on it – that ultimately we come to see ourselves tackling an adventure of choice, instead of a series of problems.

The Paradise Garden

The more we awaken, the more we become aware of the need for choice. *How* do we do it? Do we whine and wail and weep and say, 'Why should this terrible life happen to me?' Or do we ask, 'What's the meaning of this life that has happened to me?' Do we trudge it, do we dance it? The way through is to take it as an adventure, not just plod it. It takes a lot of courage. It doesn't mean we have fewer problems; it may mean we have more. This is consciousness too. In each individual, each family, there is told the whole story of humanity, of the emergence of the consciousness of the human race out of the deepest depths. We come out of the flesh, we are born into the mass, we're in unconsciousness. As children, we're in a deep sleep till we begin to build little islands of personality within the profound depth of the dream of those very early days, the *participation mystique* of the original oneness. The baby is not just in the mother's womb, it's in the womb of life itself; not just born to a particular mother, but a human being born out of the amniotic fluid of unconsciousness, beginning to be born from the dream.

And a lot of us want to stay in that dream. As we've seen, this is Paradise Garden, this is innocence, this is our beginnings. If everything were still lovely, still paradisaical, if there were no serpent in the garden, no choice to be made, we'd probably stay there for ever, just responding, lulled and enwombed and cosy and safe.

'Rock-a-bye baby in the tree top,

When the wind blows the cradle shall rock;

When the bough breaks – '! Yes, but up till then we're lulled, longing for the original peacefulness, being cradled and held and cosied, simply reacting to the ebbs and flows: 'Let the others do it –'let the parents decide – let it all happen. I just want to stay asleep – I want to dream.' We may have a vested interest in staying in that lethargy and inertia: it's all so wonderfully warm, isn't it, a nice safe place to be. A lot of us re-enact it every morning!

Awakening

But, for whatever reason, the life-force wakes certain people up. Not everybody is awake. Gurdjieff made a whole teaching on this: in an ordinary street, in the train, in the family, a number of the people will be asleep, while others are in various degrees of conscious awakening. If you have begun to awaken, you can't really go back to this deep sleep.

Choice begins to happen at the next stage, when we come out of this. Once we've woken up, the first decision is, 'Do I go to sleep again, or do I stay awake?' Before that, there's no need for choice; we remain as children, as babies in Paradise. That's fine: a lot of people do not want the responsibility of choice, and they may be very wise: 'Why did I ever begin to wake up? I was happier before, I liked being a caterpillar, or a cabbage, I don't want to be a butterfly or a rose!' Others say, 'I just can't do it, I'm so tired here I'll just let go and sink back into the mass.' But once we're awake and beginning to remember, we're caught into the inexorable pull of awakening, and it would take an act of will to choose to go back to sleep.

It's a threshold. There's a lot of anxiety and conflict set up at this threshold: 'Do I leave our cottage and follow these knights riding by?' asks the hero. 'Or do I stay here? Do I wake up, or do I risk death by inertia?' Generally speaking, at this stage it's not a conscious choice, it's a totally unconscious one. Those who've decided to stay asleep try to make everybody else into their parents, authority figures who'll take the decisions for them. They want to walk this world just like angels, without experience. But those no longer in the mass, those out in the middle ground for better or for worse, are caught immediately into the pairs of opposites, into the inevitable choices that come with being awake.

As we begin to awaken, that primary unity becomes the realm of duality – of night and day, inner and outer, good and bad, right and wrong, 'shall I turn to the left or shall I turn to the right?' Wherever there is the need for choice, there will be anxiety and fear, for the unknown enters in. Behind is the familiar, but once we're beyond the impasse, we're out into the unfamiliar. That's why, when we have to make conscious choices, we may duck and weave and try to get back into unconsciousness. Or we may go on, and have to face the fears of being out over the threshold into the middle ground, becoming an individual: 'I don't know what to choose – I want to go back – I need to change but I'd much rather not – what I choose may be taken away from me, so I prefer not to choose – I'll stay with what I know, what's familiar – better the devil I know...'

The Garden of Eden

In this lovely story, once the choice had been made over the eating from the Tree of Good and Evil the two were turned out, and the angels set so that they wouldn't get back in again. But in the Paradise Garden there was another tree, the Tree of Everlasting Life. The suggestion here is that eventually they would be able to come back in. It's a wonderful creation myth: the emergence from Eden, then the moving out into the world of experience and choice that is the individual. And the ultimate return to the One will be the return to Paradise Garden, coming into it again by a different gate, to eat of the Tree of Everlasting Life.

And presumably it was God who put the snake in the garden, otherwise it wouldn't be there. Is the snake not Saturn the tempter, tester, opener of doors? Were not man and woman created to make choices? It's all about the raising of consciousness. We are put here to make choices, otherwise we would not be able to grow towards the light. So the snake was put there and the angels said 'Great!' and Adam and Eve went out holding the light. For some extraordinary reason we tell the story of the Fall as all Eve's *fault*! Looked at in this other way, it's the most exciting story in the world.

Because of the later suppression of the Flesh, the Devil and the Feminine, the Earth herself is seen as temptress. James Joyce called the Feminine 'a rib-size cutlet': Adam's cutlet, nicely blamed for everything. It's the very love of Earth, love of the senses, desire – desire for life, the life-force – that's been put down, set aside all through the ages. People gave up the pleasures of this world in order to go on; they took the sacrifice path of giving up, rather than the path of making sacred.

The Prodigal Son

Here's another who left the father's house, went out on the wheel of experience, and was at last drawn back – to be not the person who set out, but a different person. These two stories are also realities of the human psyche, told in all creation myths right across the world. Would any of us ever leave Paradise Garden without something causing us to set out on the journey? How many of us started in Paradise Garden and – went on in Paradise Garden? The adventure's not there; that's why we set out in the first place, to discover what it's like on the middle ground. Here's the choice: shall I go on into adventure? Or shall I go back? For a while we have the illusion that we can decide to commit a kind of long-term *hara-kiri*, decide to go back, not to take the choice.

The Grail quest

What are the challenges of the Middle Ground? Can I fall asleep again or do I have to continue to come awake? The Knights of the Round Table are in quest of the Holy Grail, with Galahad the prime figure. Joseph Campbell tells how they would be ashamed to set out together. Not wanting to go as a group ('group' in the mass sense) they go by their own way into the deepest part of the forest, each one entering alone at the most mysterious point, where there is no path. Any path is someone else's. Entering the forest, each knight follows his own intuition. What happens is entirely unique; what he brings forth was never before seen on earth. His potentialities, different from everybody else's, are fulfilled. He is helped only by tiny clues and if he starts to follow the trail of another knight, he goes altogether astray.[62]

It's lovely; as good as the original Grail legend. We know that isolation. One of the big choices of the Middle Ground is deciding what to leave behind: 'I used to be so cosy, everyone thought as I did, and now no one seems to think as I do.' Can I take this challenge? As the ego develops, as duality looms on either side, we are all at once in light and dark, the known and the unknown, safety and danger, and the longing for the old familiar devil-we-knew gets stronger and stronger. I'm sure Adam and Eve yearned many times for the original unity of the Paradise Garden.

The hero's journey

But the Serpent is the life-force. It is the life-force itself that drives and pushes us on, forcing us to develop. The Kundalini energy, which is also the Serpent, begins to rise. The further we go on this path the more we begin to awaken, whether we wish to or not, and have to take the responsibility of choice. We fear reality: 'I'll make mistakes, I'll make a wrong choice, it won't work'. We fear the loss of the mass, loss of face, the loss of our previous identity; we fear failure, rejection, social ridicule; we fear being scapegoated, seen as a renegade or a heretic. The word *hero* comes from the same Sanskrit root as the words *heresy* and *heretic*;

---

62   That's the Mediaeval view, the Middle Ages story, rather than the *Quest de Sangrail*.
      See Campbell, 1968, Page 540.

somebody who sets themselves apart from the mass is always in danger. That's the risk of individuation, of becoming an individual. Lots of people limit themselves so as not to upset those around them, staying smaller than they really are. And yet, as the life-force drives us on, the development of individuation pushes us further into the Middle Ground.

Those who stay in the mass want as many people as possible to be the same as they; that guarantees their existence and their identity. So by nature they feel that someone who stands apart has to be scapegoated: 'They're different from me, don't think the same as I do; it frightens me, because I have no sense of identity' – which is very dangerous stuff.

If we're driven further into the adventure, we can choose not to go. I think that at any point we can still decide to come off the spiral and continue to go round and round and round. Only later will we be impelled on to the next stage by another force which comes to collect us: the Self, or Soul, beginning to *insist* that we go on. But that's later. At the early stages we do have this choice. And lots of people choose to stop; they repeat the same patterns, the same jokes, the same stories, round and round and round. For those of us out on the adventure, that looks like a very good place to be – back and around the whirligig again and again – because it's cold out here on the next turn. How lovely to stay in the known and familiar!

But of course, if we are truly on the journey, if we have any sense of vocation (conscious or not) then after a while our nature will give us no choice but to go on. This is what vocational calling is about: to be called forth by a voice. Though we may have to repeat the old patterns till they're imprinted in us, eventually they fall apart. The symptoms in our bodies tell us that we can't stay where we are. We try to live by the same projections till our failing relationships call to us that we can't keep on with them. We have to find other ways of being, now.

If we've been chosen to travel, called to the journey, we'll inevitably be faced with an intractable problem, one that we *can't* solve. It forces us to discover new skills, new techniques, new ways of being, new attitudes, new perspectives, and at the same time it forces us to turn inward towards something greater than ourselves. And inevitably our anxiety and fear will grow as we become aware of the quality of choosing involved. The more awake, the more prone we become to almost existential all-human fears: 'Will I make the right choice? And what will happen to me if I don't? What may I have to give up?' – the pain and sacrifice of it? Moments of joy come but, though we can handle quite a bit of pain, we don't know how to handle joy, enjoyment. We avoid it, or turn it into desire, try to hang on to it, and lose it.

The choices get more and more subtle the further one goes on. When first we step over the threshold they're much more black and white: 'Is this right or wrong?' – 'Shall I go forward, shall I go back?' Later, it becomes something of 'OK against OK-est', grey or coloured, nothing like so marked and clear. The need to work that one through causes us eventually to call on something else. Remember the old saying: 'If in doubt, sleep on it'– pray on it, even at the beginning, toss the dice on it. Thus we hand over to something greater than ourselves.

Many wrong choices are made because we felt we *ought* to do something. Letting some of that guilt go, we can now come into a place of kindness to ourselves and *it* will pardon many a shortcoming if we stay there. Being friends with ourselves is as important as being friends with anybody else. 'Love thy neighbour *as thyself*,' said Christ. It's the quality of the Self that we aim at, taking as much interest in that Self as in the other. Self-abnegation can be an easy path. Out of our solar plexus we construe our bodies as desire and self-indulgence, and the mass always agrees: 'You are so selfish, you ought to look after *me*!' Parents have said to their children, 'You ought not to think of yourself; it's *me* you should be thinking of!' That's a lovely one, I like that one! Where's the equality, where's the parity of choice there?

The Self comes seeking

So in the beginning we were held by the group, and so we emerged from the One. Now we return more consciously. And the later consciousness is that the One comes seeking us; the same Love comes to meet us. In the past we didn't question the authority of the 'shoulds' and the 'oughts'; when we began to, it was usually easier to stick with them, since scapegoating and humiliation would follow if we went with the awareness, the awaken-ness. It's only when we've gone through this middle ground, begun to 'extrapolate out', that our Self will find us. Now we return more consciously to the Paradise Garden, return to eat of eternal life; but we've had a long journey in between. This is what the creation myths are about.

So when we get to a certain cross-over point the One comes searching for us. God comes searching for us. It's as old as dreams. It's a very solitary journey, because of the warmth and ease of the original group we've left. We're beginning to move towards the real group, the true group. One by one, we find someone who speaks the same language. It's as though we've been living for many, many years in a foreign country, having to learn the language of that people. Then suddenly we hear the language of our homeland; somebody really speaks it! Often we're blown apart; we run and hide from them for quite a few years, because we can hardly withstand the impact. Can this be somebody from our group, can somebody be speaking *that* language? We may not be meant to marry them, come into everlasting happiness with them, but the fact that they exist – well, if they are there, then all is well. And others will come. Certainly it is said that on the path of Wisdom we do find our own kind. We begin to speak the language of our homeland, the place from which we originally came, and give it voice. Having for long years lived far from home on what may have been quite alien soil, we've also learned different languages, and can now become translators.

So at last we begin to come home. Coming back to ourselves, we are met by the One. And very often as we come back we trip over the doorstep, catch our toe on the stopper at the threshold! This can be a painful period. The threshold may appear frightening, the threshold of pain, the threshold of a near-death experience. We probably have to reach out beyond ourselves, not only Self-loving but going beyond the limits of personality. Even our staying-power, even all those values and virtues of the journey, have to be put aside. Our truths have to be reduced, the exalted personality has to give way to something greater. We may call it God, we may call it the Self, we may call it the Soul, we may give it no name at all. We may be like the monk who, falling over the precipice, cried up from the abyss, 'Is there anybody there?' and God replied, 'Have faith, my son.' Pause: 'Isn't there anybody *else* up there...?'

At a certain point, choice is forcibly taken from us. In the earlier part of the journey, *holding on*, doing the heroic stuff, taking full responsibility, was important. Now, our attitude changes; *letting go* becomes vital in this part of the journey, when the Self begins to come closer. It's quite an advanced stage, I think. Now the choice is made by that part of us – our Soul, our Self, our spirit – that *remembers*. All the time we were struggling, it remembered; while we were forgetting, it remembered. The statement, 'Lo, I have been with you all the days' is not just from the Bible, but from most bibles of most peoples. That which we've come through has been valued. It hasn't been just us; we've been part of the *human* struggle to awaken.

The way of the Boddhisattva

Those who come to this may always come back to teach and help others, if they're still able to hold incarnation in this world, and haven't gone through Death's threshold to the next bit of the adventure on a different turn of the spiral. These are the Returning Ones, the Boddhisattvas. The Boddhisattva is the Buddha saying, 'Although I am enlightened, I will nonetheless return to help those who are seeking.' The Buddha under the Boddhi Tree, although he was being invited into the pantheon of immortals to become an Enlightened One – 'Buddha, the Awakened One' – is believed to have taken the Boddhisattva vow: 'So long as one blade of grass cries out for love, I shall come back and walk again.' This is the Boddhisattva tradition. Christ is one of them, Buddha, Shri Krishna; figures who have returned in order to walk in the company of human beings on their journey.

This is why it's so helpful to read myth, story, fairy tale, to heed the artists, the poets and playwrights and musicians. Listen to Beethoven and his last quartets, to Mozart and his Requiem; watch and sense all great art, and you have it – the same journey, which comes from the One. Forgetting, experiencing, remembering, we come from the One. After which we have no choice but to return; the pull is so strong all choice is taken from us. Of this again, the greatest freedom in life is to do *willingly* that which I must. It's not 'my will' but 'thy will'. It is a handing over, said to be the most joyful, blissful thing. This is heaven, this is bliss, this is the return to the Oneness of life. One doesn't have to choose, one stands and is chosen through. Duality stops, Oneness comes in, and it ceases to be an issue of choice. Rather, 'Into thy hands...' and then choices are made quite spontaneously. We stand by the integrity of our nature and know what to do and how to act. The decision which is no decision is without thought. We become instruments. A good definition of service is 'the spontaneous out-flowing of an overbrimming pot'.

So, if we are awakening, we can enter the spiral of life, conscious that we are returning to the One. Evolution has brought choices. We awaken by varying degrees. Those who've been chosen may either go willingly, or screaming and reluctant. Yet others are not necessarily on this journey at all. That's all right. We should never judge another human being, thinking they ought to be like us. Our only concern is, are we waking up, are we making our choices, taking the responsibility for all the mishaps and joys *en route*? If other people wish to stay asleep, fine – don't wake them! Don't say, 'Oh, this is what I've discovered; you must do what I've done!' which is like slapping the face of a sleeper or clapping your hands in their ear. It's fine to be asleep; and when they do awaken they may take off like hares, and our tortoise be well and truly overcome. Jung would say, 'Use your breath to cool your *own* parsnips', and leave them to get on with theirs; we can trust that the One has them in hand too.

That's the map. People have talked about the different ways of working up through it, and what it's like to come out on to the middle ground: the Dark Night of the Soul, the Labyrinth, the Wasteland, entering the Belly of the Whale, the Place of the Unknown. We have plenty of stories, legends and myths telling us how other people have fared on that way and giving us hope. Sometimes we come to places where what we feel is more like loss of self-authority; it's depression, not enlightenment, going to sleep rather than awakening, loss of Soul, burnout. All these things are *en route*. But if we stay with it, if we can dance it, keep travelling, if, like the knights in the Grail story we do not expect to be walking a footpath that's already been way-marked, then we're creating paths for those who follow after us. Although we may not realise it, we're helping others to follow, as we are following the footsteps of those who've gone before us, carrying us over the River Styx – carrying us until eventually we ourselves truly join the group. And one day we will recognise it, and remember.

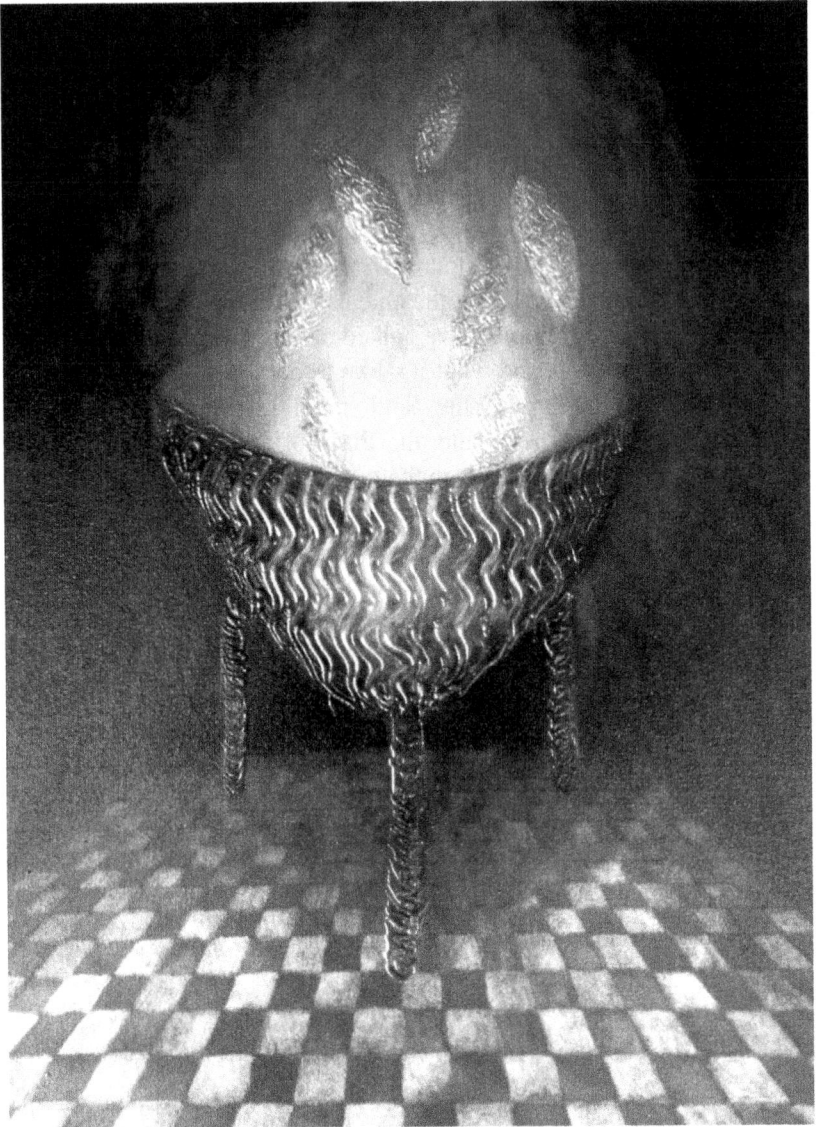

Plate 15

Fusion

POSTSCRIPT

Anthony Thorley

Transpersonal psychology serves to remind us that the human condition is much greater than the sum of its parts, and that our lives are a vivid lifelong developmental journey from a first seed of wisdom to the profound fruiting of elderhood. The magic of this inspired oral teaching is that it produces, out of the alchemy of the anxiety of presentation and the confidence born of experienced practice, a dimension of creativity and synthesis that is rarely caught or communicated in the same way by the written word. The essence of this teaching often bubbles with infectious humour and stunning originality. We are reminded, just as we were by the original seminars: 'I have been here before'. There is nothing arcane or exclusive in this material. Indeed, in its avoidance of prescription and dictum it kindles our natural insights and confirms the therapeutic wisdom that we all carry within. The spiritual and the secular are seen as one.

It is clear that the psychology presented here does not try to be an end in itself but is a stepping off point for further development and practice. No one – no psychologist, no counselling practitioner, no pained individual looking for a new understanding in life – who reads this uniquely informative book and absorbs but a little of its optimistic wisdom can ever be quite the same again.

Dr. Anthony Thorley
Addiction Psychiatrist
BATH
Somerset
9th April, 2002

"Barbara Somers and the late Ian Gordon-Brown are two of the great pioneers and spiritual representatives of transpersonal psychology in Great Britain. The high standard of their work and teachings is reflected in the quality of this book. It skilfully integrates the personal with the Transpersonal, allowing readers insight into their childhood and the greatest challenges they face on their psycho-spiritual journeys. If you are interested in finding a depth of understanding for your biography, your relationships, your greatest issues and obstacles, as well as your purpose in life – this book is a *must read*."

Diana Whitmore
The Psychosynthesis and Education Trust

"I know of few works that are so profoundly and meaningfully human, and at the same time so intensely spiritual. It offers a safe haven, a harbour amid the seas of uncertainty, tumult and internal storm on which so many of us today drift. The timely appearance of this book is an apt manifestation of the synchronicity with which Barbara and Ian were always so in touch. We are indebted to Hazel Marshall for making this wisdom accessible to all, enabling it to radiate ever further outwards, like ripples in a pool."

Sacha Abercorn
Initiator of the Pushkin Creative Writing Prize for children. This Prize brings together Catholic and Protestant children from both Northern Ireland and the Republic of Ireland.

BIBLIOGRAPHY

Roberto Assagioli 1975, '*Psychosynthesis: A Manual of Principles and Techniques*', London, Turnstone 1975.

Connie Bensley 1981, '*Progress Report*', Cornwall, Peterloo Poets, 1981 and Northumberland, Bloodaxe Books Ltd, 1990.

Joseph Campbell 1968, '*The Masks of God: Creative Mythology*', New York, Viking Press, 1968, London, Penguin, 1982.

Chuang Tsu 1974, '*Inner Chapters*', A New Translation by Gia-Fu Feng and Jane English, London, Wildwood House, 1974.

Irene Claremont de Castillejo 1973, '*Knowing Woman: a Feminine Psychology*', London, Hodder & Stoughton, 1973.

Edward Edinger 1972, '*Ego and Archetype*', London, Shambala, Random Century Group, 1972.

Adolf Guggenbühl-Craig 1971, '*Power in the Helping Professions*', Zürich, Spring Publications, 1971.

Nor Hall 1980. Pausanias, quoted in '*The Moon and the Virgin*', Nor Hall, London, The Women's Press, 1980. Taken by her from 'Description of Greece', Tr. J.G. Frazer, New York 1965, 6 vols. 9.39.

Joseph L. Henderson 1967, '*Thresholds of Initiation*', Connecticut, Wesleyan University Press, 1967.

James Hillman 1971, '*The Puer Papers*', Dallas, Spring Publications, 1991.

James Hillman 1996, '*The Soul's Code: In Search of Character and Calling*', London. Bantam Books, 1996, see his chapter on the Parental Fallacy.

Ted Hughes 1998, '*Birthday Letters*', London, Faber & Faber, 1998.

Jolande Jacobi 1942 '*Psychology of C.G. Jung*', London, Routledge & Kegan Paul, 1942.

Jolande Jacobi 1965, '*The Way of Individuation*', London, Hodder & Stoughton, 1965.

C.G. Jung 1953, '*The Collected Works of C.G.Jung*', London, Routledge & Kegan Paul, 1953, revised 1968:

C.G. Jung 1921, '*Psychological Types*', Collected Works Vol.6.

C.G. Jung 1928, '*The Psychology of the Unconscious*', Collected Works Vol.7.

C.G. Jung 1929, '*The Secret of the Golden Flower: A Chinese Book of Life*', Richard Wilhelm & C.G. Jung, London, Routledge & Kegan Paul, 1931. Also in Collected Works Vol. 13, Commentary on 'The Secret of the Golden Flower', 1929.

C.G. Jung 1930-34, '*The Visions Seminars*' Vols.1 & 2, Lectures given 1930-34, Zürich, Spring Publications, 1976.

C.G. Jung 1938-54, '*Four Archetypes: Mother, Rebirth, Spirit and Trickster*', London, Routledge & Kegan Paul, 1972. Lectures extracted from 'The Archetypes and the Collective Unconscious', Collected Works Vol.9 Part 1.

C.G. Jung 1963, '*Memories, Dreams, Reflections*', London, Collins and Routledge & Kegan Paul, 1963. Fontana, Harper Collins 1995.

C.G. Jung 1977, '*The Symbolic Life: Miscellaneous Writings*,' Vol.18, Paras. 1552 and 1607.

Sheldon Kopp 1974, '*If You Meet the Buddha on the Road, Kill Him!: A Modern Pilgrimage Through Myth, Legend, Zen & Psychotherapy*', London, Sheldon Press, 1974.

Robert Graves 1959, '*New Larousse Encyclopaedia of Mythology*', London, Hamlyn, 1959, 1979.

Abraham H. Maslow 1954, '*Motivation and Personality*', New York, Harper & Row 1954, 1970.

John G Neihardt 1932, '*Black Elk Speaks*', 1932, 1959, University of Nebraska Press 1961, London, Barrie & Jenkins Ltd 1972. ISBN 0 349 12522 8

K.R. Pelleier 1977, '*Mind as Healer, Mind as Slayer*', New York, Delta, 1977.

Skynner & Cleese 1983, '*Families and How to Survive Them*', London, Methuen, 1983.

Marie-Louise von Franz 1970, '*Puer Aeternus: A Psychological Study of the Adult Struggle with the Paradise of Childhood*', Santa Monica CA, Sigo Press, 1970, 1981.

Frances Wickes 1927, '*The Inner World of Childhood*', London, Coventure 1977.

Frances Wickes 1963, '*The Inner World of Choice*', London, Coventure 1977.

INDEX

9 781906 289423